Hudson Institute Series on National Security
and International Order

Number 1

On Escalation

Metaphors and Scenarios

HERMAN KAHN

On Escalation

Metaphors and Scenarios

FREDERICK A. PRAEGER, *Publishers*
New York • Washington • London

FREDERICK A. PRAEGER, *Publishers*
111 Fourth Avenue, New York 3, N.Y., U.S.A.
77-79 Charlotte Street, London W.1, England

Published in the United States of America in 1965
by Frederick A. Praeger, Inc., Publishers

Library of Congress Catalog Card Number: 65-18080

Printed in the United States of America

Acknowledgments

The research reported on in this book was originated by the Hudson Institute under a contract with the Martin Company, the aerospace division of the Martin Marietta Corporation, to study "The National Interest in International Order." Some earlier work was discussed in *Thinking About the Unthinkable* by Herman Kahn (New York: Horizon Press, 1962). The material was elaborated on in work done on various government contracts, and some of this was included in two unpublished Institute reports, *A Study of Escalation: The Use of Force in Peace and War* by Morris Isom, Herman Kahn, Robert Lawrence, William Pfaff, and Edmund Stillman, and *Crises and Arms Control* by Anthony J. Wiener and Herman Kahn; and in a contribution to the book *National Security: Political, Military, and Economic Strategies in the Decade Ahead* (New York: Frederick A. Praeger, 1963) under the title "Escalation and Its Strategic Context." The present book makes use of all three of the above documents, other work done at the Hudson Institute under various contracts and grants, and additional work done under the Martin contract. The Martin Company did not, of course, influence the character of this work, and the findings should not be construed as necessarily representing the views of the company. The company is responsible only for making this research possible.

The author would like to acknowledge his debt to William Pfaff, who read the entire manuscript critically and made innumerable substantive and editorial suggestions. Crises and tension contexts and programs have been the subject of many Hudson Institute studies, and this book rests on much work done by others of the

Hudson organization, including Francis Armbruster, Robert Axelrod, William Brown, Sara Dustin, Raymond Gastil, Morris Isom, Morton Kaplan, Felix Kauffman, Jeremy J. Stone, and Martin Zlotnick. The author would like especially to thank William Katz, Max Singer, Edmund Stillman, and Anthony J. Wiener. However, the author is solely responsible for the substantive judgments included.

H.K.

Preface

In September, 1961, the Martin Company gave a contract to the Hudson Institute to study "The National Interest in the International Order." According to the work statement of this contract, the Institute was to:

> explore the complex interrelations of national and international security, including but not necessarily limited to the following specific areas of study:
>
> 1. An examination of the long-run implications of the arms race.
> 2. An investigation of the ways in which improvements in international order might be brought about and of the political, military, social, and economic consequences of different modes of transition.
> 3. Identification of areas of opposition and areas of compatibility and the general interrelations between the national interest and international security.
> 4. A consideration of the applications to the tasks of international order and development of the intellectual and material resources currently used for military purposes.

It should be clear that this is a very large subject. In the two to three man-years of research available under the contract, it was not envisaged that the Hudson Institute would do even a modestly systematic study of the range of problems. The Martin Company's intention was to focus attention on issues that might be of special interest to defense planners in the United States and to utilize the other contract work at the Institute as a basis for additional studies.

The contract was given by the company as a contribution to the public interest. There was no attempt to direct the work in the company's special interest. There was, however, a definite attempt to do the work in such a way that long-range planners in government and in aerospace and related industries would be able to make use of the results. In particular, there was an attempt to fulfill all the objectives listed below:[1]

1. Stimulate and stretch the imagination.
2. Clarify, define, name, expound, and argue major issues.
3. Design and study many alternative policy "packages" and contexts.
4. Create propaedeutic and heuristic methodologies and frameworks. We use these unfamiliar words because they fit Hudson's objectives so well.

    "Propaedeutic" pertains to introductory instruction, although there is no suggestion of the elementary. Because creative integration of ideas can normally be accomplished only in a single mind, even a very sophisticated and knowledgeable policy-maker, analyst, or long-range planner must absorb many ideas from unfamiliar fields. Hence, propaedeutic techniques are vital.

    "Heuristic" refers to that which serves to discover or to stimulate investigations, or to methods of demonstration that lead a person to probe further. While heuristic techniques are not necessarily scholarly or rigorous, their value needs no explanation.

5. Improve intellectual communication and cooperation, particularly by the use of historical analogies, scenarios, metaphors, analytic models, precise concepts, and suitable language.
6. Furnish specific knowledge, conclusions, recommendations, and suggestions.
7. Clarify current choices, with emphasis on those that retain flexibility for a broad range of contingencies.

[1] This list comes from a current Hudson Institute brochure. It is one on which we have long pondered because it seems valuable to be consciously and intellectually aware of what one is trying to do.

8. Increase the ability to identify and understand the significance of new patterns and crises.
9. Improve the perspective of decision-makers and increase their ability to react appropriately to the new and unfamiliar.

A number of briefings and informal consultations were held with Martin personnel during the course of the work. In addition to these sessions, we are providing a final report in four documents and an additional summary report. The four documents are:

Technological and Doctrinal Lags by Herman Kahn
Escalation: Metaphors and Scenarios by Herman Kahn
The National Interest in the Future of the International Order: A Heuristic Treatment by Andrew Caranfil, Herman Kahn, William Pfaff, and Edmund Stillman
Aspects of International Order by Joseph Allen, Robert Axelrod, Felix Kaufmann, Morton Kaplan, William Pfaff, and Martin Zlotnick

The first document, *Technological and Doctrinal Lags,* is mostly an expository account of work that had been done preliminary to the Martin contract, rather than original research. It attempts to consider the rate at which technology changes, and how this does and should affect our intellectual and conceptual framework. It particularly concentrates on the difficulty of keeping up with all the consequences of technological change. The paper was originally produced as a background document for other researchers on the study.

The second document (and the original study on which this book is based), *Escalation: Metaphors and Scenarios,* is an attempt to treat those aspects of international relations in which the role of escalation and negotiation is important. It tries to summarize effectively much of modern escalation theory, possibly treating some aspects more systematically and intensively than has been customary. Its approach, in particular, is propaedeutic and heuristic, so that individuals who are not specialists in internationl relations can more easily use the results.

The third document, *The National Interest in the Future International Order: A Heuristic Treatment,* attempts to give a substantive and contextual account of current and likely developments in international relations. It is not only a mixture of research and exposition, but contains some research in exposition. To the extent that it succeeds, this report is, among other things, a kind of high-level "college outline" of international relations for the nonexpert in international relations, as well as a reasonably systematic account, of possible interest to the expert, of some basic factors and tendencies in the current international situation.

The last report, *Aspects of International Order,* is a collection of individual documents produced under the contract at various times for various purposes. The unifying theme is the control and use of force, and it represents an attempt to get some idea of the proper directions, routes, and destinations for the United States in trying to do this better.

* * *

This book, like my *On Thermonuclear War,* is the outgrowth of a series of lectures or briefings. The origin still shows in some of the emphasis and structure, yet this residual legacy of the briefings is, I believe, of some value, since the lecture form is particularly useful in presenting the relatively technical and dry "methodological" issues that are the book's subject.

The lectures were given mostly to expert military or civilian audiences. Many members of the audiences had a quite different set of biases, attitudes, and beliefs than is commonly encountered in public discussions. While the members of these specialist audiences are, in my opinion, generally much sounder on most questions of military policy than many liberal intellectuals, on the wider issues being discussed in this book my own views are often much more in accord with generally recognized liberal positions than with the opinions of many in my audiences. As a result, these lectures were, in effect, a "left-wing" presentation to audiences inclined to question much of what was being said.

In the interests of saving space and focusing attention on major points and ideas, this book deliberately begs many questions of feasibility and practicability. However, as far as I know, I have avoided academic or "scholastic" discussions of possibilities that in the real world are simply not worth serious attention. I realize, however, that many will disagree with this judgment.

While the Hudson Institute research on which this book is based has as its major emphasis the synthesizing and integration of diverse scholarly areas, technical skills, and practical experiences, this particular publication is deliberately focused on a narrow range of issues that arise in escalation situations or crises. In particular, such factors as technology and technological innovations, various military capabilities, cultural backgrounds and national styles, the role and use of force in bringing about changes in the international system, the basic controversies that give rise to crises and escalation situations, the psychological and emotional influences upon individuals who direct the military-political decision-making apparatus of governments are considered either perfunctorily or not at all. Other Institute research (soon to be published) does give serious attention to all of these issues.

While an understanding of the need for control, caution, prudence, understanding, restraint, and rationality in international conflict is widespread in the United States, and received particular attention during the (relatively superficial but still educational) 1964 campaign debate, it seems likely that the further study of conflict and crisis policy may be seriously neglected while the East-West *détente* endures. There is something to be said for letting it decline—since that is part of what makes up a *détente*—but there is much to be said, too, for persisting in the sober study of the risks of a nuclear world. It does not, in any event, seem likely that the systematic discussion of escalation theory can have a very adverse effect on world *détente*, and it may have an extremely important and beneficial effect upon our government and society in improving our ability to control violence. A lack of competence in this, above all areas, could have disastrous consequences—and not only for us.

HERMAN KAHN
Director, Hudson Institute

January, 1965

Contents

On Escalation

Metaphors and Scenarios

I

Introduction

Escalation in Brief

Escalation, in the sense used here, is a relatively new word in the English language.[1] In a typical escalation situation, there is likely to be a "competition in risk-taking"[2] or at least resolve, and a matching of local resources, in some form of limited conflict between two sides. Usually, either side could win by increasing its efforts in some way, *provided that the other side did not negate the increase* by increasing its own efforts. Furthermore, in many situations it will be clear that if the increase in effort were not matched and thus resulted in victory, the costs of the increased effort would be low in relation to the benefits of victory. Therefore, the fear that the other side may react, indeed overreact, is most likely to deter escalation, and not the undesirability or costs of the escalation itself. It is because of this that the "competition in risk-taking" and resolve takes place.

There are many reasons why a nation might deliberately seek to escalate a crisis. Each of the criteria given later to measure the de-

---

[1] It is not found at all in the *Oxford English Dictionary* (1961), and *Webster's New International Dictionary* (3d ed., 1961) defines it only in the noninternational sense. Yet the word is now familiar and can be used without apology to describe an increase in the level of conflict in international crisis situations.

[2] I believe this is Thomas C. Schelling's phrase (though he does not recall inventing it).

3

gree of escalation might also be a means or objective that one side or the other seeks. That is, one side might wish to escalate specifically to threaten the other side with all-out war, to provoke it, to demonstrate committal or recklessness, and so forth. A nation may also escalate for prudential as well as coercive reasons: to prevent something worse from happening, to meet a problem, to prepare for likely escalations on the other side, and so on. A nation might evacuate its cities simply because it wished to protect its people, without necessarily thinking through or even facing the thought that by making its people less vulnerable it increases its bargaining and military power, perhaps to such an extent that the other side may feel under pressure either to take some direct action or to back down. Sometimes the reasons for escalation, whether prudential or pressure-producing, will affect the technique and consequences of the escalation, and other times they will not.

As indicated in Figure 1, there are at least three ways in which a would-be escalator can increase, or threaten to increase, his efforts: by increasing intensity, widening the area, or compounding escalation. For example, let us assume that there is some kind of limited conflict or "agreed battle"[3] going on. The most obvious way to escalate is by a quantitative increase in the intensity of the conflict by doing more of what one already is doing—perhaps using more equipment, using new equipment, or attacking new targets such as the enemy's logistics. A large intensive increase, or escalation, would be the use of nuclear weapons against these targets. The area of the conflict may also be increased; in particular, some local sanctuary could be violated. This could mean taking such actions as "crossing the Yalu," retaliatory raids or bombings of North Vietnam or hot pursuit, or other violations of geographical sanctuaries. It could constitute a permanent widening of the area

[3] Max Singer's term. It emphasizes that in an escalation situation in which both sides are accepting limitations, there is in effect an "agreement," whether or not it is explicit or even well understood. Thus the term does not have any connotation of a completely shared understanding, an intention of continuing indefinitely with the limitations, or even a conscious *quid pro quo* arrangement.

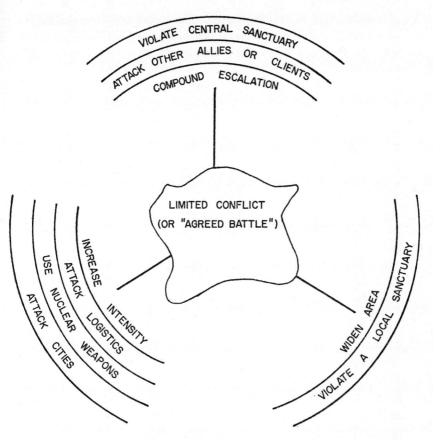

FIGURE 1

THREE WAYS TO ESCALATE A LIMITED CONFLICT

of conflict or simply of the area of a local battle. In almost all the intense conflicts and crises that have occurred since World War II, there have been important local sanctuaries. There have also been pressures—usually, one assumes, on both sides—to violate such sanctuaries.

Finally, one can escalate by precipitating a new crisis or conflict elsewhere than in the local area. This "compound escalation"[4] could consist of an attack on an ally or client of the principal opponent—though it could also be an attack on troops or colonies of the principal, but geographically outside the central sanctuary. The compound escalation might also violate the central sanctuary, but in the case of such opponents as the Soviet Union and the United States, this would be a very high-level escalation. Even in a conflict between, say, the Soviets and a powerful country such as Japan or a West European nation, this would be considered a high escalation.

Thus, in any escalation, two sets of basic elements are in constant interplay: the political, diplomatic, and military issues surrounding the particular conflict, and the level of violence and provocation at which it is fought. The latter merges with those considerations raised by the possibility of escalation to higher or more extensive levels of violence, including the possibility of a deliberate, provoked, or inadvertent conflict eruption[5] leading directly to central war.

[4] The focus of our analysis is on deliberate compound escalation. But it must be remembered that in a tense situation or a confrontation, the whole relationship of the contending states is specially charged and acts no longer will necessarily be accepted by an opponent at their "normal" valuation or significance. A "normal" troop or fleet movement, a conventional and unrelated diplomatic act by one party may be interpreted by the opponent as an escalatory act. Moreover, third parties may take advantage of a tense situation to gain ends of their own and in fact escalate the big-power crisis. The British-French-Israeli attack on Suez in 1956, while not planned to take advantage of the Hungarian crisis, actually affected the behavior of the U.S. and the U.S.S.R., and itself was affected by the crisis situation of the great powers. The Turkish air action against Greek Cypriotes in August, 1964, was probably influenced in its character and timing by the crisis between the U.S. and North Vietnam and was probably made more "acceptable" because of the precedent set by the U.S. in striking against North Vietnam a few days before. The importance of such precedents will be discussed later. If the Cyprus crisis had continued—had escalated—with greater Soviet involvement, this crisis could have constituted an inadvertent compound escalation of the great-power crisis.

[5] Morton H. Halperin has suggested (in his *Limited War in the Nuclear Age* [New York: John Wiley & Sons, 1963], p. 3), that two terms should be used to describe different kinds of escalation:

. . . *explosion*—the sudden transformation of a local war into a central war by the unleashing of strategic nuclear forces . . . and *expansion*—a gradual increase in the level of military force employed.

Just as there are two basic sets of elements in the escalation situation, so there are two basic classes of strategies that each side can use. One class of strategies makes use of features of the particular "agreed battle" that is being waged in order to gain an advantage. The other class uses the risks or threat of escalation and eruption from this agreed battle.

Users of the second class of strategies can deliberately try to eschew the ultimate eruption threat by establishing a fixed limit on how high they will go. This limit can be kept secret, in which case one side may run some risk of a full-scale pre-emptive eruption by the other side; or it can be announced in advance, with varying degrees of solemnity and credibility.

Strategies that emphasize the possibility of escalation or eruption are associated with the term "brinkmanship." (We will sometimes refer to the game of "chicken" when the brinkmanship is overtly two-sided.) They include strategies that use the risks of escalation to induce an opponent to let one maintain a position that cannot be maintained solely by use of local capabilities and actions. But whatever is emphasized, some mixture of both classes of strategies is combined in almost any move by either side.

Thus, the conditions of two-sided escalation situations can be summarized as follows:

1. Either side can usually put enough into the particular battle to win if the other side does not respond.
2. The value of victory is usually great enough so that it would be worth while for either side to raise its commitment enough to win the escalation *if it were certain that the other side would not counter the rise.*

He then points out:

> These two processes, "explosion" and "expansion," are frequently discussed together as "escalation." However it is important to keep the two processes separate. The considerations that go into the decision to begin a central war would be very different from the considerations that have gone and will go into decisions to expand a local war. These latter decisions will be influenced by a number of factors, including the foreign-policy objectives of the two sides, their estimate of the risk of central war, their images of the role of force, and their domestic political objectives.

Our term "escalation" covers Halperin's terms "expansion" and "escalation" (according to context), and our "eruption" is similar to his "explosion."

3. Upper levels of escalation are both dangerous and painful, and each side wishes to avoid them. Therefore, the risks of escalation even to limited heights, as well as to undetermined heights, and the risks of direct "eruption" to general war are all major deterring elements in almost all decisions about escalation or de-escalation—even when one expects to be able to "prevail" at the upper levels.

4. Typically, both sides are interested in "systems bargaining" —in preserving precedents (thresholds) that reduce the likelihood of escalation, eruption, or other undesirable long-term effects.

5. There are two basic types of escalation strategies that each side can follow:
   a. strategies based on factors relating to particular levels of escalation (agreed battle) or the specific situation.
   b. strategies based on manipulation of the risks of escalation or eruption.

6. Generally, each side will attempt to avoid looking like a cool mathematician or cynical blackmailer in its tactics, and will emphasize the agonistic, stylistic, or familial aspects of its behavior (as discussed later).

Escalations are thus relatively complex phenomena. They are not to be ordered in a simple fashion, yet for some purposes we wish to do exactly this, even if it does some violence to reality. Very roughly, at any particular instant in a crisis or war, the degree of escalation might be measured by such things as:

1. Apparent closeness to all-out war.
2. Likelihood of eruption.
3. Provocation.
4. Precedents broken.
5. Committal (resolve and/or recklessness) demonstrated.
6. Damage done or being done.
7. Effort (scale, scope, or intensity of violence).
8. Threat intended or perceived.

In practice, the "measurement" of the degree of escalation at any particular instant will depend on the criteria used. Thus, there is no objective reason why the apparent closeness to all-out war (as measured by popular concern) need be a very good measure of the objective likelihood of eruption. This is clearly true for accidents "out of the blue," and it may be true for many other situations. In fact, in a crisis, concern over the possibility of eruption may make the probability of eruption very much less. There may also be a great deal of provocation without much likelihood of eruption or much apparent closeness to all-out war. In general, the criteria given above measure different things, but all have been used by various authors as measures of escalation. For our part, we will be deliberately vague and not usually specify the criteria being used to determine the degree of escalation. However, in most situations the context (or the correlation between the possible criteria) will be clear enough to avoid confusion.

The Strike and "Chicken" Metaphors

There are two interesting analogies, or metaphors, that one can apply to escalation: the strike in labor disputes and the game of "chicken." Neither of these analogies is entirely accurate, but each of them is useful in explicating the concept of escalation and in conveying a feeling for the nuances and tactics.

The strike analogy operates primarily on the lower levels of escalation. In a strike situation, labor and management threaten to inflict harm on each other, do so, and under pressure of the continuation of this harm, they seek agreement. It is usually assumed that events will not escalate to the limit (i.e., erupt): we do not expect workers to starve to death or businesses to go bankrupt. In a strike, each side is expected to hurt or threaten to hurt, but not to "kill" or even permanently injure the other side. Under pressure of continuing threats of harm, it is assumed that some compromise will be arrived at before permanent or excessive damage is incurred. Occasionally, these expectations are not fulfilled; a business does go bankrupt, or the workers do look for jobs elsewhere. But this is rare. Usually, the strike is settled long before such limits are approached.

In this context, the question immediately comes up, "Why go through this expensive, dangerous, and uncomfortable route to settle disputes? Why have a strike at all? Why not settle the dispute?" The answer is obvious. In the absence of enforceable or acceptable adjudication, the side most afraid of a strike will tend to get the worst of the bargain. A "no strike" policy—the analogy, in labor disputes, to nonviolence—rarely works for any length of time. And even when it seems to work for some years and disputes are settled without strikes, a strike situation or a serious strike threat may eventually arise. The threat of a strike or a lockout is ever present as a last-resort pressure for compromise.

Escalation has one major feature that is not present in most strike situations—the possibility of eruption. In the usual strike, the maximum punishment that the workers can inflict on the management is to deny it one day's production at a time. The maximum punishment that management can ordinarily inflict on the workers is to deny them one day's wages at a time. There is, therefore, a natural limit to the rate of punishment—an accident or spasm of anger is not likely to force either side over the brink. Escalation in international relations is quite different, since each side decides at what rate it wishes to inflict harm on the other side. This makes escalation incomparably less stable than the strike situation. A moment of anger, a surge of emotion, a seemingly innocuous miscalculation or accident, or a "wrong" decision can have catastrophic consequences.

Another useful—if misleading—analogy which brings this aspect to the fore is the game of "chicken." While it is a very popular metaphor, particularly with peace groups, the analogy to the game of "chicken" greatly oversimplifies international conflicts. "Chicken" is played by two drivers on a road with a white line down the middle. Both cars straddle the white line and drive toward each other at top speed. The first driver to lose his nerve and swerve into his own lane is "chicken"—an object of contempt and scorn—and he loses the game. The game is played among teenagers for prestige, for girls, for leadership of a gang, and for safety (i.e., to prevent other challenges and confrontations).

Escalation is much more complicated than this game. Still, the game provides a useful analogy because it illustrates *some* aspects of international relations that are important and should be emphasized—for example, the symmetrical character of many escalation situations. Some teenagers utilize interesting tactics in playing "chicken." The "skillful" player may get into the car quite drunk, throwing whisky bottles out the window to make it clear to everybody just how drunk he is. He wears very dark glasses so that it is obvious that he cannot see much, if anything. As soon as the car reaches high speed, he takes the steering wheel and throws it out the window. If his opponent is watching, he has won. If his opponent is not watching, he has a problem; likewise if both players try this strategy.

One of the reasons people do not like to use the "chicken" analogy is that it emphasizes the fact that two sides can operate in the same way. It seems to me that some who object to this label want to play a limited game of "chicken," but do not like to concede that that is what they are doing. I believe it is a good thing to label the tactics, and I also think that, under current conditions, we may have to be willing to play the international version of this game whether we like it or not.

It is clear from the above why many people would like to conduct international relations the way a teenager plays "chicken." They believe that if our decision-makers can only give the appearance of being drunk, blind, and without a steering wheel, they will "win" in negotiations with the Soviets on crucial issues. I do not consider this a useful or responsible policy. We may be willing to run some risks, and we may not want to hem ourselves in tactically by seeming completely sober, clear-visioned, and in full control of ourselves, but we will obviously benefit by having a reasonable degree of sobriety, a reasonable degree of clear vision, and a reasonable degree of self-control. The Soviets are likely to pursue a similar policy.

But escalation often has a crucial point of similarity to the game of "chicken": one side must convey the impression to the other side that the opponent must be the one to give way, or at least accept a reasonable compromise, yet both sides are trying to get this message across.

The strike and the game of "chicken" both cast some light on the concept of escalation. But almost any analogy can be misleading, and these cases are not exceptions. Therefore, although we will use both analogies, we must now consider some points at which these analogies break down.

In the case of the strike in labor disputes, both sides are likely to recognize their absolute need for each other, and this basic community of interest will tend to dominate the negotiations. There will be no attempt by one side to eliminate the other. In fact, no strategy that envisages a great possibility of grievous harm to the other side is likely to be acceptable. Thus, while we will point out later that "familial" considerations may play an important part in escalation situations, the strike analogy probably overstates the shared sense of a community of interests in international conflict.

In the "chicken" analogy, the difficulty is the exact opposite. This involves no give-and-take bargaining. There are no natural pauses or stops, or even partial damage—only all-out collisions. Even more important, the primary objective of the game is the total humiliation of the opponent. There can be no possibility of compromise or face saving.

In international relations, escalation is used to facilitate negotiations or to put pressure on one side or both to settle a dispute without war. If either side wanted a war, it would simply go to war and not bother to negotiate. For this reason, the common observation that "neither side wants war" is not particularly startling, even though it is often delivered with an air of revealed truth. Neither side is willing to back down, precisely because it believes or hopes it can achieve its objectives without war. It may be willing to run some risk of war to achieve its objective, but it feels that the other side will back down or compromise before the risk becomes very large.

"Chicken" would be a better analogy to escalation if it were played with two cars starting an unknown distance apart, traveling toward each other at unknown speeds, and on roads with several forks so that the opposing sides are not certain that they are even on the same road. Both drivers should be giving and receiving threats and promises while they approach each other, and tearful mothers and stern fathers should be lining the sides of the roads urging, respectively, caution and manliness.

There is another way in which escalation differs from these analogies. In escalation situations, both sides understand that they are likely to play repeatedly. Therefore (as discussed below), "systems bargaining" is important. Neither side wishes to gain an advantage at the cost of creating a psychological or political situation that will make eruption probable on the next play. Indeed, both sides may become anxious to work out some acceptable methods of adjudicating the game or to adopt general rules embodying some principles of equity or fairness. In fact, both sides may become so interested in getting such rules of procedure or rules of adjudication accepted that either side might be willing to lose a particular issue occasionally simply because trying to win that issue would set a precedent that would reduce the applicability of the basic rules.

In any case, the balance of terror is likely to work well enough to induce some degree of restraint and prudent behavior on each side. Precisely because both sides recognize that deterrence strategies are unstable, they are likely to refrain from testing the stability of the situation too often or too intensely, and to avoid the kind of behavior that might provoke an imprudent response from the other side. Both sides will understand that a strategy of deterrence requires the support of precedents and depends on widely understood and observed thresholds if it is to be reliable for any length of time.

One may still ask why we are buying this time. Why don't we settle these matters now, without running such great risks? Unfortunately, in this respect, the situation is much like the "chicken" and strike analogies. There is no reason, in principle, why manufacturers and workers should not be able to reach settlements without threatening or undergoing the great mutual harm of the strike. But, unfortunately, if either side desperately desires to make a settlement without harm or risk of harm, it is likely to get a very bad bargain. In fact, if one side does this repeatedly, it is possible that both sides might suffer harm: the manufacturer might go bankrupt through repeated concessions, or the workers might receive such low wages that they would be forced to leave the industry. The analogy in escalation would be to one side or the other becoming rigid or desperate as a reaction after having made repeated concessions, even though these were made in the hope of conciliation. In the absence of accepted or compulsory peaceful methods of adjudication, both sides must be willing either to escalate or to endure the settlements imposed upon them.

Thus, even if a nation is not willing to run great risks to achieve positive national goals and objectives, it may be willing to run great risks in order to prevent disasters or costly imposed settlements. In general, it is easier for a community to agree on what it is against, even if it cannot agree on what it is for. But we need alternatives other than all-out spasm war or peace at any price—i.e., war or surrender.

Conceding all the above, we see that the probability of war eventually occurring as a result of "chicken" being played once too often may be very high. In particular, in any long period of peace, there may be a tendency for governments to become more intransigent as the thought of war becomes unreal. This may be the case especially if there is a background of experiences in which those who stood firm did well, while those who were "reasonable" seemed to do poorly. After a while, the hypothetical danger of war may look less real than the tangible gains and the prestige that are being won and lost. It may turn out that governments learn only after peace has failed that it is not feasible to stand firm on incompatible positions. Today there is reason to hope that we can reduce the dangers of the game of "chicken" by considering carefully how wars might start and how they might be fought. Thus, our serious study of escalation. But escalation obviously is dangerous. Unless workable arrangements are made for effective adjudication, someone may play the international analogue of this game once too often. To rely even on slow, rung-by-rung escalation in international crises is a dangerous strategy.

No nation wishes to play the game of "chicken" in the same spirit as teenagers play it. One major alternative is to have sufficient capabilities on the lower escalation levels so that the opponent is not tempted to play even a limited game of "chicken." One side must not be given reason to believe that he can outdo the other in low-level escalations since this might tempt him to risk such escalations in the belief that the other side will capitulate before it escalates higher. And indeed the alternative to having significant capabilities for low-level escalation is to make sufficiently credible threats of going higher. However, there is a temptation to rely on this tactic too heavily, and it may be well to remind ourselves that in dealing with violence there is a tendency in the United States to take strong moral stands and then, because we have defined the issue as a moral one, to make excessive threats and take excessive risks.

It is because of this tendency that I have been so blunt in referring to the use of threats of escalation as playing or intending to play some version of the game of "chicken." To the extent that we are serious, or to the extent that our pretense creates seriousness, we will have to face the consequences of being on the escalation ladder. And when one competes in risk-taking, one is taking risks. If one takes risks, one may be unlucky and lose the gamble. It may be that, unilaterally or bilaterally, we should agree not to play the game of "chicken." This could be encouraged (as discussed below) by increasing the instrumental, agonistic, or familial restraints against eruption, thus converting escalation into something more like a labor strike, and by reducing the role of escalation threats in settling international disputes. But there are likely to be limits as to how far we can go in this direction.

Sources of Control and Cooperation in International Society

This book deals mostly with the "political" use of force, although we will also consider the military uses of political techniques. The potential, as well as the actual, uses of force in both peace and war can be for the purposes of defense, denial, punishment, destruction, warning, bargaining, fining, deterrence, and so on. We will examine all these possibilities, giving primary attention to the threat or reality of force or coercion as a factor in negotiation.

Thus, I will be looking at the international order from a rather specialized and technical point of view. This focus will cause my consideration of international order to have many distortions, and biases, since factors that regulate international behavior other than force, coercion, and threat will be slighted.

We can, for example, distinguish the following aspects of national conduct in trying to study the behavior of nations in conflict: (1) contractual, (2) coercive, (3) agonistic, (4) stylistic, and (5) familial. For the purposes of this book, we can think of these as rough, overlapping categories or as different aspects of a unified whole. It would be much too ambitious to try here to define the above terms in such depth and clarity as to resolve all the conceptual and semantic difficulties, but a brief discussion is appropriate and useful.

The first two aspects, contractual and coercive, involve *instrumental* motivations—narrow considerations of profit and loss. Contract, of course, involves the *quid pro quo* exchange of promise and benefits. A coercive relationship can also be considered as a *quid pro quo* exchange, but now it is an exchange of threats and punishments. A threat can be regarded as a negative promise: Unless you do so and so, I promise to hurt you; or if you do not do so and so, I promise not to hurt you. For our purposes, it seems better to separate instrumental motivations and exchanges into the more or less artificially distinguished areas of contractual and coercive dealings.

The contractual concept is particularly consistent with American and Anglo-Saxon traditions of civil law, public life, and business. *Quid pro quo* is an eminently reasonable basis on which to conduct affairs if there is no special reason to do otherwise. While Americans tend to believe that it is useful and important to have friendly personal relations among potential contractors, they recognize that there is no absolute necessity for such special relationships. In American culture, even two very hostile people can arrive at a mutually beneficial agreement—one in which there is an adequate compromise between advantage and disadvantage—and yet remain hostile after the agreement has been concluded. Indeed, many of the approaches to arms control in the West that de-emphasize political aspects and concentrate on technical issues are pursuing a strictly contractual point of view—one that may not be as practical as it appears, since these contracts are so difficult to negotiate.[6] If

[6] Arms-controllers sometimes do not realize how difficult. For example: Assume there are two individuals who are going to fight a duel to death with blow torches. The duel is to be conducted in a warehouse filled with dynamite. One might conjecture that they could agree to leave the lights on. There is undoubtedly powerful motivation for them to do so. While both are agreed that only one is to survive, they would each like some chance of being that one; neither prefers an effective certainty of both being killed. Yet they might still disagree on: How many lights? Where? How bright? Should the one with greater visual acuity handicap himself in other ways? And so on.

In short, despite urgent and overwhelming reasons for agreement, the basic animosity may make it impossible for the two to agree on details and then arrive at a "contract."

the two sides are relatively hostile or suspicious, the advantages and disadvantages are much harder to balance.

Coercive bargaining is the negative aspect of the same continuum since, as we have noted, it involves threats and violence. It uses dissuasion as opposed to persuasion, the stick as opposed to the carrot.

Most Americans are not entirely comfortable with the concept of "cool," or businesslike, negotiations in an atmosphere of some degree of physical threat or coercion. For the most part, they do not consciously assign to force any rational or reasonable role in "ordinary" negotiations. In the recent past (except in the case of "just" revolutions), we have tended to the view that only a criminal or a sick or insane person initiates the use of force. Therefore, we are inclined to believe that someone who uses force is not only our enemy, but an enemy of humanity—an outlaw who deserves extermination, imprisonment, or medical constraint and treatment. The "crusade," and even an initial pacifism as well, comes more naturally to Americans than the kind of cool, restrained, and moderate willingness to threaten or use force that will be suggested in this book.

The common American attitude toward force is somewhat naïve. Force is a permanent element in human society, used by good, bad, and indifferent nations and people. It has been used rationally as well as irrationally, wisely as well as foolishly, moderately as well as extravagantly, virtuously as well as maliciously. Even if we unreasonably or even immorally institute the use of force, coercion, violence, and threats, it is entirely possible to go on to use these things in a reasonable fashion. At least there is no inevitable necessity to use them in a wildly unreasonable or reckless fashion.

There are thus two traditional American biases: an unwillingness to initiate the use of moderate levels of force for limited objectives, and a too-great willingness, once committed, to use extravagant and uncontrolled force. Both biases are potentially dangerous and should be guarded against. They could have most serious consequences unless we deliberately and consciously think about ways in which violence may occur and still be kept relatively limited.

The other three aspects of international conflict in our list—agonistic, stylistic, and familial—particularly the first two, can be thought of as cultural factors. I will use the word "agonistic"[7] to cover prescriptive behavior in a somewhat wider sense than usual. While instrumental behavior can be thought of as a calculated act committed in order to gain access to values (which may or may not be controlled or influenced by one's opponent or partner in conflicts and negotiations), agonistic behavior can be thought of as "decent" or correct behavior between partners or opponents who act in accordance with the "rules of the game," whatever their instrumental or emotional motivations may be.

I am probably stretching the word "agonistic" to make it cover almost all behavior in which such factors as custom, precedent, sense of fairness, religious injunctions, and codes of conduct or of *noblesse oblige* or chivalry affect actions strongly, but no other word seems as appropriate. Much behavior is regulated by such normative influences and ideals, even among the most cynical or depraved.

Thus, particularly when the opponents or partners are of the same culture or respect common cultural values, even if they are representative of quite different societies, the existence of these common bonds and values can make it possible for conflicts and negotiations to be carried out as a "contest" or "game" (i.e., according to more or less absolute rules). Because of the common respect for the values that neither can control, both sides accept restraint and regulation. These values (customs, morals, laws, codes of honor, etc.) can transcend any conflicts, no matter how desperate or bitter.

Occasionally, of course, the rules may be transgressed. But, paradoxically, both opponents may have instrumental reasons for preserving agonistic restraints and are likely to recognize that if the customs, laws, and codes are transgressed too often, the system will disappear. Thus, even if they are not willing to obey the rules blindly, if they value the system, this instrumental reinforcement of the agonistic motivation can greatly strengthen the force and reliability of the code. In any case, both sides are likely to be willing to accept large disasters or lose great opportunities for gain rather

[7] It seems to have been first used in much this way by Hans Speier, in his *Social Order and the Risks of War* (New York: George W. Stewart, 1952), p. 255.

than transgress or risk certain systems or codes. Therefore, what is sometimes called "systems bargaining" contains both instrumental and agonistic considerations.

"Systems bargaining" is used here as a general expression for situations in which all or almost all members of a system would be better off if every individual abided by certain rules. It is a characteristic of such situations that while all members would be worse off if the rules were generally broken, individual members of the system could gain great individual advantages by breaking them, provided that this were not done by too many other members of the system. That is, from the viewpoint of any individual, A, who is making purely selfish calculations, situations are usually preferred in the following order:

1. A "cheats," but nobody else is induced to cheat by his example.
2. A cheats, and only very few are induced to cheat by his example.
3. Nobody cheats.
4. Others cheat, but if A were to join them, this particular precedent would endanger the stability of the system, so A does not cheat.
5. Everybody cheats.
6. Everybody cheats but A.

In some sense, all human societies contain elements of such systems and are concerned with seeing to it that desirable rules and standards are generally obeyed. Various societies have achieved adequate degrees of conformity, unity, and discipline by different combinations of all five of the motivations we have listed. But almost invariably there is a good deal of familial, agonistic, and stylistic influence even in societies whose main emphasis is on instrumental motivations—on contractual and coercive behavior— and vice versa.

There is thus, typically, a mixture of agonistic, familial, and instrumental considerations in the attainment and maintenance of any systems bargaining. In particular, large nations with a great stake in the *status quo* may find it instrumentally useful to attempt to conserve and extend agonistic constraints. Unfortunately, agonistic rules, no matter how sacred or prized, cannot be relied upon to be observed by all peoples at all times. A large *status quo* nation may therefore, along with its interest in "conservative" behavior, be concerned about the possibility of accepting disastrous unilateral handicaps. It can and perhaps should be prepared to live with some cheating, but may also consider it necessary to be prepared to modify its own norms to some degree, even though such readiness may in itself weaken these norms despite the absence of "provocation."

In addition to rules followed as moral injunctions, there are rules, traditions, or patterns that are followed simply because they seem appropriate or proper or are satisfying in various ways, but which do not have moral force behind them. We will refer to these behavior patterns as "stylistic." They are related to or are part of what is sometimes thought of as culture, national character, national style, and the like.

Such stylistic questions can be important. Throughout history, wise men have attempted to "know" themselves and their enemies (where the term "know" referred as much to style and personal characteristics as to equipment and capabilities). An early manual on this subject, which illustrates extremely well what we mean by "style," was prepared by the tenth-century Emperor Leo of Byzantium. This manual discussed the style and capabilities of the various enemies of the Byzantine Empire. C. W. C. Oman[8] quotes Leo's assessment of the Franks, the West European opponents of Byzantium:

> The Frank believes that a retreat under any circumstances must be dishonorable; hence he will fight whenever you choose to offer him battle. This you must not do until you have secured all possible advantages for yourself, as his cavalry, with their long lances and large shields, charge with a tremendous impetus. You should deal with him by protracting the campaign, and if possible lead him into the hills, where his cavalry are less efficient than in the plain. After a few weeks without a great battle his troops, who are very susceptible to fatigue and weariness, will grow tired of the war, and ride home in great numbers. . . .

[8] *The Art of War in the Middle Ages: A.D. 378-1515* (Ithaca, N.Y.: Cornell University Press, 1960), p. 34.

You will find him utterly careless as to outposts and reconnaissances, so that you can easily cut off outlying parties of his men, and attack his camp at advantage. As his forces have no bonds of discipline, but only those of kindred or oath, they fall into confusion after delivering their charge; you can therefore simulate flight, and then turn on them, when you will find them in utter disarray. On the whole, however, it is easier and less costly to wear out a Frankish army by skirmishes and protracted operations rather than to attempt to destroy it at a single blow.

In part, the first paragraph, at least, still holds as an appraisal of the Western (European and American) style of war. It is also interesting to note what Oman had to say about the Byzantine style:

One of its most striking points is the utter difference of its tone from that of contemporary feeling in the rest of Christendom. Of chivalry there is not a spark in the Byzantine, though professional pride is abundantly shown. Courage is regarded as one of the requisites necessary for obtaining success, not as the sole and paramount virtue of the warrior. Leo considers a campaign successfully concluded without a great battle as the cheapest and most satisfactory consummation in war. He has no respect for the warlike ardor which makes men eager to plunge into the fray; it is to him rather a characteristic of the ignorant barbarian, and an attribute fatal to anyone who makes any pretension to generalship.

He shows a strong predilection for stratagems, ambushes, and simulated retreats. For an officer who fights without having first secured all the advantages to his own side, he has the greatest contempt. It is with a kind of intellectual pride that he gives instructions how *parlementaires* are to be sent to the enemy without any real object except that of spying out the number and efficiency of his forces. He gives, as a piece of most ordinary and moral advice, the hint that a defeated general may often find time to execute a retreat by sending an emissary to propose a surrender (which he has no intention of carrying out) to the hostile commander. He is not above employing the old-world trick of addressing treasonable letters to the subordinate officers of the enemy's army, and contriving that they should fall into the hands of the commander-in-chief, in order that he may be made suspicious of his lieutenants. Schemes such as these are "Byzantine" in the worst sense of the word, but their character must not be allowed to blind us to the real and extraordinary merits of the strategical system into which they have been inserted. The art of war, as understood at Constantinople in the tenth century, was the only scheme of true scientific merit existing in the world, and was unrivaled till the sixteenth century.[9]

I must add, even if reluctantly, that these lines suggest to me a certain empathy or identity between these ancient Byzantines and the modern systems analyst, even though large portions of the Byzantine philosophy must be rejected. The Byzantine attitude of professionalization without heroics, in particular, seems far and away the most reasonable position to be adopted in the latter half of the twentieth century.

The last motivational category, familial, includes both instrumental and cultural aspects. It occurs when there is a sense of love, good will, community, shared fate, or basic common interests and goals among negotiators or rivals.

The familial context is a normal and comfortable one for Americans. Such considerations play a large role in the American political viewpoint and even in national-interest calculations. Indeed, familial considerations usually exist in any negotiations among nations, even those with very different national characteristics. Today they seem to be acquiring a larger role in international relations. For example, there is now a widespread understanding that the rich and better developed countries have an obligation to help the poorer and less developed ones, and, to a lesser extent, that the powerful must protect and defend the weak.

Most important of all, there is a widespread consensus about the necessity for controlling force and weapons of mass destruction. To a startling extent, the "arms race" has been pictured as a common enemy that promotes among those threatened a sense of community.

These five terms—contractual, coercive, agonistic, stylistic, and familial—can be used to describe either objectives or tactics. Rather than characterizing separate and distinct categories, they describe different elements which can be blended in different ways. While they do not lend themselves to sharp and firm distinctions, they are still convenient to use.

[9] *Ibid.,* pp. 43–44.

The Question of Who, Whom, and Why

In a more complete discussion of the role of force in international affairs, we would tend to ask a question like the following: . . . *Who* deters, influences, coerces, or blocks *whom* from what *actions* (*alternatives*), by what *threats* and *counteractions* in what *situations,* in the face of what *counterthreats* and *counter-counteractions?* . . . And why does he do it? This is a paraphrase of a comment by Raymond Aron,[10] who was trying to illustrate the richness and complexity of the deterrence concept. The ellipses have deliberately been inserted to indicate that there are many other things going on before, during, and after the time being examined. It is only by examining all these aspects that one can explain many real situations. For example, we may consider several recent situations in which one side enjoyed a clear military superiority over its opponent, but for various political or other reasons did not, could not, or would not use its military superiority to impose its will, although a narrow calculation of the force relationships clearly indicated that to do so was within its power.

It should be clear from the following examples that mere military superiority will not necessarily assure "escalation dominance." Escalation dominance is a complex concept in which the military calculations are only one element. Other elements are the assurance, morale, commitment, resolve, internal discipline, and so on, of both the principals and their allies. This does not mean that pure calculations of force capabilities and abstract escalation tactics might not determine the result of a given situation, or that, at other times, while they might not be as important as the specific and "characterological" aspects of the conflict, they might not nevertheless influence the situation in very important ways.

[10] Aron's original comment appeared in *Survival* (published by the Institute for Strategic Studies, London), January–February, 1963, p. 40. It can be translated from the French as: "Who deters whom, from what actions, by what threats . . . in what circumstances?" We have expanded this relationship among four variables to one that involves a dozen or so to emphasize the continuing nature of the relationship (such as the effects of counterthreats and counter-counteractions) and the importance of motivation.

Some Examples of the Importance of Who, Whom, and Why

The Soviet Union certainly has the military power today to over-whelm Albania, a state whose defiance has been a serious embarrass-ment to Soviet policy. The Soviet Union also has military domi-nance over China. The United States has the power to invade Cuba and overthrow the Castro government. The Soviet Union had the sheer power to invade Yugoslavia and depose Tito in 1948, when he defected from Cominform policy. In 1945, the Soviets possessed the power to annex all of Finland, something they had attempted after the 1917 Revolution and again in the "winter war" of 1939-40. The Soviets also had the power to invade Poland in 1956, when the October uprising took place.

The British and French Suez expedition of 1956, in conjunction with the Israeli invasion of the Sinai Peninsula, had the potential power to take over the Suez Canal and occupy Cairo, and it was reasonably clear at the time that the Soviet Union, despite the heavily qualified warnings it issued, would not have effectively intervened militarily on behalf of the Egyptians. In all the colonial conflicts that have taken place in the decade and a half since World War II, there has hardly been one in which the colonial power did not have the physical power, or at least the potential physical power, to suppress indefinitely the nationalist movement or uprising.

Finally, the United States had the power to expel Chinese forces from Korea in 1953. It could have invaded Iraq in 1958 to restore a pro-Western government that had been overthrown by a Com-munist-supported revolution. Today it has the power to conquer North Vietnam.

In none of these cases—and they are by no means the only ones that could be mentioned—did the militarily dominant power act on the basis of its military capabilities alone, although in each case it was presented with a threat or challenge of significant character. These states could not use their physical superiority to achieve escalation dominance; they were restrained by such inhibitions as fear of disproportionate costs or excessive involvements, partic-ularly fear of great-power involvement or further escalations, by moral (or agonistic) qualms, and so on. It is clear that there are many cases in which the who-whom-why and the situation-alterna-tive analyses cannot be fully isolated, even in a narrowly technical discussion of the escalation possibilities, and even less in a discussion focused on the restraints and thresholds that are inherent in any escalation situation.

Any analysis that tries to treat the who-whom-why and situation-alternative questions as seriously or as well as the actions, threats, counteractions, and counterthreats (and counter counters) is, of course, going to be very complex indeed. Much of the seeming artificiality and abstractness of this book comes from the fact that I will necessarily tend to ignore or de-emphasize the who-whom-why aspects, consider only briefly situations and alternatives, and focus most attention on actions, threats, and counters. As a result, some considerations and possibilities will appear unmotivated and unrealistic, but this is inevitable in a relatively technical document whose aim is to focus attention on some of the less discussed aspects of the use of force and coercion. And while I will try to avoid discussing "academic," logical, but unrealistic possibilities, I will tend toward discussion of possibilities *as* possibilities, without giving full attention to their credibility or likelihood.

Thus, in many cases, I will ask the reader to suspend disbelief while I talk about these possibilities, and, after he has considered the range of things that could happen (a range much larger than what has already occurred or is usually thought of), to judge the importance of an awareness of these possibilities and to make his own decision as to their likelihood. I am trying to concentrate on relatively general principles, more or less true for all the interactions of escalation and negotiation in which a fear of further escalation and a desire not to set undesirable precedents or to weaken desirable restraints are present.

Let us consider two examples—a historical one from World War II and a typical artificial scenario in which the interaction between who-whom-why factors and "more objective" factors is well illustrated—and then I will go on to abstract and general considerations.

An Example of Restraint and Negotiation in Total War (World War II)

World War II usually is regarded as a virtually total conflict. While it is generally remembered that poison gas and bacteriological weapons were not used, these limits upon the maximum use of the belligerents' destructive capabilities are usually cited as great exceptions to the general rule of the war. Relatively little notice has been taken of the restraints on the use of conventional high-explosive and incendiary bombs in aerial bombardment in Europe, restraints that remained in effect for a notably long time after the start of the war. Actually, the war was in many ways limited, and a great deal of implicit and some explicit bargaining and negotiation went on during its course. The limitations existed despite the fact that the intention of both sides was to devote all possible resources to the effort.

In considering this example of limitations and negotiations in World War II, I will rely heavily on an article by George Quester.[11] Before the war, the French and British (at least) were committed to the airpower theory of the "knockout blow"—which held that bombing could rapidly and decisively knock a country out of a war. Mr. Quester describes the September, 1939–May, 1940, or so-called "phony war," period:

> Despite many dire prewar predictions of a total conflict leaving no sanctuary for civilian populations, and despite the existence of a German force of over 1,100, bombing aircraft and of an Anglo-French force of approximately 1,000, the opening rounds of the Second World War witnessed no bombing raids at all on the populated areas of Germany, Britain, or France.
>
> On the first day of the war, September 1, 1939, President Roosevelt had addressed an appeal to the belligerent powers for a restriction of aerial warfare to strictly military targets, the formal acceptance of which appeal was announced on the 2nd by the Allies, and on the 18th of September by the German government. Yet all evidence indicates that orders to this effect had been issued to each of the air forces in question even before the appeal.[12]

[11] "Bargaining and Bombing During World War II in Europe," *World Politics,* April, 1963. Excerpts reprinted by permission.

[12] One can easily imagine that if there were ever again a formal declaration of war, as is suggested later, a similar plea might be made and accepted. Today's potential belligerents are no less fearful than Germany, England, and France were of the potential effects of unrestricted strategic bombing. (H. K.)

During the German September campaign in Poland, the Luftwaffe was used primarily in close support of army units, or in attacks on the airstrips of the Polish Air Force. A series of attacks was carried out on Warsaw itself in the first week of the war, and again in the final siege of the city, but orders were issued to all crews in the first raids to aim with care at bridges and communications targets, and the bombings of the final siege were explained by the Germans as close tactical support against resisting enemy positions.

Whatever the implications of the Polish campaign, German operations in the West were limited to reconnaissance flights and to mine laying and attacks on coastal shipping. Orders to the Luftwaffe in this early period were so strict as to preclude almost any attack which would be likely to result in bombs falling on British or French soil. Allied bombers, similarly restricted, conducted only reconnaissance missions, some leaflet raids, and a few attacks on ships and bases of the German fleet. Even the raids made against naval shore bases on both sides were limited to targets well isolated from populated areas.

The German invasion of Norway in April 1940 saw a use in that country of both bomber forces, again in a tactical role. No expansion of the air war in the West was to occur, however, until the invasion of the Low Countries on May 10, more than eight months after the outbreak of the war.

For these first eight months, then, the exemption from air attack applied not only to the capital cities of Berlin, London, and Paris, but to all other populated areas of the three countries, however close to military or industrial targets. . . .

Allied offensive attacks did not promise to save London and Paris, defensive measures seemed able to help these cities only to a slight degree, and *the holding of German population centers as intact hostages appeared to be the sole possible means of sparing them.* [Italics added.] The British and French governments therefore saw the gains of restraint, the avoidance of horrible destruction to their cities, as outweighing the costs, the missed opportunities for a strategic weakening of Germany; no reversal of this option was to take effect until May 1940.

The German decision, on the other hand, to hold back the Luftwaffe in 1939 stemmed from calculations quite different from those of Chamberlain and Daladier. . . .

Hitler was nevertheless very anxious to avoid any bombing of Germany at all, not for fear of the total breakdown envisaged in London and Paris, but because of his personal desire to spare Germany all possible wartime hardship, and because of a fear that the enthusiasm of the German people for his regime might not survive the rigors of war. . . .

Much of Mr. Quester's discussion of the developing scale of air warfare is summarized in Figure 2, making use of terms drawn from this book and from strategic discussions generally. As indicated in the first eight months (the "phony war"), the central sanctuaries of both sides were almost meticulously observed. (Technically, raids on isolated naval shore bases did violate the central sanctuaries, and if they had been conducted with nuclear weapons, or had even been very large conventional raids, we would say today that the central sanctuary had been violated by a "constrained force reduction salvo" or "constrained exemplary central attack," but the actual raids were so small and tactically oriented that the sanctuaries may be regarded as essentially unviolated.) The tactical operations carried out by the German Air Force in the Polish and Norwegian campaigns were done in such a manner as to avoid collateral damage to civilians as much as was practical.

The war heated up on June 10, 1940, with the invasion of the Low Countries, and on June 15 the Germans destroyed a considerable portion of Rotterdam. The German Government argued that this was a justifiable attack upon military targets in a defended town (and thus did not constitute a change in the air-war policy). But German propagandists attempted to exploit the shock of the event and to emphasize the power of Germany's air arm by publicizing the attack as a terror raid. This attempt to have it both ways (with the propagandists' statements running counter to the official explanations) succeeded in obscuring the limits the Germans believed themselves to be observing—obscuring them, in fact, for many Germans as well as for the Allied governments and populations. The Rotterdam attack was generally understood as an arbitrary terror attack upon civilians. Mr. Quester describes the situation as follows:

> The German restraints observed throughout the campaign in the Low Countries and France demonstrated a continuing German desire to impress distinctions on the Allies which would prevent a heavy assault on German cities—a desire which at times however was crossed

FIGURE 2

ANGLO-GERMAN WORLD WAR II ESCALATION

Phase	German Actions	British Actions
"Phony war" (September 1, 1939– May 9, 1940)	Central sanctuary "observed" Tactical symbolic attacks	Central sanctuary "observed" Tactical symbolic attacks
Poland and Norway	Tactical bombing with avoidance	
Defeat of France	A noncentral exemplary attack Counterforce with avoidance	Strategic with avoidance
Air-superiority battle	Counterforce with avoidance Limited strategic with avoidance	Strategic with avoidance
Aerial blitz (1940)		
a. August 24–September 6	Strategic with avoidance	Exemplary reprisal plus
b. September 7–October 29	Strategic	Strategic
c. October 31–December 11	Strategic	Augmented strategic
d. December 11 on	Strategic	Countervalue
Lull	Precise reprisals	Experiments
One-sided eruption		
a. 1942	Exemplary reprisals ("Baedeker raids")	Selective . . .
b. 1943–45	Countervalue devastation and exemplary reprisals	Countervalue devastation, strategic and counterforce

by the irresponsibility of German propaganda agencies, and by the inherent haziness of the distinction between tactical and strategic operations.

It was the case, moreover, that Hitler again had high hopes of negotiating an end to the war with Britain after the defeat of France, and that he hoped to make such a settlement easier by showing restraints in his conduct of the campaign. It was possible that the possession of intact cities might make the British feel that they had more to gain by a peace. The restraints shown in the sparing of French cities similarly served to give the French a stake in an early surrender, a stake which the Luftwaffe could easily deny them if it desired, but which would be retained by a speedy French capitulation.

The extreme British fears of a "knockout blow" had however been considerably moderated over the period of September 1939 to May 1940, as civil defense and air defense preparations in the United Kingdom began to show some progress, as newer and more sober estimates were made of the nature of aerial bombardment, as new perils arising for Britain tended to reduce the relative importance of the aerial threat, and as Winston Churchill replaced Chamberlain as the British Prime Minister.

A segment of the RAF Air Staff moreover still felt (as it had before the war) that significant results might be achieved by a precision assault on a few "key" targets in Germany; these planners had continued to press for permission to begin such an offensive, to put Bomber Command to some use at last. The fate of Rotterdam and the ambiguity of German declarations about this instance of bombing moreover reduced British prospects of being forever spared; in view of the German successes on the ground, it was felt that it might, in fact, be advantageous to bait the Luftwaffe onto military targets in Britain (thus easing pressure on the forces in France, and bringing to action those RAF fighter squadrons which had in any event to be held in Britain).

For all these reasons, the order to commence a program of "precision" night bombings of military and industrial targets in Germany was given on May 15. The British had not yet lost all hope of being spared severe bombardment of their cities, nor had they decided to end all their self-restraints; the prospect of German bombardment had merely become a less terrifying one, while the hope of avoiding it was no longer as bright, thereby making lesser British restraints now seem appropriate. The exemption of Berlin from attack was still maintained, in hope that London might yet be spared and in face of the physical disadvantages of long-range strikes against eastern Germany. While it was thought necessary to attack by night to avoid high casualties, it was still intended that target discrimination would be practiced; the extent to which inaccuracies at night would weaken this distinction in the eyes of the attacked country was not appreciated (an error which was to be repeated by both sides at several more critical points in the exchange of blows).

Until the very surrender, the French government still lived in real terror of the fate that might befall its undefended and unprepared cities, and the British raids on Germany throughout the campaign were conducted against French desires. *The projected raids against northern Italy were thus forcibly stopped by the French to prevent a feared massive Italian retaliation against Nice and Marseilles.* [Italics added.]

According to Mr. Quester, there were a number of mistakes made in interpretation of the motivations and capabilities of each side. He argues that in the summer and fall of 1941:

Bomber Command's offensive . . . had been limited in size and scope only by technical capacity; yet the British inability to mount severe raids into Germany in fact led Hitler to see supplementary advantages in the restricted air activity imposed on him by the Russian campaign. It is likely that Hitler saw himself as the beneficiary of voluntary British restraints during the latter portion of 1941, and that he was in fact overestimating the technical ability of the RAF to mount an offensive at this time. Luftwaffe assaults on Britain in late 1941 were limited to reprisal attacks designed to give an impression of precise reciprocity for British raids on Germany, and thereby perhaps to continue a deterrence of such raids.

There is no evidence to indicate that the Luftwaffe lull or the reprisal raids had any actual deterring effect on the British leadership. German radio broadcasts about "reprisal raids" were often interpreted simply as morale boosters for the German people, while the lull in the Luftwaffe attack on Britain was attributed entirely to a German overcommitment to the Russian front. The possibility that the Germans were (or would be) exercising restraints was given little credence, and the failure of the RAF to go over completely to area bombing was due only to a few lingering uncertainties as to the form of attack offering the greatest practical results.

One of the most interesting tactics, from our point of view, was that initiated by the Luftwaffe on April 14 with a series of reprisal raids calculated to inflict maximum shock on the British population. These raids were designed to be dramatic retaliations for British attacks and did not provide the Germans with any direct military advantages. Towns of great historical and cultural importance but little or no military or industrial value were hit. These "Baedeker raids"[13] continued into the summer of 1942, but their significance as more or less specific retaliations for various British raids was never understood by the British public. Rather, these attacks were taken as especially malevolent acts by the Nazis—simple manifestations of brutality—and the effect was to strengthen rather than weaken British morale and assurance.

Mr. Quester's article concludes:

> In the early stages of the Second World War a long series of limits to aerial warfare was proposed on both sides, by word and, often more significantly, by deed. Of these, some were accepted, some were not recognized, and some were rejected. Rated roughly in order of stringency (although not in order of precision or intelligibility), they ran: "no air raids at all," "air raids only on targets away from civilian population," "attacks only on tactical targets," "attacks only on military and industrial targets, by day," "the same by night," and "no raids on national capitals."
>
> The extent to which the mutual recognition of such limits was due to prior deliberations and declarations is not easy to determine. Various proposals for rules of aerial warfare had been put forward (but never ratified) at the Hague in 1923, and at the Washington Disarmament Conferences, generally making only the distinction, however, between "strictly military" targets and targets close to civilians, which were not, therefore, "strictly military." Hitler himself had in 1935 proposed limits to the areas open to aerial bombing, such as the area of "tactical combat" or, more specifically, the area within the range of both sides' artillery; at other times the Führer alluded to a total abolition of aerial bombing to be agreed to by all sides.
>
> Yet while the "words" of the prewar period may account for the general intelligibility and acceptability of certain distinctions of limitation, others, such as "no capital cities," were simply *evolved in practice*, being communicated and accepted by "deeds." [Italics added.]

[13] So called after the well-known traveler's guidebook.

It is probably fair to say that Nazi Germany had an interest in limits on aerial warfare for a longer period than did the Allies. For reasons of genuine lack of opportunity, or for failure to see opportunity, the German leadership did not count on winning its war by aerial bombardment, and with its strong aversion to domestic austerity it preferred a limited air war instead. It may be the case that Germany could not have overcome the handicap in aircraft development and production imposed prior to 1935 by the Versailles Treaty, without giving up the heavy bomber; it may also be true that Germany completely missed the significance of the bomber. In any event, Germany desired limits; but, unfortunately for the Germans, their bargaining for such limits was poorly executed in several respects.

German propaganda under Goebbels was not fully harnessed to the task of communicating the nation's intent; Luftwaffe complaints of misinterpretations and distortions of its campaigns were recurrent, and on crucial questions of fine distinction, such as Warsaw and Rotterdam, broadcasts threatening other cities with similar imminent fates served to undermine the general German purpose. *The deliberate prewar tendency (in pursuit of lesser objectives) to threaten all-out air attack if German wishes were not granted, similarly made ambiguous the wartime German intention to abstain from such attack except in retaliation.* [Italics added.]

Beyond the distortions of propaganda, however, the Germans *chose rather incautiously at several points to interpret borderline opportunities in their own favor,* opportunities which might not appear so "tactical" or "strictly military" to the other side. [Italics added.] For a nation as averse to bombing as Germany, the severity of the final raid on Warsaw and the dive-bomber attack on Rotterdam were precarious moves, as was the decision to add a night offensive against Britain, based, as it was, on a serious overestimate of bombing accuracy.

Thirdly, if the Germans really hoped thus to limit the war, it would seem that a careful measure of the values of the opponent should have been taken before threatening its very existence. While France proved willing to surrender before expanding the air war, Britain preferred, under Churchill, to drop limits when the national existence was threatened, and when a dropping of such limits offered a contribution to survival. By threatening to invade Britain, Germany exposed herself further to air assault.

Finally, to the extent that a German ability to limit the war depended on inflated foreign beliefs in the awesome capabilities of the

Luftwaffe, it was unwise to demonstrate how limited these capabilities were. It seems very likely, for instance, that if the British had known what the Blitz would be like, they would not in 1939 have been restrained by fear of a "knockout blow."

The severity of the later Allied air offensive came as a surprise to Hitler, although it was still not a "knockout blow." Perhaps the German aversion to air attack would indeed have been fortified if there had been foreknowledge of its actual severity, and perhaps the bargaining for limits might then have been conducted with more care. As it was, the Germans did seek limits fairly consistently, but also quite ineptly.

Thus, the restraints and limitations that were observed in World War II were more often unplanned or even inadvertent than calculated, and there were fewer of them than might be expected today. Throughout the war, one side or the other was generally so grossly inferior to the other in strategic air power that there not only was no equality of threat, but the absolute level of threat on the inferior side was relatively low. While the inequality could obtain again, it is likely that the absolute level of the inferior in the nuclear future will be high enough to command respect.

We turn now to a scenario drawn from contemporary conditions. In it, no one can doubt that great devastation could be inflicted by either side.

A "Standard Crisis" Scenario

Here, in outline form, is a "standard crisis" scenario which has been used in some Hudson Institute studies. The scene is Germany, not because we believe that this currently is an unusually dangerous area of the world, but out of the conventional assumption that Germany's division is the most obvious and plausible source for a European crisis.

The following steps occur in our scenario:

1. Unrest and precipitating incident of violence in East Germany or Berlin.
2. A high level of popular agitation with street violence follows in East Germany.

3. The East-West German border (or the Berlin Wall) is opened up at various points by East German insurgents.

4. There is a limited but important degree of intervention by West German "volunteers."

5. The Soviets deliver a warning to West Germany and NATO.

6. Limited evacuations in Europe and the United States.

7. NATO replies to the Soviet warning with a warning against Soviet intervention.

8. Violence and border crossings continue, with West Germans involved in large numbers.

9. The Soviets intervene, launching a limited foray across the border or initiating other major violence, or perhaps making a nonlethal demonstration of nuclear force.

10. Further exchange of messages.

11. A cessation of or abatement in hostilities.

12. "Armistice" is violated.

13. More evacuations and the initiation of other emergency readiness programs.

14. More border crossings by both sides.

15. One side issues an ultimatum.

16. Preparation and completion of emergency readiness programs.

17. Either the Soviets make a limited attack on Western Europe, designed to display resolve and to split NATO (with the hope of gaining capitulation, or pressure for capitulation, by one of the major participants), or the U.S. makes a limited attack to deter the Soviets.

18. U.S. announcement of open cities and a city-avoidance strategy.

19. Similar NATO announcements of an open Europe west of the Rhine, with likely selective announcement of open areas in Germany.

20. Either the U.S. or the Soviets make a large counterforce strike with very careful avoidance of collateral damage, simultaneously issuing either a further ultimatum or an offer for a peace settlement.

21. . . .

This scenario needs little discussion. Many readers will doubtless find it implausible, since it is quite clear that in most circumstances this crisis would more likely be stopped at any given point in its development rather than pass on to the next point. Nevertheless, it is a conceivable development, since real or imagined technical problems, official or unofficial sabotage, defiance or unauthorized behavior, misunderstandings and miscalculations, and so on, could interfere with attempts to arrest the crisis—and there would, of course, be significant popular and political obstacles to any decision to stand aside from a "Hungary" in East Germany. It could take more political courage to stop the crisis than might be available in the crucial government offices. Indeed, there undoubtedly would be some officials who would see in the crisis as much an opportunity as a danger.

There are, of course, a large number of different ways in which this crisis could continue. Some of them are indicated below.

1. Local (pre-emptive?) surrender by either side.
2. Local (pre-emptive?) accommodation by either side.
3. Surrender or accommodation by the Soviets or NATO.
4. Revolution or disarray in NATO or the Warsaw Pact.
5. Stabilized front—cease-fire.
6. *Quid pro quo* settlement.
7. Quick restoration of *status quo ante*.
8. Sustained conventional fighting.
9. "Pause"-type conventional fighting.
10. Local victory and local retreat.
11. Short tactical nuclear war.
12. Sustained tactical nuclear war.
13. Central escalation.
14. Negotiated peace treaty.

Some of these possibilities will be discussed in later chapters.

II

The Rungs of the Escalation Ladder

A Useful Metaphor

In treating the coercive aspects of international relations, this study analyzes a spectrum of international crises and a selection of mechanisms for dealing with them. It will focus attention on the use and misuse of escalation tactics and strategies, rather than consider sustained conflict at any given level. The study will not deal with all aspects of escalation, but will focus on the escalation-ladder metaphor, a methodological device that provides a convenient list of the many options facing the strategist in a two-sided confrontation and that facilitates the examination of the growth and retardation of crises. Most important of all, the ladder indicates that there are many relatively continuous paths between a low-level crisis and an all-out war, none of which are necessarily or inexorably to be followed.

Metaphors, of course, can be misleading. Studying the ladder is supposed to stretch and stir the imagination, not confine it. Thus, I would not argue with analysts who wish to use more nuances and complexities, but I am convinced that, except for special purposes or specific situations, they should not normally try to do with fewer.

Of course, decision-makers and their immediate advisers may not have to consider a large range of alternatives in dealing with special purposes and specific situations. They may find it perfectly satisfactory to deal with a simple and limited number of options, but except for such special purposes and specific situations it is important to be aware of a full range of possibilities and considerations. As always, this makes the job of the analyst and the staff planner more difficult than that of the decision-maker in a crisis who is dealing with the special and specific and is not further handicapped by a sense of disbelief and incredulity. Hence, a decision-maker may, in a crisis, be able to invent or work out easily and quickly what seems in normal times to both the "academic" scholar and the layman to be hypothetical, unreal, complex, or otherwise difficult.

Figure 3 depicts an escalation ladder, a linear arrangement of roughly increasing levels of intensity of crisis. Such a ladder exhibits a progression of steps in what amounts to, roughly speaking, an ascending order of intensity through which a given crisis may progress. Any particular ladder is intended as an archetype that can serve as a pattern and context for the study of a certain class of international crises. Specific crises in this class do not necessarily follow any step-by-step progression and they may never escalate very far, but the escalation ladder provides a useful framework for the systematic study of the possibilities, both realized and unrealized.

I would like to emphasize again, though, that escalation ladders are metaphorical tools that have been found useful in preliminary studies of escalation. No particular ladder should be considered as being a theory of international relations, although it may be a fragment of such a theory. Its utility derives partly from its provision of a convenient list of some of the options available, and partly from its ordering of escalatory activities in a way that facilitates examination and discussion.

The escalation ladder also may be used to set a context for the discussion of escalations in terms of regions of the ladder, steps up and down the ladder, rungs of the ladder, and so forth. The ladder concept is particularly useful when one attempts to examine the interrelations between the two basic sets of elements in any escalation situation—those related to a particular region on the ladder and those related to the dynamics of moving up and down the ladder.

We will defer detailed discussion of the value of this methodo-

FIGURE 3

AN ESCALATION LADDER

A Generalized (or Abstract) Scenario

─────────────────── AFTERMATHS ───────────────────

CIVILIAN CENTRAL WARS	44. Spasm or Insensate War 43. Some Other Kinds of Controlled General War 42. Civilian Devastation Attack 41. Augmented Disarming Attack 40. Countervalue Salvo 39. Slow-Motion Countercity War

(CITY TARGETING THRESHOLD)

MILITARY CENTRAL WARS	38. Unmodified Counterforce Attack 37. Counterforce-with-Avoidance Attack 36. Constrained Disarming Attack 35. Constrained Force-Reduction Salvo 34. Slow-Motion Counterforce War 33. Slow-Motion Counter-"Property" War 32. Formal Declaration of "General" War

(CENTRAL WAR THRESHOLD)

EXEMPLARY CENTRAL ATTACKS	31. Reciprocal Reprisals 30. Complete Evacuation (Approximately 95 per cent) 29. Exemplary Attacks on Population 28. Exemplary Attacks Against Property 27. Exemplary Attack on Military 26. Demonstration Attack on Zone of Interior

(CENTRAL SANCTUARY THRESHOLD)

BIZARRE CRISES	25. Evacuation (Approximately 70 per cent) 24. Unusual, Provocative, and Significant Countermeasures 23. Local Nuclear War—Military 22. Declaration of Limited Nuclear War 21. Local Nuclear War—Exemplary

(NO NUCLEAR USE THRESHOLD)

INTENSE CRISES	20. "Peaceful" World-Wide Embargo or Blockade 19. "Justifiable" Counterforce Attack 18. Spectacular Show or Demonstration of Force 17. Limited Evacuation (Approximately 20 per cent) 16. Nuclear "Ultimatums" 15. Barely Nuclear War 14. Declaration of Limited Conventional War 13. Large Compound Escalation 12. Large Conventional War (or Actions) 11. Super-Ready Status 10. Provocative Breaking Off of Diplomatic Relations

(NUCLEAR WAR IS UNTHINKABLE THRESHOLD)

TRADITIONAL CRISES	9. Dramatic Military Confrontations 8. Harassing Acts of Violence 7. "Legal" Harassment—Retortions 6. Significant Mobilization 5. Show of Force 4. Hardening of Positions—Confrontation of Wills

(DON'T ROCK THE BOAT THRESHOLD)

SUBCRISIS MANEUVER-ING	3. Solemn and Formal Declarations 2. Political, Economic, and Diplomatic Gestures 1. Ostensible Crisis

─────────────── DISAGREEMENT—COLD WAR ───────────────

logical tool and some of its pitfalls to later chapters, merely noting here that neither the particular ladder described nor the ladder concept should be taken too literally. The order of the rungs is not to be regarded as fixed, since in practice the circumstances of any particular escalation can cause important changes. There is also no necessity that one inexorably go *up* the ladder—rung by rung. One can go down as well as up, or even skip steps. In short, the ladder is intended to describe only a class of situations, and that from a single point of view. Perhaps most important, the ladder indicates that there are many relatively continuous paths between a low-level crisis and an all-out war—paths that are not inexorable at any particular time or place, and yet that might be traversed.

The particular ladder we will use has forty-four rungs. It is bordered by a pre-escalation stage called "Disagreement—Cold War," and a post-escalation stage called "Aftermaths." Methodologically, the ladder can be considered a scenario generator that connects subcrisis disagreements or incidents of the Cold War with some kind of aftermath.

The forty-four rungs of the ladder have been grouped into seven units (including varying numbers of rungs):

1. Subcrisis maneuvering.
2. Traditional crises.
3. Intense crises.
4. Bizarre crises.
5. Exemplary central attacks.
6. Military central wars.
7. Civilian central wars.

These seven groups are separated from one another on the diagram by six spaces that represent (mixing metaphors) "firebreaks," or thresholds, at which very sharp changes in the character of the escalation take place. The six basic thresholds are:

1. Don't rock the boat.
2. Nuclear war is unthinkable.
3. No nuclear use.
4. Central sanctuary.
5. Central war.
6. City targeting.

I will discuss the thresholds as thoroughly as the rungs, since they are equally important.

Another metaphor as useful as the escalation ladder would be that of an elevator stopping at various floors. We can think of a typical escalation situation between the United States and the Soviet Union in terms of a department store with seven floors, each offering a number of options of varying intensity, but still appropriate to that floor, from which the decision-makers on one side or the other may choose.

Description of the Rungs and Thresholds

The following discussion will, in effect, provide a summary of the entire book, introducing the most important vocabulary and concepts. I will then be able more easily to refer to the full range of considerations. In this chapter, I will not try to supply many of the motivations and contexts for discussing these forty-four options; the reader is urged to suspend disbelief until he has reached the more systematic discussion in later chapters.

SUBCRISIS MANEUVERING: We are interested here not in day-to-day maneuvers that do not raise the possibility of escalation, but only in the ones that manipulate, either deliberately or otherwise, the fear of escalation or eruption. It will be one of my theses that remote as the middle and upper rungs of the escalation ladder may seem, they often cast a long shadow before them and can greatly influence events well below the violence threshold, or even below that point in a conflict when the explicit threat of violence is voiced.

Rung 1. Ostensible crisis. At this stage, the language of crisis is used, but with some degree of pretense. Either one or both sides assert, more or less openly and explicitly but not quite believably, that unless the dispute is quickly resolved, rungs of the escalation ladder will be climbed.

Rung 2. Political, economic, and diplomatic gestures. Legal but inconveniencing, unfair, unfriendly, discourteous, inequitable, or threatening acts are carried out against the opponent to punish, apply pressure, or convey messages. If this becomes very hostile, these acts are called "retortions" (see Rung 7).

Rung 3. Solemn and formal declarations. These are purely verbal but explicitly solemn and formal actions intended to demonstrate resolve and committal. They may be in the form of legislative resolutions, formal executive announcements, diplomatic notes, or other very explicit and obviously serious declarations. Such a resolution or proclamation may be a simple notice to other nations of one's policy in a certain geographical or other area, or it may address a conflict or dispute more directly. It may often be thought of as a pre-emptive or preventive escalation that tries to forestall escalation by the opponent.

TRADITIONAL CRISES (THE BOAT IS ROCKED): In a thermonuclear balance of terror, both nations will be reluctant to start a crisis that could escalate, perhaps inadvertently, possibly even going beyond control and erupting into an all-out war. There is, therefore, a tendency not to let even a low-level crisis start—a constraint not to rock the nuclear boat.

Rung 4. Hardening of positions—Confrontation of wills. When the situation becomes coercive rather than contractual, the antagonists often attempt to increase the credibility of their commitments by "bridge-burning" acts, a deliberate increasing of the stakes, perhaps a joining together of several issues with the deliberate purpose of making it harder for the other side to believe that one can be made to back down.

Rung 5. Show of force. One side or the other may hint, or even make clear, that violence is "thinkable." If it does this by acts rather than words, we call it a "show of force."

Rung 6. Significant mobilization. The accompaniment of a show of force by a modest mobilization that not only increases one's strength but also indicates a willingness to call on more force or to accelerate the arms race if necessary.

Rung 7. "Legal" harassment—Retortions. One can harass the opponent's prestige, property, or people legally. That is to say, one may act in a very hostile and provocative manner, but within the limits of international law.

Rung 8. Harassing acts of violence. If the crisis is still not resolved, more or less illegal acts of violence or other incidents designed to harass, confuse, exhaust, violate, discredit, frighten, and otherwise harm, weaken, or demoralize the opponent or his allies and friends may be carried out through clandestine or unattributed channels, or through limited paramilitary or other overt agencies.

Rung 9. Dramatic military confrontations. If there is a direct ("eyeball to eyeball") confrontation that appears to be a stark test of nerves, committal, resolve, or recklessness, all participants and observers will take an intense interest in the proceedings.

INTENSE CRISES (THE UNTHINKABLE NUCLEAR WAR BECOMES CREDIBLE): Exactly where this threshold occurs is variable and very dependent on a specific course of events, but at some point the "nuclear incredulity"[1] that all of us share may be sharply decreased, if not eliminated. The popular sense of security ends or is shaken, and the "unreal" and "hypothetical" nuclear stockpiles may suddenly be perceived as real threats. This change will not come all at once, and may not be extreme, but it may occur to a large enough degree that a percentage of the population and a majority of decision-makers seriously envisage the possibility of a nuclear war actually occurring.

Rung 10. Provocative diplomatic break. This act would be intended to communicate to the opponent that one's reliance on the traditional peaceful measures of persuasion or coercion is at an end and that acts of force may now be resorted to.

Rung 11. Super-ready status. Placing military forces on super-ready status automatically involves dangerous or costly actions. If it did not, we would be doing these things normally.

Rung 12. Large conventional war (or actions). Casualties may occur in these acts—a significant deepening of the crisis. But even should these contests reach the level of open and continued fighting, neither side will use its more "efficient" or "quality" weapons— the nuclear, bacteriological, or chemical weapons—unless it wishes to escalate much farther up the ladder.

Rung 13. Large compound escalation. One side may demonstrate its resolve by reacting to an opponent's escalation with actions that raise issues not involved in the original conflict—the posing of a threat in a new area.

Rung 14. Declaration of limited conventional war. A declaration of limited conventional war would be an attempt to achieve one or

[1] Raymond Aron's phrase.

both of the following objectives: to give the enemy an incentive to reciprocate by making a clear-cut, unilateral announcement of "no nuclear first use"; to limit the conventional war geographically or otherwise in a manner considered most favorable or stable by the side making the declaration. In addition, such a declaration would have grave symbolic, political, and moral effects upon one's own country and the opponent.

Rung 15. Barely nuclear war. During a conventional warlike act (Rung 12) or the super-ready status (Rung 11), one or more nuclear weapons may be used unintentionally (accidentally or unauthorizedly). Or one of the antagonists may make military or political use of a nuclear weapon but try to give the impression that the use was unintentional.

Rung 16. Nuclear "ultimatums." Whether or not there is a conventional or barely nuclear war, the crisis could enter a stage of such increased intensity that the state of nuclear incredulity would not merely be weakened but would vanish. This could occur when one side or the other seriously considered the possibility of a central war and communicated this fact convincingly to its opponent.

Rung 17. Limited evacuation (approximately 20 per cent). This would most likely be at least a quasi-official move ordered by a government for either bargaining or prudential reasons, or both. The difficulties, and possible public and political reactions, make such an evacuation a momentous decision, and one whose consequences could not reliably be predicted. I would also include at this rung serious efforts by one or both sides to prepare for both large-scale evacuation and improvised protection.

Rung 18. Spectacular show or demonstration of force. A spectacular show or demonstration of force would involve using major weapons in a way that did no obvious damage, but appeared determined, menacing, or reckless. The purpose would be to punish the enemy for a previous act, or pre-emptively to punish him for an anticipated one (with the intention of establishing a precedent to deter later provocations), or to intensify the fear of war in the hope of frightening the enemy into backing down.

Rung 19. "Justifiable" counterforce attack. A "justifiable" attack would be sufficiently specialized and limited to seem a reasonable response to provocation, and yet it might significantly, or even decisively, degrade the military capability, prestige, or morale of the opponent.

Rung 20. "Peaceful" world-wide embargo or blockade. This would be an extreme measure of nonviolent coercion brought to bear against an opponent. It is more escalatory than the previous rungs because of its continuing nature.

BIZARRE CRISES (NUCLEAR WEAPONS ARE USED): Up to this point, while nuclear incredulity would have been shattered, nuclear weapons would not have been used extensively. Even if the barely nuclear war had occurred, it presumably would have been accepted as an accident or limited episode, and even a nuclear show of force or "justifiable" counterforce attack might have been understood as a limited action rather than serious nuclear warfare. Now we move wholly into what many consider an entirely bizarre range of possibilities, the very limited and restrained use of nuclear weapons.

Rung 21. Local nuclear war—exemplary. Almost every analyst now agrees that, with the possible exception of Rung 19–type tactics, the first use of nuclear weapons—even against military targets —is likely to be less for the purpose of destroying the other side's military forces or of handicapping its operations than for redressive, warning, bargaining, punitive, fining, or deterrence purposes. As this would be the first unmistakably deliberate use of these weapons since World War II, it would be a profoundly consequential act, even if very limited and specialized.

Rung 22. Declaration of limited nuclear war. At this point, it might be judged desirable to make a formal declaration of limited nuclear war—perhaps in hope of setting out relatively exact limits and establishing expectations about the types of nuclear action that the declarer intends to initiate and that he is prepared to countenance from the enemy without escalating further himself.

Rung 23. Local nuclear war—military. It is also possible that nuclear weapons could be used in a local situation for traditional military purposes such as defense, denial, destruction, or degradation of the opponent's capability, and so on, and that, within the established limits, the scale and targeting would be, and would be acknowledged to be, dictated by wholly military and "tactical" considerations.

Rung 24. Unusual, provocative, and significant countermeasures.
One side might carry out redeployments or maneuvers that would
have the effect of shifting the balance of power by increasing an opponent's vulnerability to attack or otherwise degrading its capability, morale, or will.

Rung 25. Evacuation (approximately 70 per cent). At this point,
the situation may be very close to large-scale war. It may now seem
advisable to evacuate a large number of people from cities. The
total would probably amount to between two-thirds and three-
fourths of the population—women and children and those men who
are not essential to the functioning of the cities. I would judge that
all important industries, communications, transportation facilities,
etc., could be operated by about a quarter of the population or less.

EXEMPLARY CENTRAL ATTACKS (VIOLATING THE CENTRAL SANC-
TUARY—NUCLEAR GUNBOAT DIPLOMACY): Attacks that avoid the
zone of interior of the enemy observe a salient threshold: the one
dividing the categories of "homeland" and "not-homeland." To
cross this threshold would open the way to large-scale violence.

Rung 26. Demonstration attack on zone of interior. A "harmless"
attack (perhaps on an isolated mountain top or empty desert)
which does dramatic and unmistakable physical damage, if only to
the topography.

Rung 27. Exemplary attack on military. One side might begin
destroying portions of the other side's weapons systems, but in a
relatively careful way so as not to cause much collateral damage.
These attacks could be launched primarily to exert psychological
pressure or to reduce the defender's military capability significantly
by finding leverage targets.

Rung 28. Exemplary attacks against property. The next step
would obviously be to increase the level of these limited strategic
attacks. One possibility would be attacks on such expensive installations as bridges, dams, or gaseous diffusion plants. More damaging
and dangerous would be limited attacks on cities, presumably after
warning had been delivered and the cities evacuated; the purpose
would be to destroy property, not people.

Rung 29. Exemplary attacks on population. In any crisis of the
mid-1960's, this attack would probably be much higher on the

ladder than I put it here, but if the balance of terror becomes sufficiently stable, and governments are believed to be under intense and graduated mutual deterrents, even this attack could occur without an eruption to spasm or other central war.

Rung 30. Complete evacuation (approximately 95 per cent). But at this point, large-scale warfare has either begun or is imminent. If at all possible, each side is likely to evacuate its cities almost completely, leaving 5–10 per cent of the population behind for essential activities.

Rung 31. Reciprocal reprisals. This is a war of almost pure resolve, with more or less continual tit-for-tat exchanges, whether limited to purely symbolic attacks or more destructive exemplary attacks. Many strategists believe that reciprocal reprisal wars— "resolve against resolve"—might be a standard tactic of the future when the balance of terror is judged, whether correctly or not, to be almost absolute or when, because of strategic invulnerability, no other choices are available to desperate or gambling decision-makers.

MILITARY CENTRAL WARS (THE "NEW" KIND OF ALL-OUT WAR): Two groups of central-war rungs lie above the traditional threshold between war and peace (a distinction that has not been obliterated by new developments). In military central wars, the military authorities, or commanders in chief, have access to all the resources of the nation, although their intention is to utilize tactics that avoid or limit damage to an opponent's civilians.

Rung 32. Formal declaration of "general" war. An esoteric possibility, almost completely overlooked in modern defense planning, is that one side will respond to provocation with a formal declaration of war but without immediate acts of large-scale violence. An ultimatum or declaration of war might, as in World War II, be followed by a "phony war" period, in which there was some limited tactical or strategic harassment but no large attacks.

Rung 33. Slow-motion counter-"property" war. In this attack, each side destroys the other's property in tit-for-tat fashion. We sometimes refer to this as a "war of resolve," since each side is attempting to force the other side to back down and there is a naked matching of resolve against resolve. If the exchanges are few in number, and for limited purposes, we call them "reciprocal reprisals" (see Rung 31).

Rung 34. Slow-motion counterforce war. This is a campaign (which could either precede or follow a large counterforce attack) in which each side attempts attrition of the other side's weapons systems over time. One can conceive of a slow-motion counterforce war lasting for weeks or months during which Polaris submarines are hunted down, hidden missiles found, land bases dug up, and so on.

Rung 35. Constrained force-reduction salvo. The attacker here attempts to destroy a significant but small portion of the defender's force in a single strike while avoiding undesired collateral damage. It is especially likely to be used against weak links or high-leverage targets at the outbreak of a war.

Rung 36. Constrained disarming attack. One of the major arguments for the counterforce-with-avoidance attack (see Rung 37) is that not much is lost by narrow military calculations, and with populations spared, the possibility that post-attack blackmail would work is increased enormously. In the constrained disarming attack, one may follow the same logic further. Tremendous military disadvantages might be accepted in order to spare people and improve the possibilities of successful negotiation to determine the war on an acceptable basis. In this attack, the attacker tries to destroy a significant portion of the defender's first-strike forces and even some of his second-strike forces, but avoids civilian targets as much as possible. This might make it disadvantageous for the defender to launch a counterstrike, since his damaged forces might be only partially effective, even in countervalue targeting, while his attacker might be able to deliver an annihilating second blow against the enemy population with his withheld and regrouped forces.

Rung 37. Counterforce-with-avoidance attack. This attack differs from a constrained disarming attack in that it is less scrupulous about avoiding collateral damage to cities and does not deliberately spare much, if any, of the enemy's second-strike forces. This counterforce attack targets everything that does not involve major collateral damage to civilians. In the case of a Soviet strike against the United States, such an attack probably would include hitting Tucson (a city of 250,000 population, completely ringed with Titans), but probably would avoid the San Diego Naval Base, the Norfolk Navy Yard, and the Pentagon in Washington. If it did hit these targets, or the SAC bases near very large cities, 20-kiloton rather than 20-megaton weapons might be used in order to limit the collateral destruction. After such an attack, one must assume a counterattack, but one may still try to use counter-counterthreats of further escalation into countervalue war to limit the defender's response.

Rung 38. Unmodified counterforce attack. Here, no degradation of the counterforce attack is accepted to spare civilians, but there is no deliberate attempt to enlarge such collateral damage as a "bonus."

CIVILIAN CENTRAL WARS (VIOLATION OF THE "NO-CITY" THRESHOLD): The example of strategic city bombing in World War II is so firmly held in many people's minds as "proper" action that they cannot visualize a large strategic war in which cities are not priority objectives. Yet thermonuclear wars are likely to be short, lasting from a few hours to, at most, a couple of months. In such a war, it is unlikely that cities would in themselves be of any great military consequence: factories would not have time to turn out weapons; millions of men would not be drafted and trained; there probably would not even be elections in which the fears or suffering of the civilian population could generate direct pressures to change established national policies. Thus, cities are no longer urgent military targets; they may be destroyed in a strategic war, but there is no military reason to do so, or to do so quickly. Populations, of course, may be evacuated, but buildings cannot be, and it is unlikely that one side or the other would feel so strongly motivated to destroy civilians early in a war that they would attack to pre-empt such an evacuation.

None of the above is necessarily clearly understood by the governments and war planners of either side. If one side or the other decided to go to war, it might, simply because of this lack of thought, attack cities. Of course, the United States has more or less formally enunciated a strategy of "no cities except in reprisal," but this strategy is neither widely understood nor very firmly held even here. And it remains true that if intrawar deterrence were to break down, or "bargaining" seemed to require it, cities might get hit anyway.

Rung 39. Slow-motion countercity war. A war of resolve (see Rung 33) carried to an ultimate form—"city trading."

Rung 40. Countervalue salvo. It is, of course, always possible in fighting a slow-motion counterforce, slow-motion countervalue, or other kind of war, that one side will fire a large number of missiles at civilian targets, in either inadvertent or deliberate eruption.

Rung 41. Augmented disarming attack. This would be a counterforce attack deliberately modified to obtain as a "bonus" as much collateral countervalue damage as could be achieved without diverting significant resources from the military targets.

Rung 42. Civilian devastation attack. An effort to destroy or gravely damage the enemy's society, distinguished from spasm war only by its element of calculation and the fact that there may be some withholding or control.

Rung 43. Some other kinds of controlled general war. It is possible to have many kinds of "all-out" but controlled, as well as "all-out" uncontrolled, wars. (The term "all-out" is enclosed in quotation marks to emphasize again that this is not necessarily a spasm war in which each side strikes indiscriminately against the other's cities and military bases; "all-out" refers to a level of effort, not to whether there is or is not discrimination in targeting, or negotiation.) In a "rational," "all-out," but controlled war, military action would be accompanied by threats and promises, and military operations themselves would be restricted to those which contributed to the achievement of victory (an acceptable or desirable peace treaty), to the limiting of the damage the enemy could do, to the improvement of the nation's postwar prospects (perhaps by worsening the enemy's prospects), or to the gaining of a measured amount of revenge or punishment.

Rung 44. Spasm or insensate war. The figurative word "spasm" is chosen because it describes the usual image of central war in which there is only a "go-ahead" order; all the buttons are pressed, and the decision-makers and their staffs go home—if they still have homes; they have done their job. A spasm war may occur, of course, but to the extent that there is any art of war possible in the thermonuclear age, the attempt must be made to prevent it, to try to get the losing side to cease fire before he has used up his weapons. In a "moment of truth," and particularly if there has been a preliminary crisis that has educated the leaders, all decision-makers are likely to understand at least to some degree that there need be no compulsion to wreak useless and contraproductive destruction just because one has weapons that can be used.

III

Disagreements and Subcrisis Maneuvering

Basic Description and Definition

Among the most important questions I will consider is the effect the threat or danger of escalation has on the negotiation and settlement of low-level crises and disagreements, and the influence such crises and disagreements can have on further escalation. Such situations and tactics are included in the first three rungs of the ladder: ostensible crisis; political, economic, and diplomatic gestures; and solemn and formal declarations. (See Figure 3, p. 39.)

All three rungs can be well below the "Don't rock the boat" threshold or well past it, depending on details. Thus, there is no absolute necessity for a dispute to raise questions of coercion or to lead to a crisis or even to strained relations, particularly if the disagreement takes place within a contractual or familial relationship. The antagonists may be able to resolve the dispute, may be able to leave it unresolved hoping that time will bring some sort of decision, or may have some mutually acceptable way of conducting arbitration or continuing negotiations, perhaps to arrive at some temporary *modus vivendi*. It obviously is possible for two nations to disagree sharply, even bitterly, on some issues, and still be friendly in other matters. However, if a disagreement takes place between nations that have a recent history of coercive negotiations, the dispute is more likely to escalate.

Thus, in the past, there have been many people in both the U.S.S.R. and the U.S. who seemed to believe, even without resort to the escalation ladder, that there was essentially nothing wrong with the world except that the other side existed and had goals that interfered with "peace" and with one's own legitimate aspirations. Under such circumstances, every retreat or advance was taken to be a notable occasion—a precedent and a prognosis. But today, of course, there is a substantial *détente* between the U.S. and the U.S.S.R. Some tend to think of the Cold War as near the point of fading away. Others believe that the situation remains basically unstable, that so long as the other side does not experience major internal changes, regardless of what its leaders do or say and regardless of the current relaxation of tensions, there remains a basic disagreement about the future of the world, and that we and Russia exist in at least a subcrisis stage of conflict, with escalation only a matter of time or opportunity.

In any case, the environment is still such that any disagreement could easily result in either a slow or a rapid climb up the ladder. It is also possible that, with time, *détente,* or the "agreement to disagree peacefully," will become so firm, the rivalry between the U.S. and the U.S.S.R. so channeled, that both sides will firmly and reliably agree on how to coexist peacefully, with each side negotiating, maneuvering, and conspiring, but without using the language or techniques of escalation, even though these will always necessarily remain in the background. While this situation would start as an "implicit contract," it presumably would eventually become more normative—i.e., agonistic or familial.

Whatever happens to this particular Cold War, escalation ladders are, of course, applicable to confrontations other than that between the United States and the Soviet Union. However, I have not explicitly tried to generalize these considerations to include other cases, so, while the ladder I discuss may be of interest in connection with these other cases, I have made few concessions to this interest. In fact, as I will discuss below, the particular ladder considered here is in some senses an American rather than a Soviet ladder.

The Rungs of Subcrisis Maneuvering

RUNG 1. OSTENSIBLE CRISIS: In this stage, one or both sides assert, more or less openly and explicitly, that unless a given dispute is resolved in the immediate future, the rungs of the escalation ladder will be climbed. Vague or explicit threats may be made that one will take extreme measures rather than back down. These threats are made credible by various hints as to how important the government considers the issues. There may be officially inspired newspaper stories to the effect that the chief of state takes a serious view of the matter. There may be explicit announcements or speeches by other important officials—but none of them of the bridge-burning variety, none deliberately designed to make it really difficult for these same officials to back down later.

Extremist groups may be urging decisive action, and there may even be newspaper headlines, but most people probably will not be worried. The "crisis" looks more like a "play" to them than a serious endeavor to put pressure on the opponent, although decision-makers may also join, more or less openly, in the "play-acting." However, neutral, "hysterical," or alienated groups may become extremely concerned. Thus, there may be pressures put on either or both sides to meet or to moderate their demands, or at least to have them mediated, perhaps through United Nations or other international auspices. In fact, one of the main reasons for the "play-acting" is to raise such apprehensions and generate such pressures.

We might conjecture, for example, that since Khrushchev's November, 1958, speech (or ultimatum), the Berlin crisis has vacillated from an ostensible crisis to a real one, but has been more ostensible than real. Similarly, we would argue that in the escalation in the Gulf of Tonkin in the summer of 1964, once the United States had carried out its raid and announced that it was satisfied with this reprisal, the crisis dropped from a real one to an ostensible one, even though most of the language used for some weeks afterward was designed to sound appropriate to a real crisis, particularly in the releases from the Chinese Communists.

One real problem in a balance-of-terror environment is that, with time, a nation's decision-makers may become so confident of the stability of the situation that in a real crisis they will misjudge some of the language and acts and take them as "ostensible" rather than real. Making explicit the knowledge that "play-acting" takes place should increase one's skill in recognizing the real thing when it occurs.

RUNG 2. POLITICAL, ECONOMIC, AND DIPLOMATIC GESTURES: If the other side does not look as though it is going to be reasonable, one can do more than drop hints of trouble to come. One can perform legal but unfair, unfriendly, discourteous, inequitable, or threatening acts to put pressure on an opponent—to carry unmistakable (or at least relatively clear) messages. Acts by one government to seek redress for, or prevent recurrence of, an undesired act by another government are often called "retortions." We will restrict that term to acts that are quite hostile (see Rung 7) and exclude the kind of thing that could occur, for example, in an intensified tit-for-tat argument between the U.S. and the Common Market. At this lower level one can: (1) recall an ambassador for lengthy consultation; (2) refuse to facilitate negotiations on other issues; (3) make overtures to the other side's enemies; (4) denounce a treaty; (5) make a moderate but unmistakable legal or economic reprisal; (6) push resolutions in the U.N. against the other side; (7) replace an official in a key spot by one who is known to be "hard" or "tough"; (8) start a violent publicity campaign, encourage mass meetings, "spontaneous" public demonstrations, and so on. If the public becomes involved, the tone of castigations of the "enemy" will tend to be shriller than before. Or most of the accompanying communications may be made privately. The private threat, though, may carry less weight because the side making it has revealed an unwillingness to make a public commitment. However, if the other side yields to a private threat or accepts some face-saving compromise, it has not lost as much prestige as might otherwise have been the case.

It is also possible for government officials to arrange for deliberate newspaper leaks. This can be done in a number of ways— from the formal public gesture (as discussed at Rung 3) to the relatively private and "unofficial" acts. Even in the former case, when everyone knows the source of the leak, a government is not usually as committed as if a senior official had made a formal speech (as in Rung 3). Thus, a semiofficial Tass dispatch or an interpretive column in *The New York Times* is still at Rung 2.

In the summer of 1964, the United States and the Chinese engaged in a series of such semiformal leaks and announcements about the war in Vietnam. Since the technique used was so typical, and in this case so well reported, I have included at the end of this chapter an example of such a news story.

Political and military gestures can be part of an escalation process and still be justified or motivated for reasons other than escalation. The creation of the NATO alliance, an alliance clearly designed to fight a defensive battle against the Soviets if need be, was a military as well as a political and diplomatic act to counter the Berlin blockade and the Communist coup in Czechoslovakia. Yet it could also be justified as a reaction to postwar technology, to the existence of two superpowers and of a power vacuum in Western Europe.

RUNG 3. SOLEMN AND FORMAL DECLARATIONS: We do not generally include in this category a press conference or even the usual speech in which some executive or senior decision-maker may draw an opponent's attention to the fact that one will react in a way the opponent will not like. To be at Rung 3, the declaration has to be of such a nature that it is almost impossible to argue that a binding and honorable commitment has not been made. Typical of such a commitment would be a resolution formally passed by the legislature and concurred in by the executive, a solemn executive declaration in which there was a deliberate attempt to heighten the importance of the occasion, a formal diplomatic communication between the heads of state, and so on.

Such declarations go much further than Rung 2 in demonstrating resolve and commitment, but they need not be deliberately hostile. They may provide merely a simple notice to other states of a nation's policy in a certain geographical or other area, as the Monroe Doctrine did; or the declaration may deliberately avoid a precise statement of its applicability and limitations. An example of such ambiguity could be the Congressional Resolution of January 28, 1955, which authorized in advance any military action the President might take outside Formosa proper and the Pescadores in order to defend Formosa, without actually committing the U.S. to take any action. Another example could be the resolution passed by Congress in August, 1964, at the request of President Johnson as a result of the escalation in the Gulf of Tonkin: Congress resolved that "the United States is, therefore, prepared, as the President determines, to take all necessary steps including the use of armed force, to assist any member or protocol state of the Southeast Asia Collective Defense Treaty requesting assistance in defense of its freedom."

One of the most famous Rung 3–type gestures was the guarantee by the British to Poland in 1939 that they would declare war on Germany if Hitler invaded Poland.

Such a proclamation or resolution is usually a warning to a potential opponent not to climb farther up the escalation ladder, at least in the area covered by the announcement. The declaration may be thought of as pre-emptive or preventive escalation which tries to forestall further escalation by the opponent. The possibility of such pre-emptive escalation falls into the general category of "rationality-of-irrationality" and "committal" strategies.

Rationality-of-Irrationality and Committal Strategies

The term "rationality-of-irrationality" describes a class of bargaining or negotiating tactics or escalation situations whose common characteristic is that there is a rational advantage to be gained from irrational conduct or from the expectation of irrational conduct.

In a deterrence context, rationality-of-irrationality usually refers to a current rationality of planning future irrationality. Sometimes, however, it means the present rational advantage of present irrational behavior. Thus, if one wants to buy a valuable object at a low price, and there are no other prospective buyers, one is more likely to succeed if one seems too stupid to realize the real value of the object and if one can communicate this "stupidity" to the seller. More subtle and sophisticated forms of this kind of rationality-of-irrationality are very common.

Rationality-of-irrationality plays an important part in deterrence. For example, in most deterrent situations, once deterrence has failed, it is irrational to carry out the previously made warnings or threats of retaliation since that action will produce an absolute or net loss to the retaliator. Thus the threat of retaliation, in order to be believable, must depend upon the potential irrationality of the retaliator.

There are at least three basic kinds of "irrationality" used to enhance deterrence, as well as other rationality-of-irrationality tactics. One is the expectation of the real human irrationality—that is, the possibility that decision-makers will act from such "irrational" motives as outraged honor, shock, rage, vengeance, confusion, or stupidity.

The second "irrationality" is an arrangement that prevents rational decision-makers from wholly controlling the system: if the system is not likely to be controlled, then rationality cannot be expected from it. Thus, the teenager's tactics of being blind, drunk, and without a steering wheel in the game of "chicken" are all chosen to lessen the degree of control and are generic examples of how to go about doing so. Rationality may also at least be degraded or reduced by the introduction of special factors that change the calculations in certain situations. The paradigm of this is a bargaining situation in which one of the bargainers unconditionally establishes a high penalty against himself if he pays too high a price to get a settlement, even though it may be a price that otherwise would be a reasonable one for him to pay. If enough such additional values are created that will be served by the activation of threats or warnings, then it can be made "rational" to carry them out, even if, in the absence of the additional reasons, it would be "irrational" actually to carry out a given threat. These techniques all are used (or misused) for committing oneself.

A committal strategy is one that involves some element of more or less irrevocable commitment to a contingent action. If it is reasonable or advantageous to make the commitment, but irrational in the absence of the commitment to carry out the action if the contingency occurs, then such a strategy is an expression of rationality-of-irrationality. However, not all committal strategies are examples of rationality-of-irrationality. It may be irrational to make the commitment itself, or it may not be very irrational to carry it out. Committal strategies are sometimes called "resolution strategies," but this is poor terminology because it is too easily confused with the term "war of resolution," a quite different thing.

The Rung 2 Escalation of the Summer of 1964

One of the most interesting recent examples of subcrisis maneuvering was the series of leaks and announcements issued by U.S., Chinese, and North and South Vietnamese leaders in the summer of 1964. While it would take too much space to discuss in detail the various messages and gestures that were delivered and made, I do consider it worth while to reprint a story by Arnold Beichman that appeared in *The Washington Post* on July 10, 1964 (p. A-15).

U.S. REPRISAL RAIDS IN NORTH VIETNAM KEPT AS LAST RESORT

SAIGON, July 9—Specific details of a United States contingency plan for American bombing raids on Communist North Vietnam have been revealed here.

Such contingency planning inevitably accompanies the conduct of military operations, and whether this particular plan would ever be implemented depends on the course of the fighting during the months to come. If the latest U.S. and South Vietnamese tactics show signs of turning the tide against the rebels, air raids on North Vietnam would undoubtedly be ruled unnecessary.

According to reliable sources, the plan aims at producing a minimum number of civilian casualties together with maximum military and industrial damage. It has been carefully prepared by U.S. military experts both in Saigon and in Washington.

Political Solution Stressed

It should be stated clearly that the new U.S. diplomatic team here, Ambassador Maxwell D. Taylor and Deputy Ambassador Alexis U. Johnson, is persuaded that the biggest part of the problem in beating the Communist Viet Cong—"60 to 70 per cent of it," in the opinion of one high U.S. official—is political, the remainder military.

But there is another school of thought here, both U.S. and Vietnamese, that believes no matter how successful the political effort in South Vietnam, the Communist regime in Hanoi cannot accept peaceful coexistence with a non-Communist southern neighbor.

Therefore, it is argued, so long as North Vietnam remains a privileged sanctuary providing inspiration for insurrection there can be no peace in the strategic sector of Southeast Asia.

How Plan Works

The reprisal plan, designed to deter North Vietnam from such a policy, would work as follows:

If the Viet Cong overruns and destroys a government-held village in South Vietnam, the U.S.–South Vietnamese forces then will announce publicly that a village in North Vietnam will be bombed from the air on a given day the following week as a retaliatory measure.

Since to announce the name of one village would merely give the enemy an opportunity to concentrate all his ack-ack guns against the U.S. aircraft, the announcement would list 200 villages, only one of which would be bombed.

This public notice would give the inhabitants of the villages named one week to evacuate and to take provisions with them. Since any one of 200 villages might be hit, counterinsurgency planners here envision civilian panic over a large part of North Vietnam.

The "village-for-village" advance warning would be made by radio broadcasts beamed to North Vietnam, plus the dropping of hundreds of thousands of leaflets by U.S. aircraft overflying enemy territory. And on the specified day or night, bombers would wipe out the selected target.

Lists of Targets Ready

Two lists—List A and List B totaling 400 villages—already exist and their use awaits the day when the White House decides that Hanoi can no longer be immune from reprisal.

Another part of this plan envisions the infliction of economic damage through bombing of selected North Vietnamese industrial targets. This tactic will be adopted only in reprisal for the murder of anti-Communist village leaders in South Vietnam.

One of the most successful tactics of the Viet Cong has been the killing of village chiefs loyal to the Saigon government. The inability of the present Saigon regime to guarantee the security of these village leaders has led to the seesawing of villages from one side to the other.

As it stands now, government forces often enter an area, mop up the Viet Cong and leave after a week, having installed a new pro-government administration. In a day or so, the Viet Cong reinvade the village and shoot the village leader after suitable torture.

Under the U.S. counterinsurgency plan, the price for such execution of a village leader will be the destruction of a major industrial or strategic installation of North Vietnam. A list of potential targets will be announced in advance through leaflets scattered over the target areas. Thus, workers will be given warning of the possible bombing.

This "early warning" tactic, it is argued, would do serious damage to industrial production in North Vietnam since it is hard to envision workers, who know that on a given day they might be bombed at any time during a work-shift, willingly remaining on the job.

Since the above was obviously "leaked," it was likely to be understood by Hanoi and Peking as semiofficial, if not official. It would be difficult to give a more detailed, specific, and expository threat and account of the theory. However, the extent to which such stories may have influenced the behavior of Hanoi and Peking is an open issue. It clearly did not prevent the later attack on U.S. destroyers in Tonkin Bay.

IV

Traditional Crises

Basic Description and Definition

In this chapter, I want to consider Rungs 4–9, which fall between the "Don't rock the boat" and "Nuclear war is unthinkable" thresholds. (See Figure 3, p. 39.) Thus I will examine what happens when a disagreement is allowed to reach a crisis stage[1]—where opponents do not agree to disagree peacefully, and both sides feel that something will happen before the disagreement is laid to rest.

[1] As discussed in Anthony J. Wiener and Herman Kahn, *Crises and Arms Control* (Hudson Institute publication, HI-180-RR, October 9, 1962), pp. 7–16, a crisis can be defined as an intense confrontation in which the various participants believe that there is going to be an important turning point in history; thus the participants also believe or feel there is an important degree of threat, warning, or promise that will emerge or be fulfilled as soon as the events take their course. The outcome is thought to be to some degree indeterminate; since if it is determined, there is no crisis action to be taken. Finally, there are usually important points of decision or crucial times. As further discussed in the report, crises frequently have the following characteristics:

1. Events often converge to cause a high degree of complexity.
2. Time pressures increase.
3. Adequacy of information seems to decrease.
4. Uncertainties seem to increase.
5. Instrumental control is decreased.
6. Decision-makers are under extreme personal stress.
7. Internal decision and bargaining relations change.
8. Alliance decision and bargaining relations change.

We will not discuss the above in this book, which concentrates on options and tactics rather than on administration or command, control and communication.

Of course, in a world in which there is a thermonuclear balance of terror, large nations are likely to be reluctant to start a crisis that could escalate, perhaps inadvertently, possibly going beyond all control and erupting into an all-out war. A nation is especially likely to be careful if it feels that its potential nuclear opponent has, or could have, an important commitment to the issue. In that case, it will realize that the other may be willing to escalate before backing down. Therefore, it is likely to judge that even if it finally wins the escalation the risk may be too great in comparison to what it might gain. Even worse, the "victory" might turn out to be Pyrrhic. There is thus a tendency not to let crises start—a strong pressure not to "rock the nuclear boat."

This fear of inadvertent eruption can be used to influence the behavior of the opponent. While the deliberate use of such a strategy is old and has been considered many times with varying degrees of sophistication, the first serious modern treatment of it seems to have been in an article by Thomas C. Schelling, "Threats Which Leave Something to Chance," which is included in his book *The Strategy of Conflict*.[2]

In its most extreme form, the manipulation of the fear of inadvertent eruption might go as follows: Let us assume that two nations have such strategic systems and war plans that all-out war between them would be mutual homicide. Let us imagine that these two systems are built so that in a tense situation there is some probability, say one chance in a thousand per week, that they will go off accidentally. Assume also that both nations insist on maintaining this probability of total and mutual homicide until the other side backs down or compromises. We now have a situation in which there is an intense "competition in risk-taking."

An actual crisis situation would not be this stark. Nobody really knows what the probability of war is under different circumstances. We do not even know whether it goes up or down in a tense situation. It is, for example, quite conceivable that the extra care and concern associated with a tense situation might more than make up for the seeming extra danger that arises from weapons being on alert, from men operating under strain, and from the weaken-

---

[2] Cambridge, Mass.: Harvard University Press, 1960.

ing which takes place in that important safeguard against accident, that high degree of "nuclear incredulity" which influences operators and decision-makers to disbelieve orders or signals that a nuclear war is under way. In practice, this strategy depends on an apparent increase in the probability or the risk of war, whether or not this actually occurs: it gives the impression that it is dangerous to allow the situation to drag out. In some cases, this apparent probability may in fact be a good objective estimate of the actual situation. In other cases, large and frightening as the apparent probability might be, it might be a serious underestimate of the actual risk of war. And in still other cases, it might be an overestimate of it.

While this concept of manipulating the risk of war in order to obtain foreign-policy advantages seems bizarre, the bizarreness comes from the scale of the threat and from its being made explicit. The tactic itself is used regularly, as the name of the threshold, "Don't rock the boat," suggests. Short of absolute surrender, or unilateral disarmament, there is always some probability, no matter how small, of inadvertent eruption, and whatever a nation does must affect this probability. It is also clear that affairs cannot be conducted in such a way as invariably to minimize this probability. Indeed, it sometimes is impossible to know for certain what actions would, in fact, minimize such a probability.

Fear of inadvertent war can be a very effective pressure partly because everybody knows that neither side really understands its present weapons systems or really appreciates the various ways in which an inadvertent war could occur. A rigorously realistic estimate of the risks that are run daily is impossible. Imagine, for example, that an accidental war actually occurred and someone then tried to persuade an investigating committee that the system had, in fact, been quite safe, but that there had been an incredibly unlucky event, rather than that the system had been dangerous and the inevitable had happened. It would be almost impossible to convince anyone after the fact that a system with literally thousands of armed and alert missiles and planes widely distributed actually was safe, and that extremely bad luck had occurred, even if it were true. And it probably would not be.

The only point I am trying to make here is that no one really knows what the probability is that things will go wrong. In particular, no one could put together a completely persuasive story to a hostile and skeptical audience. We do know that a number of useful safeguards (and probably a sufficient number) have been procured and today the U.S. system seems, to expert observers, to be quite safe—much safer than it was in the 1950's. Some of the things that have contributed to this increased safety are:

1. Current U.S. forces are relatively invulnerable. Although details of many of the changes are classified, we can point out, for example, that in early 1951 all the U.S. strategic forces were stationed at only twelve bases and all the strategic weapons were in a very small number of buildings.[3] The Soviets would have had to drop only twelve or possibly fewer bombs effectively to disarm U.S. strategic forces. Today our strategic forces are so hardened and dispersed that many analysts believe the U.S. could give the Soviets days to try to destroy these forces and they would not be able to do so. Therefore, there need be no rush for the President to retaliate. He could wait until the attack was finished and then decide on the nature of the retaliation. For example, he could communicate with the Soviets to find out if the attack was accidental or deliberate before striking back. Furthermore, he would feel little or no pressure from the possibility of a disarming "Pearl Harbor" attack even in an intense crisis.

2. Many organizational and technical safeguards to prevent accidental or other unauthorized use of nuclear weapons (as in recent novels and movies) have been installed .These include codes, "combination locks," and double-key arrangements.

3. The current strategy of controlled response, which, among other things, tries to assure deliberate and effective control of weapons by the President of the United States under all circumstances, is another important safeguard against the initiation of an accidental war. It also increases the probability that if a war started, it could be conducted with restraint and terminated relatively soon, thus avoiding much "unnecessary" damage.

4. As part and parcel of the above, a greater understanding of nuclear war and of the concept that one should fight a war with the

---

[3] See Herman Kahn, *On Thermonuclear War* (Princeton, N.J.: Princeton University Press, 1960), pp. 423–26.

idea of how to terminate it (as discussed in Chapter X) means that if an accident occurred, it might be much less destructive than it would have been in the 1950's—even if it caused an all-out military war.

Admitting all of the above, we still do not know how safe the system is. Neither does an opponent. We may both believe it to be safe in normal times. But we cannot help worrying whether there are conditions during alert status that seem to make the system more war-prone—even if they do not. There is also a question of what the Soviets have done along the same lines. Thus, in a crisis, both the Soviets and the U.S. may be worried about the accident-proneness of the Soviet system. It would be of little consolation to the Soviets if they were destroyed in an accidental war that they had started. Thus, even if they have faith in the U.S. system but do not have faith in their own, the fact that they might have to go on alert could put them under extreme pressure.

An inadvertent war, of course, could be only partially inadvertent. As a crisis developed one side could become so desperate that it actually would calculate (or miscalculate) that its least undesirable alternative was to go to war, even though, if it had realized earlier that it was going to be driven to such a point, it would have accommodated rather than let itself be "locked in."

There are a number of ways to exploit this situation. Unpleasant and reckless as such exploitation may seem, it is necessary to realize that it is regularly done to some degree, since the competitive risking of inadvertent war is unavoidable so long as weapons systems and confrontations exist. In addition, whatever the risk may be in normal times, almost all believe it is increased when there is tension or crisis, and yet almost no one is invariably willing to allay tension by automatically accommodating to all of the opponent's demands in every crisis. Thus, our willingness to undergo tension or crisis inevitably involves some increased threat to the other side.

The Rungs of Traditional Crises

RUNG 4. HARDENING OF POSITIONS—CONFRONTATION OF WILLS: As soon as negotiations take on much more of a coercive than a contractual character, I would argue that we have reached Rung 4. Certainly this is true if either or both of the antagonists attempt to increase the credibility of their resolve and committal by "bridge-burning" acts. These could include a public and irrevocable increase in the stakes or a joining together of other issues—all done with the deliberate purpose of making it harder for the other side to believe that it can make its opponent back down.

In particular, under modern conditions, either side could point out vividly to the other side's population or to its allies the totally destructive character of thermonuclear war. It could now be stressed that nobody would survive, that there is no alternative to peace—with the clear implication that, unless the madmen on the other side come to their senses, all will be lost. Alternatively, one can reassure one's own side by pointing out that the other side is not mad and will therefore back down.

Accompanying this "locking in" process, there may be a great increase of activity at Rungs 2 and 3, such as angry and bitter outbursts in the press against the other side, bellicose or jingoist speeches by prominent individuals or government leaders, possibly even including the chief of state, and detailed speculation on the possible military measures that could be implemented if events proved them necessary—all designed to deter the other side from acting in any way that it might later regret.[4]

RUNG 5. SHOW OF FORCE: As the crisis intensifies, one side or the other may display or draw attention to the fact that it does have the capability to use force if need be. There are various ways of showing such force—direct or indirect, silent or noisy. A direct show of force might be the publicized movement of naval or air units, the mobilization of reserves, provocative military exercises or maneuvers, particularly in sensitive areas, or even the "routine" deployment of naval and military units in such areas. An indirect show of force might be the testing of missiles in a provocative way, the conduct of normal maneuvers but with possibly abnormal publicity, the publicized use of military equipment in "normal" but

---

[4] Such detailed speculation also has the deliberate or accidental by-product of educating the other side's decision-makers in military realities and the "sophistications" of escalation and perhaps "controlled war."

special maneuvers which in an important way simulate an aspect of an attack possible in the current crisis, and so on.

The show of force may be silent, in an attempt to impress directly the other side's decision-makers and military and political advisers without necessarily arousing the general public. Or it may be accompanied by a press campaign and official speeches in which it is specifically stressed that the "enemy's" behavior, or the need to rectify injustice, has "forced us to do what we are doing."

As part of a show of force, practice evacuations for either cadres or population can be ordered, or a limited evacuation for particular cities can be tested. Each side might accompany its demonstrations with public statements about the strategic balance of terror. These can be designed to influence one's own side, one's allies, neutrals, or the opposition. Soviet Premier Khrushchev, for example, usually in contexts that were anything but conciliatory, often pointed out the totally disastrous effects of all-out war and the impossibility of limited war.

We, on our side, often point out the enormous superiority we have in weapons. We might amplify these remarks in a Rung 5 crisis by making public relatively detailed calculations on how the United States could conduct a controlled counterforce campaign, and the extreme unlikelihood that the Soviets would actually indulge in a countercity campaign in the face of overwhelming U.S. superiority. As I will discuss later in connection with military central wars (Rungs 32–38), a credible counter-counterthreat can make a threat more credible. We could even announce that if the Soviet leaders did not understand these nuclear subtleties before, we believe they do now.

The Soviets, on their side, would possibly reply much as follows:

The American press notes that the strategy of "counterforce" has been approved by the Joint Chiefs of Staff and the White House and interprets it as some kind of recommendation to the Soviet Union concerning "rules" for the conduct of nuclear war.

The political implication of this strategy is that by conducting a so-called "controlled" nuclear war, the destruction of the capitalist system can be prevented. However, the illusory nature of these hopes is too obvious. If nuclear war is unleashed by the militarists, then no strategy, however it may be called, will save imperialism from destruction.

As a matter of fact, how can everyone be "convinced" of the necessity to adhere to the "new rules" that nuclear strikes should be launched only against military objectives when the majority of such objectives are located in large or smaller cities and populated places. . . .

Similar admissions . . . also . . . unwittingly expose the aggressive nature of the strategy of "counterforce." This strategy . . . stems primarily from the necessity for preventive war. A strategy which contemplates attaining victory through the destruction of the armed forces cannot stem from the idea of "retaliatory blow"; it stems from preventive actions and the achievement of surprise.[5]

RUNG 6. SIGNIFICANT MOBILIZATION: The accompaniment of a show of force by a modest mobilization not only increases one's strength, but also indicates a willingness to call on more force or even to accelerate the arms race if necessary. This phase of the escalation could begin with the traditional cancellation of leaves and discharges of military personnel, and the calling up of key reserve units.

If these moves are followed by a more general mobilization, they may be accompanied by an elaborate explanation of why such measures are needed. It presumably would be argued that one's own security or vital national interests were threatened by the enemy to such a degree that only a show of fighting strength, or preparations for actual fighting, could save the situation. Generally speaking, despite the current *détente,* the present and the past mood of the "public" in both the Soviet Union and the United States is such that in most contexts these measures, if ordered, would be accepted by the population. If there appears to be enemy provocation, it is likely to be taken for granted that such steps are needed.

In addition to calling on military manpower reserves, one might stop phasing out obsolete equipment, cancel previously announced cuts in arms, announce increases in the budget, increase draft calls, or deploy forces on a wartime footing.

[5] Marshal V. D. Sokolovsky (ed.), *Military Strategy* (2d ed.; Moscow, 1963); quoted from *"Military Strategy:* A Comparison of the 1962 and 1963 Editions" (Washington: Joint Publications Service, U.S. Department of Commerce, 1964), p. 83.

The next step might be to have cadres and transportation agencies take modest but serious preparatory measures to move city populations, and to make further preparations in rural areas to feed, receive, and protect evacuees from cities. These last actions can be made to appear threatening, or they can be presented as routine safety measures taken without much thought about their use as a pressure tactic. It is hard to decide in advance which image would be more intimidating to an opponent.

A good example (though taken from a "pre-crisis" context) would be the following excerpts from a speech made by Khrushchev on August 7, 1961, in reaction to budget increases in the United States:

> Khrushchev said, "The Western Powers are now pushing the world to a dangerous brink, and the threat of a military attack by the imperialists on the socialist states is not ruled out.
>
> "We shall watch developments and act according to how the situation shapes up," Khrushchev said. He added: "It may be that we shall have to increase, in the future, the numerical strength of the army on the Western frontiers by moving divisions from other parts of the Soviet Union. In connection with this, we may have to call up a part of the reservists so that our divisions have a full complement and are ready for any eventuality."
>
> The head of the Soviet Government said that these are reply measures; the United States is in effect carrying out measures in the nature of a mobilization, and is threatening to start a war. Its allies in aggressive blocs support this dangerous course.
>
> "When a situation like this arises, it would be impermissible for us to sit with folded hands. History teaches us that when an aggressor sees that he is not rebuffed, he becomes brazen and when, on the contrary, he is rebuffed he calms down," Khrushchev said.
>
> Khrushchev said that in carrying out defensive measures and strengthening the might of the socialist motherland, various rocket weapons—intercontinental ballistic rockets, rockets of various range, strategic and tactical purpose, with atomic and hydrogen warheads—were also being developed; and that the necessary attention was being paid to other kinds of military equipment.[6]

In his speech, Khrushchev went on to describe the basic strengths and successes of the Soviet Union, its firm desire for peace, and

[6] Quoted from a summary issued by the Soviet Embassy in Washington on August 8, 1961.

how imperative it was for the Soviets to match or exceed the U.S. mobilization. He noted the problems of U.S.-German and Soviet-German relationships in such a way as to maximize the divisive effect on the NATO alliance as follows:

> Referring to the recent speech of the United States President, the Chairman of the U.S.S.R. Council of Ministers stated that the President "allowed himself to resort to threats." The President did not even stop at presenting the U.S.S.R. with something in the nature of an ultimatum, in reply to the proposal to conclude a peace treaty with Germany.
>
> "It goes without saying," Khrushchev went on, "that World War III, should it start, will not be limited to a duel between the two Great Powers—the Soviet Union and the United States of America. Is it not a fact that more than one dozen states have been ensnared in the net of military alliances formed by the United States and, of course, they would find themselves drawn into the war orbit. We are taking all this into account and have at our disposal the necessary means of combat, to be able, if the imperialists do unleash war, to strike a crushing blow not only at the territory of the United States, but also to render harmless the allies of the aggressor and to suppress American military bases flung throughout the world. Any state which would be used as a springboard for attacking the socialist camp will experience the full devastating power of our blow."
>
> Khrushchev stressed that the settlement of the question of a peace treaty with Germany cannot be postponed. To put off the conclusion of this treaty for several more years, he said, would mean to connive at aggressive forces, to retreat under their pressure. Such a position would lend still greater encouragement to NATO and the Bonn Government to form more and more divisions in West Germany, to equip them with atomic and thermonuclear weapons, to make West Germany the main force for unleashing a new world war.[7]

Khrushchev next raised the question of a peace treaty with East Germany in a way that indicated resoluteness, firmness, and reasonableness, and then concluded as follows:

> He declared that to the Western Powers the question of access to West Berlin and the question of a peace treaty as a whole is only a

7 *Ibid.*

pretext. What they want is to impose their will upon the countries of the socialist camp.

He said that, had we renounced the conclusion of a peace treaty, the Western Powers would assess this as a strategic breakthrough and at once extend the range of their demands. They would demand the liquidation of the socialist system in the GDR, would set the task of annexing from Poland and Czechoslovakia the lands restored to them under the Potsdam Agreement. And had the Western Powers attained all that, they would have presented their main claim—to abolish the socialist system in all the countries of the socialist camp.

This is why, Khrushchev went on, the settlement of the question of the peace treaty cannot be postponed. The conclusion of a peace treaty with GDR will have a tremendous positive significance for the development of the entire international situation.[8]

Thus Khrushchev explained that he was, in effect, "locked in." He could not afford to back down.

As always, private communications, either direct or indirect, through principals or intermediates, or through the use of more or less deliberately arranged leaks, can all play an important role. It should be clear that Rung 6 might easily lie below Rung 5, but if Rung 5 is accompanied by significant mobilization, this is indeed a substantial increase in the level of escalation. A mobilization by itself may be much less escalatory.

RUNG 7. "LEGAL" HARASSMENT—RETORTIONS: One may harass the opponent's prestige, property, or nationals legally. These acts are called "retortions" in international law. They are deliberately designed to indicate extreme hostility, and are carried through in a manner more provocative than the gestures discussed at Rung 3.

These retortions could go all the way from the revocation of tariff concessions (presumably at Rung 2) to such things as punitive acts against the opponent's nationals, embargoes on the shipment of goods, or even "peaceful" blockades. The opponent can also be harassed with propaganda or by means of familiar tactics like the Soviet stoppages of rail and road transport to West Berlin, or interference with shipping on public-health or safety pretexts.

[8] *Ibid.*

RUNG 8. HARASSING ACTS OF VIOLENCE: If the crisis is still not resolved, one side or the other may move on to illegal acts, acts of violence, or harassments intended to confuse, exhaust, discredit, frighten, and otherwise harm, weaken, or demoralize the opponent or his allies. Bombs may be exploded by unauthorized or anonymous means. Enemy nationals within one's border can be badly mistreated or killed. Embassies may be stoned or raided. Soldiers guarding the border may be shot. There may be kidnaping or assassination of important or (more likely) unimportant personalities, or the limited covert use of guerrilla warfare, piracy, sabotage, or terrorization. Reconnaissance probing operations or other intelligence activities may be increased. There may be overflights or other invasions of sovereignty. Harassing acts can also be verbal, either abusive or threatening in nature. But then we would put them between Rungs 2 and 7, unless they were of an extravagantly provocative and abnormal sort and were, in effect, illegal acts.

The exact level of escalation that is reached by any particular harassing act of violence depends upon details. If the act is carried out clandestinely or covertly—under the guise of being an individually motivated act of banditry or some other spontaneous individual action—the escalation is relatively low.

As the size, scale, and degree of organization of these acts are increased, and their official character is made plain, the escalation is increased, until finally we reach a level at which uniformed personnel, obviously under the orders of their government, are carrying through the actions.

To some degree, there may be large cultural differences in how these things are regarded. For example, it is quite possible that the Government of North Vietnam did not completely understand the distinction the United States would make between the sinking of one or two U.S. ships by saboteurs in the harbor of Saigon and a naval attack in international waters (even if only a few miles off the North Vietnamese coast) on a U.S. destroyer. From our point of view, the latter act was indeed a very large escalation, because very important thresholds had been crossed. We reacted violently and decisively.

The North Vietnamese, though, may have been surprised that the U.S. was so provoked by the second class of acts and so tolerant of the first. One can easily imagine a high-level meeting in Hanoi at which frequent references were made to the "inscrutable Americans."

RUNG 9. DRAMATIC MILITARY CONFRONTATIONS: The existing permanent alert of U.S. and Soviet strategic forces is an almost continual global confrontation. A case may be made that this is pre-escalation (i.e., subcrisis disagreement—Cold War); generally, this is so. However, if an important or dramatic increase occurs, the situation changes. For example, American bases overseas and American targets on the mainland are at all times zeroed in by Soviet missiles, and vice versa, but this activity can be increased and made more visible, perhaps to the point where it appears quite threatening. Moreover, the military movement can be accompanied conspicuously by various forms of political warfare.

Tension can build up further, and there may be limited but dramatic military confrontations, either local (as, for example, at the Brandenburg Gate) or global. Such confrontations are direct tests of nerve, committal, resolve, and recklessness. They are also dramatic enough to make all the participants and observers take note of what has happened. Because it seems so obvious that these confrontations can blow up, and because in the past such incidents have often caused wars, many people think of them as being closer to the brink of all-out war than, in fact, they usually are.

Under contemporary conditions of a relatively firm balance of terror, it is hard to believe that a war will erupt directly from, say, a frontier incident, although the uncertainties are such that the possibility cannot be completely disregarded. However, the main purpose of such confrontations, in addition to showing the resolve mentioned above, is to indicate clearly that reasonably large acts of violence are possible, that the unthinkable all-out war is becoming "thinkable," even possible.

A Recent Example of a "Traditional Crisis" Scenario

A spectacular recent example of a traditional crisis was the Cuban missile crisis of October, 1962. Almost everything discussed in this chapter actually occurred in that crisis. Again, it would take us too far afield to discuss the crisis in detail, but because it is such an interesting and important example I have included here a lengthy quotation from a speech made by Chairman Khrushchev in November, 1962, describing the Cuban crisis quite graphically. While his account is not completely accurate, he does show how such a crisis looks to a participant. (I will also, subsequently, quote from some news stories that describe other aspects of the Rungs 5 and 6 activities that took place during the crisis.)

How the Cuban Events Developed.—The development of events in the Caribbean proved that the menace of such aggression was present. A forced concentration of large units of the navy, air force, paratroops and Marines began in the U.S. South, at the approaches to Cuba, in the last ten days of October. The U.S. government sent reinforcements to its military base at Guantanamo, on Cuban territory. Big maneuvers in the Caribbean were announced. It was planned to make a landing on Vieques Island in the course of these "maneuvers." On Oct. 22 the Kennedy government proclaimed the establishment of a quarantine of Cuba. The word "quarantine" in this instance was only a fig leaf. Actually, it was a matter of a blockade, of piracy on the high seas.

Events developed at a swift pace. The American command put all its armed forces, including troops stationed in Europe, as well as the Sixth Fleet, in the Mediterranean, and the Seventh Fleet based in the Taiwan area, in a state of complete combat readiness. Several paratroop, infantry and armored divisions, numbering some 100,000 men, were allocated for the attack on Cuba alone. In addition, 183 warships, with 85,000 sailors on board, were moved toward the shores of Cuba. Several thousand warplanes were to cover the landing on Cuba. About 20 per cent of all U.S. Strategic Air Command planes, carrying atomic and hydrogen bombs, were kept aloft around the clock. Reserves were called up.

Troops of the U.S. NATO allies in Europe were placed in full combat readiness. A joint command of the U.S.A. and Latin American countries was set up, while some of these countries sent their warships to participate in the blockade of Cuba. As a result of these aggressive steps by the U.S. government the menace of thermonuclear war hung over the world.

In the face of these intensified war preparations we, on our part, were obliged to carry out appropriate measures. The Soviet government instructed the U.S.S.R. Defense Minister to put the entire army of the Soviet Union, and above all the Soviet intercontinental and strategic missile troops, the country's surface-to-air anti-aircraft missile defenses, fighter planes of the anti-aircraft defenses, strategic aviation and naval forces, in a state of combat readiness. Our submarine fleet, including atomic submarines, took up positions as instructed. A state of heightened combat readiness was proclaimed for the ground forces, and the discharge from the Soviet Army of the older contingents of the strategic rocket troops, the anti-aircraft troops and the submarine fleet was postponed. The armed forces of the Warsaw Treaty countries were also placed in full combat readiness.

In these circumstances, if one or the other side had failed to show restraint, failed to do all that was necessary to prevent the outbreak of war, an explosion would have followed, with irreparable consequences.

Now that the tension caused by the developments in the Caribbean has been broken and we are in the final stage of settling the conflict, I wish to report to the Supreme Soviet Deputies what the Soviet government did to put out the advancing flames of war.

On Oct. 23, immediately after the United States instituted its blockade of Cuba, the Soviet government, while taking measures of a defensive nature, issued a statement in which it firmly warned that the U.S. government was assuming grave responsibility for the destiny of the world and playing recklessly with fire. We frankly told the U.S. President that we would not tolerate piratical actions by U.S. ships on the high seas and would take appropriate measures to this end.

At the same time the Soviet government appealed to all peoples to block the aggressors' way. Simultaneously it took certain steps in the United Nations. The Soviet government's peaceful initiative toward settling the Cuban crisis met with full support from the socialist countries and the peoples of the majority of the other U.N. member-countries. U.N. Secretary General U Thant made great efforts to settle the conflict.

However, the government of the United States of America continued to exacerbate the atmosphere. The U.S. military forces pushed the development of events so as to carry out an attack on Cuba. We received information from Cuban comrades and from other sources on the morning of Oct. 27 directly stating that this attack would be carried out in the next two or three days. We interpreted these cables as an extremely alarming warning signal. And the alarm was justified.

Immediate action was necessary to prevent the attack on Cuba and to preserve peace. A message was sent to the U.S. President prompting a mutually acceptable solution. It was still not too late at that moment to extinguish the wick of war that had already begun to smolder. In sending this message we took into account the fact that the messages of the President himself also expressed alarm and a desire to find a way out of the situation that had taken shape. We declared that if the U.S.A. pledged not to invade Cuba and also restrained other ally-states from aggression against Cuba, the Soviet Union would be prepared to remove from Cuba the weapons the U.S.A. calls "offensive."

In reply, the President of the United States, for his part, declared that if the Soviet government agreed to remove these weapons from Cuba, the U.S. government would lift the quarantine, that is to say the blockade, and give assurance of the rejection both by the United States and by other countries of the Western hemisphere of an invasion of Cuba. The President declared in all definiteness, and the whole world knows this, that the United States would not attack Cuba and would also restrain its allies from such actions.

But after all, this was why we had sent our weapons to Cuba, to prevent an attack on her! Therefore the Soviet government confirmed its agreement to withdraw ballistic missiles from Cuba.

Thus, in short, a mutually acceptable settlement was reached that signified a victory for reason and success for the cause of peace. The Cuban question moved into the phase of peaceful negotiations and, as concerns the United States of America, was transferred there, so to say, from the hands of generals into the hands of diplomats.

On Oct. 29 negotiations began in New York between representatives of the U.S.S.R., the U.S.A. and Cuba, with the participation of U Thant. Comrade Mikoyan, First Vice-Chairman of the U.S.S.R. Council of Ministers, flew to Havana for an exchange of views with the government of Cuba.

Meanwhile, both sides set about fulfilling the commitments they had undertaken. The Soviet Union withdrew from Cuba all the missiles that the United States called offensive weapons. The Soviet personnel servicing the missile installations also left. The United States was given the opportunity of convincing itself that all the ballistic missiles that had been placed in Cuba were really withdrawn, and this was confirmed in statements by U.S. officials.

At the same time, seeking to expedite the settlement of the Caribbean crisis, we agreed to the withdrawal of Soviet IL-28 planes from Cuba within a month's time, even though they were outdated as bombers. By Dec. 7 these planes had been withdrawn from Cuba. They had been sent to Cuba only with a view to their potential use as a kind of flying artillery for coastal defense, operating under cover of anti-aircraft weapons. On Nov. 21 the U.S. government, for its part, lifted the naval blockade of Cuba and recalled its warships from that area. The American command withdrew the troops and planes that had been concentrated in the Florida area for attack on Cuba and demobilized the called-up reserves. The additional troops that had been sent to Guantanamo in the crisis period were also withdrawn from that base. At the same time, the President reaffirmed the U.S. pledge that Cuba would not be invaded.

In view of this, we also cancelled the military measures that we had been obliged to take in the light of the exacerbation of the crisis over Cuba. The Cuban Republic, in turn, set about demobilizing those who had been called up to defend their homeland, and they are returning to peaceful work and to their families.

At present favorable conditions have been created for liquidating the dangerous crisis that arose in the Caribbean. Now it is necessary to bring the negotiations to completion, to put on record the agreement reached as a result of the exchange of messages between the government of the Soviet Union and the U.S. government, and to seal this agreement with the authority of the United Nations.

The Soviet government is convinced that it is not in the interests of peace to delay completion of the settlement of the Caribbean crisis, and we hope that the government of the United States also understands this.[9]

One of the most interesting documents that came out of the Cuban missile crisis was President Kennedy's dramatic television address of October 22, 1962. He began with the statement that the government had maintained adequate surveillance of the Soviet military buildup in Cuba and described in detail the Soviet posture and just how dangerous this posture could be. Mr. Kennedy then went on to indicate that he had every right to feel aggrieved because the Soviets had lied to and misled him:

This action also contradicts the repeated assurances of Soviet spokesmen both publicly and privately delivered that the arms buildup in

[9] *Current Digest of the Soviet Press*, XIV, No. 51 (January 16, 1963), 5–6.

Cuba would retain its original defensive character and that the Soviet Union had no need or desire to station strategic missiles on the territory of any other nation.

The size of this undertaking makes clear that it had been planned for some months.

Yet only last month after I had made clear the distinction between any introduction of ground-to-ground missiles and the existence of defensive antiaircraft missiles, the Soviet Government publicly stated on Sept. 11 that, and I quote, "the armaments and military equipment sent to Cuba are designed exclusively for defensive purposes," unquote, that there is—and I quote the Soviet Government—"there is no need for the Soviet Government to shift its weapons for a retaliatory blow to any other country, for instance, Cuba," unquote, and that—and I quote the Government—"the Soviet Union has so powerful rockets to carry these nuclear warheads that there is no need to search for sites for them beyond the boundaries of the Soviet Union," unquote.

That statement was false.

Only last Thursday, as evidence of this rapid offensive buildup was already in my hand, Soviet Foreign Minister Gromyko told me in my office that he was instructed to make it clear once again, as he said his Government had already done, that Soviet assistance to Cuba, and I quote, "pursued solely the purpose of contributing to the defense capabilities of Cuba," unquote.

That, and I quote him, "training by Soviet specialists Cuban nationals in handling defensive armaments was by no means offensive," and that if it were otherwise, Mr. Gromyko went on, "the Soviet Government would never become involved in rendering such assistance."

That statement also was false.

The President then went on to discuss how both the Soviet Union and the United States, recognizing the need for tacit rules in the postwar world, had "deployed strategic nuclear weapons with great care, never upsetting the precious *status quo* which insured that these weapons would not be used in the absence of some vital challenges." He indicated that while the Americans had always been careful, that the Soviets had now broken the rules in

. . . this secret, swift, extraordinary buildup of Communist missiles in an area well-known to have a special and historical relation to the

United States . . . this sudden clandestine decision to station strategic weapons for the first time outside of Soviet soil—is a deliberately provocative and unjustified change in the *status quo*, which cannot be accepted by this country if our courage and our commitments are ever to be trusted again by either friend or foe. The 1930's taught us a clear lesson, aggressive conduct, if allowed to be unchecked and unchallenged, ultimately leads to war.

He proceeded to describe the detailed measures that the U.S. was taking and then issued his famous warning: "It shall be the policy of this nation to regard any nuclear missile launched from Cuba against any nation in the Western Hemisphere as an attack by the Soviet Union on the United States, requiring a full retaliatory response upon the Soviet Union." (Of course, anyone familiar with current U.S. policy would note that the phrase "full retaliatory response" does not specify the form of the attack. It is still open as to whether it would be counterforce or countervalue.)

After finishing the discussion of the measures he was taking, President Kennedy issued a special appeal to Chairman Khrushchev:

I call Chairman Khrushchev to halt and eliminate this clandestine, reckless and provocative threat to world peace and to stable relations between our two nations . . . by refraining from any action which will widen or deepen the present crisis, and then by participating in a search for peaceful and permanent solutions.

Then, and possibly most important of all, Mr. Kennedy issued the following warning: "Any hostile move anywhere in the world against the safety and freedom of peoples to whom we are committed, including in particular the brave people of West Berlin, will be met by whatever action is needed." It was probably of some tactical importance that the President specifically mentioned that the Soviets could, of course, retaliate by escalating in West Berlin, but that this would be very dangerous. A quite common but probably wrong tactic would have been not to bring up the subject, avoiding calling the Soviets' attention to this option. In fact, it is quite important to show that one is willing to face the possibility of such counterescalations, whether or not one is. The speech then continued with an appeal to the Cuban people and some comments on the importance of arms control and freedom, ending finally with a moving, if inevitable, appeal to Western ideals, values, and attitudes:

> My fellow citizens, let no one doubt that this is a difficult and dangerous effort on which we have set out. No one can foresee precisely what course it will take, or what course or casualties will be incurred.
>
> Many months of sacrifice and self-discipline lie ahead, months in which both our patience and our will will be tested. Months in which many threats and denunciations will keep us aware of our dangers. But the greatest danger of all would be to do nothing.
>
> The path we have chosen for the present is full of hazards, as all paths are. But it is the one most consistent with our character and courage as a nation and our commitments around the world.
>
> The cost of freedom is always high, but Americans have always paid it.
>
> And one path we shall never choose, and that is the path of surrender, or submission.
>
> Our goal is not the victory of might, but the vindication of right; not peace at the expense of freedom, but both peace and freedom here in this hemisphere, and, we hope, around the world.

I have quoted at length from the Khrushchev and Kennedy speeches because I want to suggest the flavor of the kinds of escalation and warnings I have been talking about, and to show how they may be conveyed through the normal rhetoric of public life.

I will close this chapter with a quotation from a column by Max Frankel which makes it clear that President Kennedy understood well the necessity for a pre-emptive escalation, even if it was only a verbal one:

> Soviet officials were not forewarned either, except by the indications of crisis in the capital this weekend. It was not until 6 P.M., one hour before the President went on the air, that Secretary of State Dean Rusk received the Soviet Ambassador, Anatoly F. Dobrynin, to announce the blockade.
>
> The elaborate secrecy here in the last few days and the lack of consultation with its allies was an important ingredient of United States strategy.

Every precaution was taken to prevent premature disclosure so that Moscow would not be able to intercede with an ultimatum or new commitment to Cuba before the President spoke.

The Soviet Union is on record with a series of tough-sounding but vague commitments to defend Cuba against aggression. It has repeatedly proclaimed the right to construct bases in Cuba for "defensive purposes."

Moscow has equated this with Western rights to maintain bases in Turkey, Italy and Japan, among other places.

Mr. Kennedy's intention was to present the Russians with the blockade as an accomplished fact before Moscow and Washington became engaged in an exchange of commitments that might have made a direct clash a certainty.

The President had been prepared to advance the time of his announcement if there had been any sign of a Soviet move.[10]

[10] *The New York Times*, October 23, 1962, p. 19.

V

Intense Crises

Basic Description and Definition

I use the term "intense crisis" to mark a crisis in which a significant number of people actually envisage that nuclear war may really occur, yet nuclear weapons have not yet been employed. Of course, there are many who understand abstractly that nuclear weapons exist and may be used, but in this kind of intense crisis the nuclear incredulity that all of us share would be sharply decreased if not eliminated. The "unreal and hypothetical" nuclear stockpiles that exist would suddenly represent a real threat. This change probably would not come all at once, and it might be a limited development; but a part of the population and most of the decision-makers would acknowledge that a nuclear war might take place—that it was no longer either "unthinkable" or "impossible."

Determining the number of people who must reach this conclusion for a crisis to be "intense," the kinds of people, and the extent of their concern clearly must be an arbitrary judgment. Operationally, it would be very difficult to make such measurements, although in practice I think the operational distinction may be simpler than the theoretical one. In any case, the matter will depend on a specific course of events.

Rungs 10–20 are included in this category of intense crisis. (See Figure 3, p. 39.) We have, of course, already experienced a large conventional war (Rung 12) in Korea, and many in Washington thought at that time that it was the prelude to World War

III. While Korea can be thought of as an intense crisis, it occurred in a relatively nonnuclear period (when the Russians had little or almost no strategic capability, and relatively little tactical capability even against Europe—at least as far as nuclear weapons were concerned). Something approaching a super-ready status (Rung 11) was experienced in both the Suez and Cuban crises; but I would regard Rung 11 as a crisis rather more intense even than those two.

Thus, if one "measures" the seriousness of a crisis by Rungs 10 or 13 through 20, it is clear that we have not had an "intense" crisis since World War II. If one wants a single standard by which to judge whether a crisis is "intense," very likely Rung 17 (in which large cities are evacuated by about 20 per cent of the population) provides it (assuming, of course, that the government does not take special measures to prevent such evacuation).

The intense-crisis category brings us into the "neither-war-nor-peace" region so characteristic of much current discussion. This area is not really unprecedented, but the introduction of nuclear weapons has made it somewhat more significant. In the early years of the postwar era, an assumption was made by many analysts that once a strategic stalemate materialized, the United States and the Soviet Union would be very likely to feel that they could safely provoke each other under this umbrella of terror. They believed then that all-out war would be deterred, but that events that would fall into this intense-crisis category would occur fairly often since each side would be willing to probe or push. This has not happened. The fear of possible eruption to the upper rungs has been great enough to strengthen the first two thresholds rather than to weaken them. This is paradoxical, since one might have thought that nations might be willing to manipulate the first two thresholds when they had greater confidence in the next two. But the more terrifying the upper rungs, the more all the thresholds are strengthened—or so it seems if the experience of the last ten years is an accurate indication of how to estimate such effects.

The Rungs of Intense Crises

RUNG 10. PROVOCATIVE BREAKING OFF OF DIPLOMATIC RELATIONS: The escalatory character of this rung is difficult to estimate *a priori* because, even more than with most rungs, much depends on the circumstances of this diplomatic break. However, I would provisionally suggest that a provocative withdrawal of diplomatic relations would be just past the nuclear-incredulity threshold. After all, this act is a traditional notification that two nations are nearing war. It is a fairly persuasive communication that one nation does not intend to coexist on normal terms with another, and that something further is likely to happen before the crisis is settled. If the break were accomplished in a sufficiently provocative and dramatic manner, it probably would lead to some of the subsequent actions of intense crisis. On the other hand, a diplomatic break with Russia of the kind sometimes advocated by some right-wing groups in the United States might simply be considered a foolish or frivolous gesture, in some circumstances an indication of a lack of seriousness, rather than of seriousness.

RUNG 11. SUPER-READY STATUS: A "ready" status may be partial or total. The present handling of SAC is an instance of partial-ready status. It may be regarded as a routine precaution rather than as the highest point that escalation has reached between the U.S. and the U.S.S.R. However, Soviet-American tension is a necessary political background for partial-ready status, and the status has come about by accumulation. Ten years or so ago, a great deal of criticism would have been leveled against the idea of maintaining strategic forces with ready triggers, but now there is hardly any, at least in the United States.

However, even our routine-ready status creates problems with allies and in the United Nations. A super-ready status would produce very much more. In particular, it would automatically involve dangerous or costly actions. If it did not, we would be doing these things normally. In a super-ready status, strategic forces may be dispersed, leaves canceled, preventive and routine maintenance halted, training deferred, every possible piece of equipment and unit put in a ready status, and limited war forces deployed. All these measures are expensive to carry out, seem to involve an increase in the probability of inadvertent war, interfere with normal training, and possibly produce other political and military repercussions. Because of the relative invulnerability and alertness under normal peacetime conditions of the U.S. Minuteman and Polaris forces (and to some extent of the bombers), such actions may be of greater importance for the Soviet Union than for the United States.

To assume a super-ready status is to say: "I would not do all of these dangerous and expensive things unless I were willing to go pretty far, perhaps to the limit. Clearly, you had better reconsider your estimate of my resolve." This can be said even more emphatically and clearly if the super-ready status is accompanied by limited "spoofing" or "jamming" or other hostile acts which tend to degrade the opponent's defensive capability so that he is less able to retaliate to a surprise attack. While at this stage these acts might not be carried so far as to make a great difference in the strategic balance, they would demonstrate resolve and determination, if not recklessness, and they would also tend to weaken the resolve of the other side in the strategic balance precisely because they are so dangerous. Such preliminary spoofing and jamming are especially "persuasive" methods of bluntly asking the other side to make a choice among compromise, a dangerous continuation of the crisis, or immediate escalation to an all-out war.

RUNG 12. LARGE CONVENTIONAL WAR (OR ACTIONS): The stage has now been set for some kind of organized military violence. It may be relatively large-scale undeclared war or border fighting such as what occurred between the Japanese and the Soviets in 1939 (involving thousands of soldiers), a Trieste-type occupation of disputed territory, or a major "police action," as in Korea.

If such a war is fought with any intensity, both sides suffer casualties in large numbers, but neither will use their more "efficient" or "quality" weapons—the nuclear, bacteriological, or chemical weapons. Paradoxically, the more "useful" these weapons are in the narrow military sense, the less likely they are to be used. In any case, there would be many casualties at this rung and, at least in the initial stages of the action, a significant deepening of the crisis.

RUNG 13. LARGE COMPOUND ESCALATION: One way to achieve a high over-all level of escalation and still keep each separate act as an act relatively low on the ladder is to retaliate or escalate in a completely different theater from the one in which the primary conflict is being waged, and at a time when the primary crisis is at a fairly intense level. This may be especially escalatory if the second theater is sensitive or potentially vital.

It is interesting to note that, except in rather small-scale actions, this obvious technique has not been used since World War II, even though there has been much concern about the possibility. For example, many senior government officials were deeply concerned that the Soviets might bring Berlin or Turkey into the Cuban missile crisis of October, 1962, by saying, for example, "Whatever you do to our access to Cuba, we will do to your access to Berlin. If you stop ships, we will stop trucks. If you sink ships, we will destroy trucks and planes," and so on. I have already noted that President Kennedy, in a speech, tried to pre-empt this possibility. Secretary Dulles' massive-retaliation threats, at "times and places of our own choosing," were threats of compound escalation, but were never carried out.

Thus, nearly everyone has instinctively recognized the danger of compound escalation, even though the reasons for the danger have never been fully explicated and articulated. Starting a new crisis when another is at full force is sheer audacity and very dangerous, yet in the paradoxical world of escalation this might be the very reason it would be judged in certain circumstances to be an effective measure.

RUNG 14. DECLARATION OF LIMITED CONVENTIONAL WAR: Nearly all commentators on this subject, and to some degree the U.S. Government, agree that if limited wars have to be fought it is best to fight them with conventional weapons, and that it is unwise to try to improve deterrence by increasing the likelihood that nuclear weapons will be used. Currently, the United States tends to fight limited conventional actions in the guise of "police" actions or by employing advisory groups. These devices make it easier for the U.S. to resist or neutralize domestic pressures to escalate: police actions are normally limited. We do not usually furnish police even with tanks or planes.

A tradition of limited conventional action has now been more or less firmly established, and it might be in our interest, if we should fight another such war, to make a formal declaration of limited conventional war. Such a declaration could also be used to cover and maintain a "phony war" period in which we did not actually fight very much, or at all, but kept open the possibility of such fighting.

Such a declaration would also provide the objectives or potential advantages discussed later in connection with Rung 32 (formal declaration of "general" war). In particular, it could be used to attempt to: (1) achieve a clear-cut declaration of "no-first-use," hopefully giving the enemy clear incentives to reciprocate; (2) set the limits of the conventional actions, geographically or otherwise, in a manner considered favorable to us; (3) create a wartime psychology in the United States, facilitating and motivating major increases in the military budget and the enactment of various crash military programs; and (4) make legal and "acceptable" the inflicting and incurring of casualties.

RUNG 15. BARELY NUCLEAR WAR: It may occur at any of the previous four rungs, but most particularly between Rungs 11 and 14, that one or a small number of nuclear weapons is used unintentionally as a result of the reduced safeguards and new stresses of an intense crisis. "Unintentional" uses could also be deliberate, in that the user could try to give an impression that a deliberate use was unintentional. There are at least two reasons for such deceptions. First, the mere fact that a nuclear "accident" had occurred would indicate clearly to the opponent, and to others who could put pressure on him, that the situation was very dangerous. The fact that the incident is called unauthorized or accidental gives special point to the warning and reduces the likelihood of retaliation or other escalation. (And such a course of action is a two-edged sword; it can also deter or frighten one's own side. The differential advantages to be achieved or lost by raising such apprehensions depend in part on the details of the balance of military power and the internal discipline and control each side has.) Second, the attacker may feel that it is particularly important to destroy some key enemy installation (for example, a centralized command and control headquarters, a particularly strategic base, a warning center, or the like) and find that he can do so only with nuclear weapons. He might destroy this installation and still hope that the opponent would accept it as an accidental or unauthorized use of a weapon. The offending side could offer to punish the guilty individuals, perhaps to provide an indemnification, or to permit a reprisal (but not really a compensating one) by the other side.

Such a use of "barely nuclear war" is exactly opposite to its symbolic or communications use. One side is actually using nuclear weapons to destroy something on the other side, but attempts to disguise this act so that the other side will not consider it a true escalation to nuclear conflict. (Some members of the analytic community have become so accustomed to the idea of nuclear weapons as carriers of symbols and messages rather than as agents of destruction that when the concept of "barely nuclear war" was first suggested, by Max Singer, they had difficulty in understanding it.)

RUNG 16. NUCLEAR "ULTIMATUMS": Whether or not there is a conventional or barely nuclear war, the crisis could enter a stage of such intensity that nuclear incredulity would not merely be weakened but would vanish. This obviously would occur when one side or the other seriously considered launching a central war and communicated this fact convincingly to its opponent. Presumably, most crises will have been settled before this point, since every rung of the ladder climbed so far has increased the pressure on both sides to settle. But it is also possible that the exertion of pressure would simply provoke counterpressures. In any case, I want to illustrate how such a situation might escalate.

At this point, the decision-makers are no longer thinking, "Neither side wants war, so the other side must back down." Or even, "The current tense situation obviously increases the possibility of an accident. The other side must feel this pressure and is therefore likely to back down." Now they are announcing, "Unless *you* back down, *we* will go to war"—a quite different thing. Or perhaps, "One of us has to be reasonable before this crisis blows up, and *it won't be me.*" Hopefully, no crisis will ever reach this stage.

But one outstanding possibility in this kind of intense crisis is an ultimatum (or quasi ultimatum) with an explicit or implicit time limit. Such an ultimatum forces the side to which it is addressed really to think in terms of nuclear war. It shatters the illusion that "unthinkable" means impossible. In any case, with or without a quasi ultimatum, the populations of both sides will, at this rung, fear war and will begin to leave target areas. We have suggested that one might define an intense crisis operationally as that time when 10 or 20 per cent of the population of New York City or Moscow has left the city out of a fear of attack. The 1958 (and later) Berlin crisis did not come even close to this rung of the escalation ladder because the "ultimatums" the Soviet Union issued were vague and heavily qualified, more appropriate to the ostensible-crisis category.

RUNG 17. LIMITED EVACUATION (APPROXIMATELY 20 PER CENT): Either the Soviet Union or the United States, or both, might carry out partial official evacuation of their cities. There is no doubt that, without an intense crisis, evacuation would meet with very great resistance from part of the population. However, the evacuation order itself might generate such a sense of crisis.

The effect of the evacuation on the resolve of the people and the decision-makers might be very different. Even if the decision-makers have ordered the evacuation for prudential rather than bargaining reasons, they may still feel they can play a stronger hand if most of the population is in, or can soon be moved to, places of relative safety. The people, on the other hand, may be both frightened and resentful.

Depending on the details of the crisis, the success of the evacuation, and the appearance of the protective arrangements, popular fright and resentment may prove to be an important force for government moderation, accommodation, or even appeasement. Of course, during the most intense moments of a crisis, the public is likely to have little influence on national actions. However, as I will discuss later in the chapter dealing with aftermaths, subsequent popular reaction, if the crisis de-escalates, may be an all-important influence on the ability of a country to meet future crises or even the threat of future crises.

Preparations for large-scale evacuation and improvised protection, or the actual creation of such protection without actual evacuation, if carried through with enough official seriousness and publicity, belong very near Rung 17, and I would probably place them at this rung.

RUNG 18. SPECTACULAR SHOW OR DEMONSTRATION OF FORCE: Rather than the show of force of Rung 5, this is an actual use of strategic weapons. Even if the "physical demonstration" did no obvious damage or destruction, it would still seem extremely menacing, reckless, and determined. Such a use or demonstration could involve a harmless detonation of a big weapon high over enemy territory, or the delivery of leaflets by ICBM's.

A demonstration of force is intended to be as harmless (and as serious) as a sentry shooting in the air and crying "Halt," or a naval patrol firing across the bow of a suspicious vessel. Its purpose may be the same—to halt some kind of action. It may also be to punish the enemy for a previous act (with intention of establishing a precedent that would deter later provocations) or to intensify the fear of war. It is, in any event, an impressive, even if symbolic, act.

Such a dramatic and thoroughly provocative gesture would undoubtedly bring about mixed reactions among both decision-makers and the public. Regardless of who had caused or previously escalated the underlying crisis, many would be opposed to and angry at the country that had escalated to the use of strategic weapons. These negative reactions could create internal disunity within a nation or alliance. There would also be great pressures on the opponent to make reprisals regardless of the danger in doing so, and there would be pressure to make concessions, perhaps after a reprisal action had been taken in order to "save face."

There are obvious variations among the United States, the Soviet Union, China, France, and other nations in their ability successfully to initiate and carry through or resist this tactic. But these differences can be exaggerated. Indeed, there are probably many circumstances in which such nations as the United States or France might be able to use the tactics as well as or better than their totalitarian opponents.

RUNG 19. "JUSTIFIABLE" COUNTERFORCE ATTACKS: There are many situations that allow "legal" or extralegal local counterforce attacks in peacetime. Either strict legality is disregarded or enough of a case has been made for committing a given act so that the question of legality or illegality is controversial, or is made to seem controversial.

In most cases, of course, if one side can attack, harm, or otherwise forcibly degrade the capabilities of the other side in a significant or dramatic fashion without actually crossing clear-cut jurisdictional lines, the action is still likely to be limited and not quite as escalatory as Rung 19. Thus, one might shoot down a plane outside one's borders but claim that the plane was within one's borders.

But in more dramatic and significant acts, such as the destruction of a submarine on the claim that it had carried out threatening maneuvers, a high degree of escalation could easily be involved, particularly if it were a strategic-weapons submarine. Even more escalatory would be the destruction of a number of submarines, either all at once or over a short period of time. An excuse for such an act might be obtained by manufacturing an incident, perhaps fabricating a charge of limited use of nuclear weapons by the submarines.

Clandestine or covert, but large-scale, acts of sabotage by unacknowledged agents could make a significant difference in the performance of the opponent's defensive system, and they could also be extralegal attacks. This damage would have to be on a large scale or otherwise be more significant than, say, a Russian trawler breaking an important U.S. cable. At this escalatory level, either a large number of important communication cables would have to be cut or there would have to be physical destruction of such important installations as the DEW Line in the Far North.

Or the Soviets could launch a missile against an isolated Allied or U.S. base or aircraft carrier, claiming that a U-2 had flown from it or that it had been responsible for some other provocation. They might bomb the radar we are said to have in Turkey on the grounds that it was used for spying. The Soviets could conceivably even arrange to have a U.S. missile stationed in Europe shot at themselves, and then proceed to destroy some of our missiles in return, on the grounds that although these missiles were dangerous we refused to operate them safely and insisted on keeping them on accident-prone alert status.

A "justifiable" attack would have to be sufficiently specialized and have sufficient cause to look like a limited, reasonable response to an intolerable provocation, and yet it might significantly or even disastrously degrade the military capability, prestige, or morale of the defender or his allies.

RUNG 20. "PEACEFUL" WORLD-WIDE EMBARGO OR BLOCKADE: It has often been suggested that if the Soviets blocked access to Berlin, NATO could retaliate by closing off the Dardanelles or the Balkan Sea, or it could possibly place an embargo on all NATO trade with the Soviet Union and its satellite nations. This latter threat, particularly as applied to West German–East German trade, has already been useful in negotiations.

If the embargo or blockade were on a very large scale, perhaps even world-wide, this could create extreme pressure on the Soviet Union, and the Soviets, in turn, might feel obligated to attempt forcefully to counter the blockade, perhaps violently, perhaps covertly. In any case, there would be many incidents, perhaps daily. There might even be large air and naval actions.

The reason for putting this action at Rung 20 (i.e., extremely high on the ladder) is that a continuous series of incidents and actions would have to be expected, and there would be continuous tension as well. There would be a very real tendency for the Soviets continuously to increase their counteractions or escalate elsewhere; the continuing nature and scale of the provocation would mean that it would be a very escalatory measure. Yet, as a result of the growth of trade by the Soviet Union with the rest of the world, the value of this particular tactic is increasing rapidly.

VI

The Nuclear Threshold[1]

The Saliency of the Nuclear Threshold

Probably the most important, and certainly the most discussed, threshold in war today is that of nuclear use. Of the six basic thresholds, the nuclear seems the most salient, the most widely acknowledged, and quite possibly the most likely to be observed.

To recognize that it is so widely accepted does not, of course, necessarily imply that it is in the interests of the United States, or any other nation, either to enhance or to weaken this threshold. It is simply to observe a fact: that it is largely at this stage that the systems bargaining is done. Some readers may think of this "bargaining" as a closed issue—that all sensible men now are "against nuclear use." And indeed most are, so far as most likely crises are concerned. But the concern here is with preparations and policies for the unlikely crises in which the question might be reopened. Deputy Assistant Secretary of Defense (Comptroller) Alain Enthoven has described the nuclear threshold as follows: "In efforts to limit violence, there is and will remain an important distinction, a 'firebreak' if you like . . . a recognizable, qualitative distinction that both combatants can recognize and agree upon if they want to."

He argues that there is an exceedingly powerful motivation to

[1] Much work has been done on nuclear and other thresholds at Hudson Institute; various sections of this chapter draw on original work by F. Armbruster, R. Gastil, M. Singer, and E. Stillman.

agree on this distinction because "if they do not there does not appear to be another easily recognizable limitation on weapons—no other obvious 'firebreak'—all the way up the destructive spectrum of large-scale thermonuclear war."[2]

This is perhaps an exaggeration. Beyond the nuclear threshold there are, as we have seen, other thresholds, such as those between attacks on the homeland ("zone of interior") and the "not-homeland," between controlled strategic war (such attacks as reciprocal reprisal, exemplary reprisal, or constrained disarming) and "spasm" nuclear war, between attacking cities and avoiding them. That other "easily recognizable limitations" exist is clear; but it remains true that once war has started no other line of demarcation is at once so clear, so sanctified by convention, so ratified by emotion, so low on the scale of violence, and—perhaps most important of all—so easily defined and understood as the line between not using and using nuclear weapons.

There are, of course, criticisms of this point of view. Some of them take as their point of departure a fact of physics and engineering—that it is possible to have an extremely low-yield nuclear weapon that is no more powerful than a chemical explosive. Why, then, it is argued, should there be any horror or misgiving over using the smaller nuclear weapon in preference to its larger chemical competitor? A fair statement of this traditional critique is the following comment by the editors of *The Air Reservist*:

> That there are various kinds of nuclear weapons is not widely understood by the general public. To many people a nuclear weapon is a nuclear weapon—and it is symbolized frequently in cartoons as a giant as tall as a skyscraper.
>
> There is a vast but not widely understood distinction among various types of nuclear weapons that are theoretically possible. A hypothetical example: The difference between a .01-kiloton weapon and a 100-megaton weapon would be profound, and yet both would carry the label nuclear weapon. The former would be 10 million times less powerful than the latter, and only two times more powerful than the conventional World War II block-busters. In the popular image, however, the tactical nuclear weapon is often equated with

[2] "Enthoven Examines U.S. Weapons Policy," *Aviation Week and Space Technology*, LXXVIII, No. 7 (February 18, 1963), 39.

the superbomb. . . . When authorized by the President, the introduction of appropriate-size nuclear weapons could insure an early termination of hostilities, reduce casualties among American and friendly forces, and limit, not expand, the amount of economic disruption and destruction that has always been associated with prolonged campaigns.[3]

The issue, of course, is not so clear-cut as the editorial concludes. Whether the use of nuclear weapons "could insure" an early termination of hostilities is the subject of a vigorous running debate within the defense community on which I will comment although the substance of this controversy lies beyond the scope of the present discussion). And it is not at all self-evident that the use of small nuclear weapons against a power with equivalent nuclear resources (as against the U.S.S.R. in the case of a Soviet attack on Europe in the next decade) would reduce casualties or limit destruction.

Also pertinent is a contrary question: Would the introduction of small nuclear arms into a war with a future "Nth" country, poorer than the United States in total military and economic resources but possessing large numbers of tactical nuclear weapons, not actually work to the detriment of the U.S.? Is it not in *conventional* war that actual and potential U.S. resources are greatest?

Nevertheless, the traditional critique has a certain validity. The distinction between very small nuclear weapons and large chemical explosives does tend to narrow under analysis, although small tactical nuclear weapons are likely to use radiation rather than blast as a major kill mechanism. If there is sufficient research and development (or possibly just with the inevitable advances in weapons technology brought about through current programs), the distinction is likely to be blurred increasingly. The collateral effects of fallout and residual radioactivity from nuclear weapons, as well as the direct use of radiation in tactical weapons, are cited in arguments favoring preservation of the nuclear ban, but it seems reasonably clear that the future development of "clean" fusion weapons, leaving little or no residual fallout—and, if necessary, not using

[3] "Tactical Nuclear Weapons," *The Air Reservist,* XV, No. 2 (February, 1963), 15.

direct radiation—could weaken the force of these objections to the vanishing point, although at operational or cost disadvantages in the weapons system itself.

But any argument designed to refute the nuclear prohibition on purely technical energy-release grounds misses the point raised by the "prohibitionist." In some sense, the nuclear threshold has become a purely formal, nonlogical distinction between two types of war. Therefore, before it can be dismissed as too arbitrary, we have to ask whether or not there are, logically, functionally, or otherwise, more "objective" and salient thresholds, at least once the nuclear border has been crossed. If we do not find such thresholds, then we must ask why it is wrong to use arbitrary distinctions when they are widely accepted. Even though the distinction between nuclear and nonnuclear war may have defects from some technical points of view, it possesses a functional meaning or utility that transcends any purely technical question.

The Nuclear Threshold as a Prototype Restraint

In the rest of this chapter, I will consider the nuclear threshold as an especially stark and simple example of the role of constraints, restraints, and thresholds generally. By using this example, I can formulate some of the issues more clearly and simply than is possible with the more subtle examples considered earlier (and later). These qualities of clarity, simplicity, and starkness are advantageous from certain expository points of view. They also introduce some distortion and bias into the discussion. But this book is attempting to expose majority policy issues rather than to provide sophisticated recommendations. In such a discussion it is useful to use as a prototype an example that emphasizes and simplifies issues. Later, of course, I consider more directly some of the complexities raised in the more subtle restraints and thresholds.

Of course, some differences arise just because of the special saliency of the nuclear threshold. Thus, some would argue that unlike the less obvious "don't rock the boat" and "nuclear war is unthinkable" thresholds, the "no nuclear use" threshold would be forever shattered by a simple transgression. This seems unlikely. The nuclear threshold is not so weak that a single use of nuclear weapons would make anyone careless about crossing it a second time; it is almost always likely to be prominent. Even if it were crossed many times, it would still have some significance in a subsequent conflict. Nevertheless, I believe that two or three uses of nuclear weapons would certainly weaken the threshold, at least to a degree where it would no longer be a strong barrier to additional uses of nuclear weapons in intense or vital disputes. There would ensue a gradual or precipitate erosion of the current belief— or sentiment—that the use of nuclear weapons is exceptional or immoral. The feared uncontrolled escalation would be rather more likely to occur at the second, third, or later use of nuclear weapons than as a consequence of the first use.

One can, of course, argue, as Gallois does, that it is precisely a threshold weakened to the use and distribution of nuclear weapons that might make deterrence work so well as almost to eliminate violence in international relations. He has argued that, "Contrary to popular belief, the further we advance in the ballistic-nuclear age, the more possible it becomes to outlaw violence, even if the aggressor nation is stronger and more richly supplied with combat means than the nation it threatens."[4] He has also said, "To humanity, it seems absurd that the very omnipotence of these new weapons can, at least temporarily, create a form of peace that would be more stable—and more advantageous—than any ever known."[5] And finally, "If this must be the direction of the development, and if the

[4] Pierre Gallois, *The Balance of Terror: Strategy for the Nuclear Age* (Boston: Houghton Mifflin Co., 1961), p. 113.

[5] *Ibid.*, p. 167. One legitimate question is, "Advantageous" to whom? It might well turn out that in a nuclear world "weaker" states who were ambitious to change the situation would find the stronger but less aggressive states deterred from using violence against them. Also, we have a tendency today to think of deterrence as tending toward stabilizing the *status quo*, in spite of the experiences with Hitler from 1933 to 1939, which indicated that fear of an unthinkable war could be used to change the *status quo*. Hitler's use of terror may be thought of as *offensive deterrence* (Raymond Gastil's term) rather than defensive deterrence. The reason we do not normally think of nuclear weapons as contributing to offensive deterrence is probably that since World War II there have been no serious uses of nuclear threats for aggressive or revisionist purposes by nuclear powers; in particular, as Soviet nuclear capability has grown, the Soviets have, perhaps somewhat coincidentally, become less aggressive, at least relatively speaking.

movement is as irreversible as the one which culminated in the generalization of firearms, it would be better for the Western nations to reach an understanding . . . by distributing [the] weapons among the cooperating states."[6]

Others have argued similarly. For example, Edward Teller says:

> In a dangerous world we cannot have peace unless we are strong. We cannot be strong unless we are fully prepared to exploit the biggest modern power, nuclear explosives.
>
> Nuclear weapons can be used with moderation on all scales of serious conflict. Nuclear weapons do not mean the end of the world, but they do mean the end of nonnuclear power.[7]

Before one could take any serious position on any of these attitudes, one must make careful and explicit estimates or guesses about the future of the world, the stability of the current system, likely dangers of the arms race, and so on. In particular, the attitude one has toward medium- and long-run international possibilities will play an important role in deciding one's preferences.

While most civilian analysts (including the author—and the opinion seems representative of the "mainstream" of American politics) would tend to disagree with both Gallois and Teller, it is not as obvious and certain as many believe that they are wrong. The usual fear that any use of nuclear weapons, no matter how limited and specific, would be likely to cause immediate and total escalation (perhaps because one or more nations would rain weapons on others merely because they did not know who had attacked or why) seems far-fetched. Particularly if most or all of the nations with nuclear weapons had also instituted procedures and equipment for reliable command and control, and the controlled-response tactics (discussed later) were well understood, it would not be likely that nations would automatically involve themselves in, or escalate, a conflict simply because a nuclear exchange had taken place. It is more likely that everyone would be extraordinarily cautious of the dangers of escalation, and would be most careful not to respond blindly or emotionally to either accidental or deliberate attack.

[6] *Ibid.,* p. 229.

[7] Edward Teller (with Allen Brown), *The Legacy of Hiroshima* (Garden City, N.Y.: Doubleday & Company, 1962), p. viii.

Thus, it seems more likely that if the weapons were widely distributed the world would live in a more or less uneasy or stable balance of "terror" ("terror" is in quotation marks because most people would soon become accustomed to the situation—and indeed already have). However, one can also easily imagine that nations might violate this balance. They could attempt intense blackmail, risk limited nuclear actions, or even wreak great destruction, possibly almost total obliteration, on other nations. If the destruction were mutual, then one could imagine that after such an event the surviving nations would try to arrange things so that such an affair would not occur again. This is one route to international reform, if a hard one. One could also argue that "occasional" and "isolated" nuclear wars might cause less net destruction than might occur in the more extensive but less intense conventional wars that the nuclear system might otherwise have deterred.

Of course, if the destruction in these wars were not mutual, and the aggressive nation had come out ahead, there might be a question of containing this aggressive nation. This could mean new attempts at collective-security arrangements, new appeals to external and internal public opinion against the aggressor, retaliatory actions, mobilizations, increased arms races, new alliances, and the like. But both exposed and "neutral" nations might tend to extreme care and caution to avoid large risks: the aggressor might be encouraged to increase its demands and refine the tactics of "offensive deterrence."

Thus, nuclear proliferation can be interpreted as creating the conditions both of increased world stability (by increasing the caution of normally prudential heads of state) and of unparalleled opportunities for "nuclear Hitlers." My own conclusion is that the Gallois argument is plausible but unconvincing—and too risky to test. I think that nuclear proliferation should be resisted.[8]

[8] See Herman Kahn, *Thinking About the Unthinkable* (New York: Horizon Press, 1962), pp. 212–18, where the following possibilities that could result from extreme proliferation are discussed:
1. Greater opportunities for blackmail, revenge, terrorism, and other mischief-making.
2. More widespread capabilities for "local" Munichs, Pearl Harbors, and blitzkriegs.
3. Pressure to pre-empt because of the first two points.
4. Tendencies to neglect conventional military capabilities.

But the major point I want to make here is that whether or not Gallois and Teller are correct, few currently believe that they are —and the fears felt by governments everywhere seem sufficient justification for two of these governments, the United States and the Soviet Union, to pursue policies aimed at trying to slow the diffusion of nuclear weapons, although neither of these governments can claim to have given the question as much thought as it deserves.

The Nuclear Consensus—An Example of Systems Bargaining

There currently exists, and probably will continue to be, what might be called a "nuclear consensus"—that is, a collection of attitudes as to who should, or should not, have nuclear weapons, and how useful they might be. I would tend to argue that the U.S., the European nations, and the U.S.S.R. should prefer that this nuclear consensus hold that nuclear weapons are, by and large, not useful except as a deterrent or response to other nuclear weapons, and that these weapons are needed only by very large powers.

I do not believe that such a consensus would be a completely accurate and objective statement of the facts, but I am willing to argue that to the extent that the U.S. and other nations can make it an accurate and objective statement, they should. Thus, as its contribution to the "systems bargaining" on this matter, the U.S. should be willing to adopt the concept that the only purpose of nuclear weapons is to negate nuclear weapons, and make it national policy not to use nuclear weapons first, but only in retaliation for use by some other nation. In addition, it should not try to get any "positive" benefits from its nuclear weaponry, but be content to use this weaponry only as nuclear deterrence, not attempting to exploit it to redress differences in conventional capability or the advantages an opponent might have in manpower, geography, morale, recklessness, etc.

---

5. Greater danger of inadvertent war.
6. Internal political problems (civil war, *coup d'état,* irresponsibility, etc.) and external factors (arms race, fear of fear, etc.).
7. Diffusion of nuclear weapons to irresponsible private organizations.
8. More complicated future problems of control.
9. Intensified *agent provocateur* problems.
10. Catalytic and anonymous war.

This might eventually call for the United States and perhaps others to make their "bargaining" explicit with a "no-first-use" declaration. Before this could safely be done there might have to be some additions to NATO's conventional capability in Europe, and possibly some increased conventional capability deployed or available in Asia, but it does not seem that very much would really have to be done. This is true in part because no one could wholly trust that the United States—or any nation—would stand by its declaration and refuse to resort to nuclear means if it were presented with a vital challenge. Thus, even if the Soviets believed that they could mobilize 100 divisions and invade Europe, they would not be likely to do so on the strength of a United States announcement of no-nuclear-first-use. They might, of course, feel that it was safer to make probes with smaller forces under certain conditions. However, such probes presumably could be met by current NATO conventional capabilities. Even under current conditions, without a no-first-use declaration, I think it would not be to the advantage of the United States to violate the nuclear threshold first, except possibly in the following circumstances. To deter or stop a: (1) continuing invasion of Europe that could not be stopped by conventional forces or threats (so-called strategy of the "pause"); (2) Chinese or Soviet attack upon Japan; (3) Chinese or Soviet attack on India that looked as if it would succeed; (4) particularly flagrant act of aggression by China or the Soviet Union that clearly "violated current conventions,"[9] assuming the problem could be met by using nuclear weapons and that it could not be met, even temporarily, by conventional weapons. However, even then, in some cases, if a good resistance could be devised, it might be better to "go down fighting" locally, accept the verdict of the conventional war, and then use this defeat to motivate an increase in conventional strength (as discussed in Chapter VIII), rather than to escalate to nuclear weapons.

It is also possible that conventional attacks may grow out of a crisis in a way that is judged to be "within the rules" and so not a flagrant or drastic challenge to the international code of behavior.

[9] See comment by President Kennedy (quoted on pp. 78–79) and Chapter XIII (pp. 261–62) for some discussion of what these conventions are.

Such eventualities might include a large-scale Chinese invasion of bordering states other than Japan or India, or a Soviet invasion of Turkey, Iran, Afghanistan, or Pakistan. Any of these events would create enormous problems, although not necessarily insoluble ones, within a no-first-use framework. But conventional attacks can be met with conventional defense, and it is, in the Soviet case at least, difficult to imagine large-scale attacks of this particular kind. And direct penetration or aggression is, it seems clear, best met by other than nuclear weapons. It must also be remembered that conventional attacks can have the effect of provoking mobilization—not only increases in U.S. capabilities but also mobilization or vastly increased defensive efforts by allies or others frightened by the conflict (see the discussion in Chapter VIII). In other words, there is no inevitable domino effect from Communist aggression.

If necessary to smooth the transition from the present situation to one appropriate to a no-first-use policy, the U.S. might explicitly state that for a given period of time it reserves the right to defend certain important areas from large conventional attacks by the use of nuclear weapons. In other areas, first use could be forgone because the likelihood of attack seems low and the importance of the area is relatively low even if an attack occurs. Moreover, it would remain clear to the Soviets, surely, that whatever the U.S. declaratory policy on nuclear weapons, a "flagrant" violation of international conventions of stability which was beyond the competence of conventional weapons would compel the U.S., whether it wanted to or not, to reconsider its policy. The Korean War is often taken as a prototype of a situation in which the U.S. revised a declaratory policy which, if literally followed, would have made the North Korean invasion perfectly safe. If it can do anything about it, no state is likely to acquiesce in a vital or even a grave setback, whatever its earlier policy declarations. Indeed, this is one matter in which I would argue that the United States can have its cake and eat it, too: the U.S. could make a no-first-use declaration and still be adequately prepared to cope with its failure. The only real requirement for the policy is that we have a reasonably adequate-looking conventional capability in vital or crisis-prone areas so as to be obviously dependent on nuclear weapons.

The Considerations To Be Examined

Let me now consider more systematically whether or not the U.S., or any other nation, should prefer: (1) a world in which most or many nations have nuclear weapons and are willing to use them more or less routinely as "quality" weapons when it seems militarily advantageous to do so; or (2) a world in which most nations do not possess nuclear weapons and in which nuclear weapons are not considered usable except in the most desperate circumstances. Most analysts would argue that Hiroshima and Nagasaki did not set precedents, but that if nuclear weapons were used once or twice again there would be a seriously increased likelihood (as discussed below) of a rapid proliferation of nuclear-weapons capabilities. I will consider this argument and the possibilities of slowing down or stopping proliferation if we do not use nuclear weapons.

Some advocates of tactical nuclear weapons have argued that whether or not nuclear weapons should be used should depend mostly on the cost (which for small weapons could be less than $100,000) and on the weapons' effectiveness as measured by their casualty-producing, destructive, and interdiction capabilities. These advocates would not necessarily use nuclear weapons in every minor conflict—for much the same reason that machine guns are not used to stop street riots. But whenever there was a serious military challenge, they would let the question of nuclear use be determined by considerations of relatively simple technical cost-effectiveness (though in practice such judgments could be difficult or uncertain). If any great nation had such an attitude, and then used nuclear weapons several times, it seems likely that nuclear weapons would not only soon become widely available, but would even become articles of commerce, in the same way that tanks, fighters, and even bombers are today. As pointed out earlier in the discussion of systems bargaining, this is one of those situations in which it might not pay to "cheat" if it touched off a wave of cheating. Thus, before the U.S. or any other nation does anything that might further nuclear proliferation or weaken the "no nuclear use" threshold, it should ask whether it really prefers a "nuclear world" to the current state of "arrested nuclear development"—even if it cannot be sure that such a world will not develop anyway.

Thus, in considering the nuclear threshold and the circumstances in which one side or the other might be tempted to cross the threshold, one should deal with at least five different kinds of issues:

1. The immediate military questions involved in symmetrical tactical nuclear use.
2. The pressures for continued escalation.
3. The immediate but wider political and other consequences on the power balance.
4. The effects of using nuclear weapons on "stability," the arms race, and nuclear proliferation questions.
5. Other long-term effects.

In order to set a context for the rest of this discussion, I will assume that the net assessment of the last two points, taken by themselves (i.e., ignoring any benefits that might accrue from a combination of the first three issues), is that it would ultimately be against the national interest of any *status quo* nation (and perhaps others as well) not to weaken the nuclear threshold. This is a controversial position, and I will discuss the controversy. But because it is convenient to have an explicit point of view in the subsequent discussion, I will anticipate my judgment of this controversy and assume that unless there is a very large net benefit on the first three issues, it is not to the ultimate interest of most nations to encourage the proliferation or use of nuclear weapons by a first use.

Some Disadvantages to the U.S.

At least in peripheral and small conflicts, a practical general availability of nuclear weapons and few inhibitions against their use would seem to put a premium on good capabilities for: (1) using blackmail and threats; (2) surprise attacks "out of the blue"; (3) anonymous attacks; (4) other concealment of forces and intentions; (5) nondependence on elaborate infrastructures and logistics; (6) having very many and highly dispersed small combat units and bases; (7) being willing, politically and morally, to accept a high percentage of casualties in a few exposed units or areas (or allies); and (8) having firm, or easily controlled, allies.

It seems fairly certain that the above desiderata for waging successful limited nuclear war tend to be those in which the U.S. would most likely be weak or incompetent. There doubtless are other kinds of nuclear war that would put a premium on the qualities and capabilities for which the U.S. is better qualified or prepared than others (or at least could be, if we made the effort), but to date these other possibilities, except perhaps in the defense of Europe, have not been widely considered or explicated.

Thus, when one compares two-sided nuclear war with two-sided conventional war, one can argue that by and large the kind of war that the U.S. is most competent to fight, and for which we have a huge technical and economic superiority, is the high-explosive war.

I should mention that a once common view, that it would be impossible for NATO to match "Russian hordes" without the use of nuclear weapons, seems to be wrong and is now no longer widely accepted. As is fairly well known, NATO currently has more men under arms than the Warsaw Pact.[10] In addition, even in the crucial Central European area (Germany), currently deployed NATO forces (twelve German divisions, six American divisions, and about four French and British divisions) are probably more than a match for the twenty smaller Soviet divisions in East Germany, at least under many reasonable circumstances. One must also, of course, consider the seven East German divisions, and perhaps the role of the East German civilian population, but it is not at all clear on whose side they would be in the kinds of crises that seem possible or plausible.

The Soviets currently seem to have an advantage when it comes to mobilization capacity, except perhaps in the first few days of a crisis, but even this may not be as large as is usually believed. In any case, it could be negated by reasonable actions by the NATO powers, if they were seriously concerned by this possibility. Thus the question of how well, under varying circumstances, the West could acquit itself against the Soviet Union and its allies in a conventional war in Europe is still open. The same is true of a nuclear war.

[10] Similarly, Russian or Chinese "hordes" on the rest of the Sino-Soviet periphery suffer from serious logistical constraints when engaged beyond their borders. If they had not, we probably would have already lost these areas—perhaps even before the Cold War began.

It may also be worth pointing out that modern developments in the conventional field seem to favor the *status quo* powers of the West—in so far as they are more interested in defense than in offense—at least so long as both sides are using conventional weapons. Current ground-to-air missiles (such as the Nike Hercules, Hawk, or Bomarc) have a very impressive probability of sharply restricting enemy use of airpower, and in most situations may attain attrition rates of 10–50 per cent, even when restricted to the use of high-explosive warheads. (In World War II, 5–10 per cent attrition was enough to make an air raid prohibitive.)

Some of the same advantages of defense seem to be true against infantry and armor. Impressive defensive gains have been made in the use of mine fields, antitank missiles, and modern fortifications. In many areas of the world, these gains may be used to increase dramatically the traditional advantages of the defense.

Thus, if we feel that we can force the attacker to restrict himself to conventional weapons, we can probably hold the line[11] in most areas of the world, possibly even in the face of numerically superior and technically equal enemies; and we need to face numerically superior and technically equal enemies (except possibly in infantry only) in most of the areas we are concerned with if we make suitable preparations. It is likely that, with only modest capabilities in being and adequate mobilization bases, we could in the long run deliver more tons of ammunition and other supplies to any spot on the earth than any possible enemy could do. If we made sufficient but reasonable preparations, we could possibly do so in the short run as well. There do not seem to be any overwhelming, or even very pressing, reasons for us to depend on initiating the use of nuclear weapons.

To some degree, the above begs the question of whether the Soviets or the Chinese would initiate the use of nuclear weapons. It is difficult, however, to believe that they would. The Soviets have

---

[11] I do not mean to imply by the phrase "hold the line" that defensive tactics are always superior to offensive tactics. Even in defense, one badly needs some tactical freedom of action and ability to counterattack for either military reasons or bargaining purposes. I do mean that, by and large, the side that is mostly on the defense could achieve differential advantages in conventional war through using modern advanced technology.

not been willing in the past voluntarily to run large risks of major damage to the Soviet Union itself, and they are probably even more interested than we are in preventing nuclear proliferation.[12] Thus, Khrushchev in the past suggested that limited wars were dangerous because they *might* escalate. He gave no sign of being reassured by the possibility that they might not. It seems to be characteristic of all major nations today, including China, that decision-makers are both deterred and prudential. They have a very real tendency to ask, "What is the worst that can happen?" rather than to hope that the best will occur.

As far as the Chinese are concerned, although they might be able to hurt U.S. allies and eventually the U.S. by the use of nuclear weapons, the U.S. could annihilate them in return. Even in a limited attack, we could destroy any capability that the Chinese have to conduct nuclear war. Thus, while they may be very interested in threatening the use of nuclear weapons—as a deterrent, in retaliation for our use, or for purposes of nuclear blackmail—they presumably would desperately need to limit as closely as possible any use that actually took place; and that would be much harder to do if they were the ones who had initiated such use.

It is possible that either the Soviets or the Chinese might choose to initiate the use of nuclear weapons in some reasonably desperate situation, and this possibility must always be taken account of. But barring such situations, it seems that the initiation is as likely to

12 Of course, to the extent that the Soviets may have organized for nuclear war, they, as we did in the mid-1950's, may have given up to some degree their conventional option. However, if this is or ever becomes true, and a crisis occurs in which they have to choose between a possible nuclear holocaust and surrender, they may want to accept surrender (compromise). In addition, just as we did, they may recognize this possibility ahead of time, change their minds about relying on nuclear weapons, and procure the required conventional capabilities. This is particularly true if they face a situation in which it is very credible that a limited nuclear war in Europe would involve their heartland more than they cared to have it involved. They might then prefer, in a conventional war, to accept some degree of defeat rather than escalate to nuclear weapons and thus risk the Soviet homeland. An independent European strategic capability that could make it plausible that the use of nuclear weapons against Europe would almost certainly entail a tit-for-tat response against the Soviet heartland would very likely limit Soviet interest in tactical nuclear war. This is discussed at length below.

come from us. We certainly cannot evade the question as to whether or not we would wish to initiate the use of nuclear weapons by simply arguing that the other side will do it—unless we feel that such an action on their part is so probable that we gain nothing by withholding. Even then, one could argue that it would be desirable, for many reasons, to have the onus on the other side.

Pressures for Continued Escalation

Escalation or eruption is, of course, the most dramatic possibility faced in the use of nuclear weapons. Much current discussion concerns the possibility of battlefield limitations, by either size, target, means of delivery, or geographic area. For example, many studies consider how the use of nuclear weapons might be limited to some distance from the "forward edge of the battle area" or, if this concept of a "FEBA" turns out to be misleading because of the confused nature of the fighting, to some reasonable distance behind the "engaged battle area" ("EBA"). In these concepts, only soldiers and equipment actually engaged in or near combat would be targets, and perhaps their immediate logistic support and staging areas.

If such distinctions should be observed, the question immediately arises as to whether the side that was losing would not violate the limits, perhaps to gain an advantage, perhaps because it did not know whether there was an advantage to be gained and thought it might just as well try, or finally perhaps out of desperation and without thought. It is also possible that one side or the other, even if it were not losing, would try to steal an advantage or make up for deficiencies in capability by cheating on the limits; or one side might "cheat" because it mistakenly believed the other side had cheated, or was about to do so. This last is an especially reasonable possibility as far as arbitrary restrictions on such things as yield or numbers of weapons are concerned. There are, after all, few physicists on the battlefield to make fine distinctions and measurements.

In order to decrease the motivations for such escalatory possibilities, it might be particularly advisable for the "winning" (and presumably more conservative) side's forces to be so deployed and operated that they do not present any tempting "sanctuary" targets, and to attempt to decrease generally the advantages possible by violating other restrictions. The side that is "winning" would thus likely be penalized by being forced to bear many of the costs and degradations it would have to bear if the restraints were being violated. Usually the losing side will have less of an interest in preserving restraints and/or more reason to look, or be, reckless, so it may not feel the same pressure to pay the penalties entailed by "poor" deployment and the other measures that would be designed to avoid tempting the other side to exceed the limits. Not doing so might gain large advantages for it.

This almost automatic penalizing of the winning side, and increased flexibility for the losing side, could be another stabilizing influence leading to relative moderation and the compromising of demands and disputes. It is also likely that some of the literature overestimates the losing side's possible interest in escalations; in many cases, the losing side may simply judge that it does not have much to gain, and will increase its losses if it increases its stakes in a losing game. (Of course, even if this is valid, the losing side as well as the analyst may overlook this possibility.) Thus, so long as there are significant escalation possibilities available to the losing side, it is likely to be important not to push that side to the point of desperation. This means that the escalation and negotiation situation might generally be envisaged as the norm for cases in which there are restraints; that "winners" cannot afford to press "losers."

Another risk of excessive escalation or demands occurs because what is a moderate escalation to principals with homeland sanctuaries may not look so moderate to allies, or to the nations upon whose territory the battle is being fought. In particular, the large increase in differential risks among allies that is entailed in even moderate escalations may weaken the resolve of the nations within which the fighting is occurring and which bear most of the increases in risks. I will discuss the effects of such potentially divisive possibilities in the next section.

There is a paradox that occurs in estimates of escalation and the effects of the fear of escalation. It is the fear of eruption that makes it likely that there will be little or no escalation after the first use of nuclear weapons. Both sides are likely to be so frightened—both the attacker and the defender—that they are very likely to agree to some kind of compromise and cease-fire almost immediately after such a use. (At least, they are likely to take the first use as defining the outer limits of acceptable use in order not to risk further escalation.) Thus, a typical scenario for the first use of nuclear weapons by the U.S. might go as follows: There is some kind of intense crisis over some aspect of the German question (such as the one illustrated in Chapter I), and the Soviets take advantage of the situation or are forced, by military considerations, to invade West Germany. They are advancing rapidly. The Americans might then use two or three nuclear weapons to destroy bridges in the Soviet rear. This destruction of bridges kills few people and is relatively ineffective in interfering with the Soviets' logistics, as they may have several other bridges they can use. The purpose of the destruction is less to degrade logistics than to say, "Having used two or three nuclear weapons, are we not likely to use many more? Don't you want to reconsider putting such pressures on us?" The Soviets are then, indeed, likely to want to reconsider, but they might not be willing to admit it. They might themselves use two or three nuclear weapons, possibly on equivalent targets, possibly on other targets, in order to indicate that they have not been frightened by the American use. But they are nevertheless likely to be frightened— as the Americans are likely to be by their own temerity. One can thus easily imagine a cease-fire being called immediately after the Soviet retaliation.

Similarly, one can imagine riots in East Germany and a successful intervention by West German divisions. The desperate Soviets then explode one or two weapons over German territory, possibly not even in a way that causes damage. The act would make it clear to the Germans that unless they could rely on nuclear support from their U.S. or French allies, they had better negotiate. It is even more likely that the Americans and French would independently urge the Germans to pull back, or would suggest that the Germans would get nuclear support only if they were willing to accept "reasonable" Soviet offers for a cease-fire or other settlement.

In other areas of the world, the basic fear is not likely to be that the use of nuclear weapons would bring an immediate tit-for-tat retaliation, as in Europe, but other considerations. Thus we could probably use nuclear weapons against the Chinese if they attacked

Formosa, or conceivably in North Vietnam, and not really expect serious, if any, nuclear reply by the Soviets. But we have already pointed out that even if the first use is likely to be effective in bringing about a cease-fire or a backdown by the other side, the third or fourth use in a later crisis—perhaps by other powers—may be more likely to escalate. Despite this increased likelihood of escalation, the successful side, and others as well, might shortsightedly come to feel that it can use nuclear weapons safely. In addition, potential users are also likely to notice or judge that one reason for the first success is that the losing side gave up too quickly, was too cautious and fearful. They might (correctly) conjecture that if the losing side had responded with a few nuclear weapons of its own, or maintained its resolve and continued fighting, the side that had initiated the use might have backed down. Such conjectures would be reinforced by the inevitable "inside" reports, whether true or not, that the winning side had really intended to back down if the other side had held out longer, that in spite of appearances the winning side had not really been willing to continue a two-sided nuclear conflict of any size.

Thus, after a *successful* first use, both potential initiators and potential responders are likely to feel greater willingness to use nuclear weapons, at least as bargaining counters. Reasoning from a nonnuclear escalation, one can almost predict that the U.S. will be more willing to escalate in North Vietnam because its first escalation (the Gulf of Tonkin incident in the summer of 1964) seems to have been reasonably successful, while if the U.S. does escalate, the North Vietnamese and Chinese may feel great pressure to overreact to prevent the U.S. from acting out of such confidence a third time. In general, the more both sides feel there will not really be serious escalation, the less willing to back down each is likely to be, and thus the more one can expect further escalation. Of course, in the case of Vietnam, neither the North Vietnamese nor the Chinese can have any assurance that the U.S. will not escalate even more in retaliation to any provocations of theirs.

This is one of the main reasons so many people oppose analyses such as this one. They feel that the more both sides believe in the possibility of nuclear bargaining, of the kind I have been discussing, the more likely it is that such bargaining will be tried and that it will escalate. These objections may not be explicitly articulated, but many readers will doubtless feel, consciously or unconsciously, that not only is the threshold against the use of nuclear weapons strengthened by nondiscussion of the subject, but that nondiscussion is likely to be helpful even if nuclear weapons are used, since both sides may then be less likely to "play the escalation game."[13]

Thus, in a paradoxical way, if both sides have excessive expectations of no escalation, such expectations are as likely to lead to a self-defeating prophecy and undesired escalation as when both sides fear escalation and thus are "excessively" willing to back down. If there is asymmetry, and one side fears escalation greatly and the other side does not, the side that does not may have an important advantage. However, here, too, the precedent is dangerous, for if one side should exploit this advantage more than once or twice, it would most likely eliminate the asymmetry—and create an extremely dangerous situation as well.

Such asymmetry in beliefs can also be stabilizing, particularly if each side worries that the other side may act according to its theories. Thus the Soviets often claim to disbelieve in the reliability or even existence of "no nuclear use" and higher thresholds. To the extent that they are sincere, they are likely to be deterred from using their conventional superiority even if, according to some U.S. theories, it is relatively safe to do so. Similarly, a U.S. President contemplating the restrained use of nuclear force might well hesitate in the face of Soviet statements that they would not observe such limitations.

The possibility of escalation and eruption makes it unlikely that either side can afford to try to gain a very important or clear-cut victory in a limited war with nuclear weapons. The stresses and pressures are so great, and the situation likely to be so delicate, that the winning side is not likely to trust that the restraints will withstand the strains that would be imposed by the loser's feeling himself vitally endangered.

---

[13] The author, of course, considers discussion important—and, on balance, beneficial—enough to justify writing this book. In addition, he admits to a bias toward trying to think problems through, and an even stronger bias against efforts made to discourage such thinking—in many cases on both sides of the Cold War line.

The Immediate Consequences on the Wider Power Balance

I have already referred briefly to the possibility that alliances would be subjected to great strains by the use of nuclear weapons. It is perhaps worth while to consider this possibility in more detail (although it is equally worth while to remember that alliances would be subjected to great strains by nonnuclear defeat). Let me use again the example of some nuclear conflict in Central Europe arising out of an aspect of the German question. Again, we will assume that the Soviets have seized some initial advantage and then asked for a cease-fire in order to discuss the problem.

Particularly if the initial action involved seizure of major German territories, or the continued use of violence by the Soviets in the suppression of an East German revolt (in which the West Germans had intervened), it might be difficult for the West Germans to accept such a cease-fire. In fact, it might be politically disastrous for the government officials concerned to do so—in part because it might also be very difficult to envisage later reversing the sequence of events and negating the Soviet advantage.

In other words, the cease-fire itself would most likely be, or appear to be, a form of capitulation. But Germany's Western allies might feel much less desire or pressure than the Germans to continue fighting. The Germans, of course, would be running greater risks than their allies, but their deepest interests and emotions would be involved. Even if some German decision-makers felt that the risks of escalation were too great to be incurred, they might also feel that they could rely on others to prevent them from going too far; that it was not up to them to choose a path of moderation in this situation, but for others to make concessions to induce them into such a path.

In those cases in which German leaders were anxious to continue the fighting, either because they really felt that they should or because they felt that they could not take the lead in refusing, one could easily expect severe alliance strains. The situation would become particularly divisive if the question were less one of *continuing* the use of nuclear weapons than of the West's introducing nuclear weapons in order to rectify the initial advantage that the Soviets had obtained or to deny the Soviets the exploitation of some current advantage. Thus, it is difficult to imagine a sequence of events in which a British government would be willing to see such a first use of nuclear weapons; and in most scenarios I think it is fair to say that neither the French nor the Americans would want to permit such an escalation. In these cases, the strain on the Western alliance might simply prove to be too great for it to endure.

Whether or not the alliance was strained to the breaking point, there would likely be grave internal strains in all the countries involved. Even if an introduction of nuclear weapons were successful, not all the countries involved would be likely to feel that the risks had justified the gains achieved.

It should also be realized that restraints could go the other way; the Germans might not be the most intransigent or the most willing to run risks. Any ally onto whose territory the battle spread would run great risks. Moreover, if the war occurred over some aspect of the German question, and was in part due to "German intransigence," or the Germans felt that some of their allies would judge this to be the case, they would also realize that the possibility of division among the allies or even of desertion of the German cause would be very high. The Germans would have particular reason to fear that the Soviets might believe they could safely escalate over German territory without running great risks of United States or NATO retaliation against Soviet territory. In addition, the Soviets undoubtedly bear a very special animosity against and fear of the Germans; in a crisis, they might have a great desire to settle this German question once and for all.

It may or may not be worth noting that the author has observed several war games in which the individual or individuals who played Soviet leadership expressed a positive desire to punish the Germans for having "caused" the conflict. In one war game, the Russian "Premier" ordered an all-out attack against both East and West German territory, then immediately asked for a cease-fire, with the promise of later accommodation to the surviving NATO nations. The "Premier" not only expressed satisfaction at achieving revenge against the Germans "who had again brought the world to the brink of disaster," but also said that, having killed most of the Germans, he had "improved" the European situation not only from the Russian viewpoint but for the French and British as well—and that they would recognize this. In the particular "game" being discussed, the concessions then offered by the Soviets were held to be large enough, and the risk of retaliation so dreadful, that the NATO players accepted the *fait accompli*. I do not suggest that this "war game" was a serious description or prediction of what would happen; but it was symptomatic of possibilities that might well be present in the minds of Germans, whether or not they are present in Soviet minds.

The above, of course, is simply a special example of a very general question. Once nuclear weapons are widely available and likely to be used, there would be a premium on being able to resist blackmail, and on a willingness to accept a high percentage of casualties in a few exposed units or areas as opposed to a smaller percentage of casualties among a larger number of units and areas. I think—and the above attempts to illustrate the point—that the West is more likely than not to be vulnerable to blackmail. The side with the greatest internal control, cohesion, discipline, and resolve would have advantages. The matter, of course, is not completely one-sided. NATO ought to be able to devise a nuclear strategy that exploited strains within the Warsaw Pact and perhaps within the Soviet Union itself. U.S. use of nuclear weapons against China might well widen the Sino-Soviet division if the Soviets sought protection by disassociating themselves from Chinese policies (although it could go the other way, with the Chinese, out of fear, seeking closer relations with the Soviets).

In any case, it is clear that the use of nuclear weapons would cause internal strains in the countries involved. This could be a particularly important point in a sustained nuclear conflict. It seems less likely to be important in a brief crisis in which the government is likely to have reasonable freedom of action, at least in the short run. I will consider some of the long-term effects of such strains later.

Strains might be particularly evident in American use of Japanese bases if the U.S. resorted to nuclear weapons in some conflict in Asia, especially if the Chinese had nuclear weapons of their own and could threaten Japan. But even if they did not, the Japanese might nevertheless deny the use of these bases to the U.S.; indeed, they might do so in a conventional war because the Japanese domestic opposition to the U.S. role in that war might become so intense as to threaten the stability of the country.

This raises another class of considerations. The first use of nu-clear weapons was by a white nation against a nonwhite. Many believe that a second such use of nuclear weapons by a white nation —particularly the U.S.—might result in an intense world-wide racial reaction against that nation. While it is easy to exaggerate this possibility (the Chinese and Africans, for instance, only arti-ficially identify their interests today, if at all[14]), it clearly exists.

Perhaps more important is that new nuclear uses by the great powers might produce an increase in the relative dependence and weakness of underdeveloped states. In the eighteenth and nine-teenth centuries, any developed nation could intimidate a small na-tion with gunboats—by shelling its capital city or other territory. Today, it is often possible for a large nation to intimidate or punish a small nation only if it makes a major effort incurring the con-siderable risk of extensive casualties. A mere exemplary naval or aerial attack often will not be effective, and can and will entail many political costs. This makes large nations loath to threaten or punish small nations. To the exent that large nations accepted the idea that they could use nuclear weapons more or less freely against small nations, some of the eighteenth- and nineteenth-century conditions would be restored. Small nations would recognize this and probably would determinedly resist such an innovation. The long-run conse-quences of this are subject to controversy, but the immediate ef-fects, or at least their direction, are fairly clear. The enormous opposition of small nations to the one-sided use of nuclear weapons is firmly grounded not merely in emotion but in reasoned self-interest. It is not likely, as some analysts occasionally suggest, that these small-nation reactions could be much modified, in most plau-sible contexts, by clever propaganda campaigns.

Effects on Stability, the Arms Race, and Nuclear Proliferation

Many believe these to be the most important questions to be con-sidered in connection with nuclear first use. Many also believe that the issue is one-sided, that the effects of nuclear use would be

[14] The Chinese have recently been saying to the Africans that "we col-ored peoples of the world have to stick together." The African reaction frequently has been: "True enough, but what concern is this of yours? You're yellow."

contraproductive in all these respects. As we have seen, this is not necessarily so, and it might be useful to consider further some potential "positive" aspects of the use (or credible threat of use) of nuclear weapons.

There are many local situations that might be stabilized by some diffusion of nuclear weapons. For example, China's designs or potential aggressions against India might well be diminished or inhibited if the Indians had nuclear weapons.[15]

One might also imagine the Japanese with nuclear weapons, but a policy to use them only in self-defense. They could well provide a stabilizing influence on the Far East when the Chinese have acquired greater military capabilities. It is also true that this Japanese development would be dangerous, both inherently and because it would provide a greater precedent for further proliferation than would an Atlantic or European nuclear force (particularly if the latter resulted in the absorption or withering away of the independent British and French deterrents—a development that could strengthen a consensus that only superpowers or "supercommunities" had a "right" to these weapons).

To the argument for a "no first use" policy must also be opposed the concern many Europeans feel over the possibility that increased conventional capabilities in NATO might reassure the Soviets as to the safety of serious conventional probes or even large conventional attacks. These Europeans argue that one of the most likely ways in which nuclear war could occur would be as a result of a conventional defense strategy—even a limited one, as in the so-called "pause" strategy—as a result of which the Soviets, feeling confident that the West was deterred from using nuclear weapons, allowed a crisis to develop or continue, or actually aggressively

---

[15] It is also possible that if both sides had nuclear weapons the current stability would be weakened. Newspaper stories indicate that in 1962, when the Indians seemed to have aerial superiority over the Chinese, they refused to make air attacks on invading Chinese forces for fear the Chinese would raid New Delhi. This was a situation in which the potential damage the Chinese could do in retaliation was very limited, and the Indians had a clear advantage. Whether or not the interpretation is correct, if there were a similar situation in which nuclear weapons were threatened, the Indian, or any nation's, resolve might be completely eroded. Whether or not the above is a correct analysis of a particular situation, it is at least an analysis of a prototype possibility.

used their troops to increase pressure on the West. Such a Soviet calculation could be a mistake, for the conventional war might immediately escalate: it might go so successfully for the Soviets that the West would feel compelled to use nuclear weapons, and the crisis might then escalate further or erupt. Thus, a preparedness to use nuclear weapons, or a credible option to use them, might be the deterrent that could convince the Soviets not to allow high-level crises to escalate.

There are other mechanisms by which the nonuse of nuclear weapons might decrease stability. For example, the longer the West refuses to consider seriously the use of nuclear weapons, and the longer the nonuse tradition continues, the more likely it is that certain weaknesses in its nuclear capability will develop in the West. These weaknesses would then present the Soviets with the temptation to use nuclear weapons. They might succumb to this temptation if an opportunity arose in which they could achieve important gains by first nuclear use.

This last possibility is not limited to U.S.-Soviet relationships. As more and more countries acquire nuclear weapons, and as more and more countries fear escalation and eruption, the possibilities for large gains by either straight blackmail or blackmail combined with some calculated limited use of nuclear weapons may grow very large.

Thus we must not neglect the possibility that a sustained military use of nuclear weapons might present the side that was prepared to fight this kind of campaign with a very large advantage, and one that could not be negated by further "feasible" escalation simply because the defending powers would be too fearful of the possible consequences of further escalation. In other words, that side which is more willing to escalate, and most capable of winning at the higher levels, may have a great advantage. This advantage is perhaps more likely to accrue to aggressive and "dynamic" nations than to the relatively passive and *status quo*–oriented West. It may well be that the only way to negate this possible advantage would be for the West simply to make up its mind that nuclear weapons are part of the arsenal and are to be used if necessary.

However, most individuals who have considered this problem conclude, at least viscerally, that the dangers are simply too great.

And many have carefully compared the dangers of each path, asking in which direction safety and morality seemed to lie, fully realizing that a one-sided, or even two-sided, de-emphasis of nuclear weapons could be dangerous. Whatever the right answer may be to this difficult question, almost all decision-makers and analysts seem to believe that the "prudent" strategy is to try to retard the diffusion and acceptability of nuclear weapons. It seems all too apparent that a widespread diffusion of nuclear weapons would make the potential of violence in international relations more open-ended than it has ever been before. The possibility of immediate and cataclysmic destruction becomes ever more apparent.

The nuclear prohibition limits violence in another sense as well: without resorting to nuclear weapons, it is impossible even to wreak havoc at the 1939–45 levels quickly and easily, or without paying a preliminary price in immense social dislocation—the long, drawn-out process of mobilizing armies, production, and finance, and disrupting millions of private lives. Nuclear war can escalate to total violence without significantly involving the citizenry in the process of prewar mobilization. Their major energies are not, as in pre-atomic total war, necessary to feed the war machine. Hence, one argument against nuclear war is that it may be peculiarly unstable, or volatile, because the tendency for social lethargy to brake violence is reduced nearly to the vanishing point. Preparations for large-scale conventional war are painful; for nuclear war, they are not. The restraints on the outbreak of large-scale violence in nuclear war are therefore chiefly intellectual, ethical, or doctrinal ones.[16]

Thus, the inhibition against the use of nuclear weapons is not based on an arbitrary unwillingness to compress high-explosive

[16] The apparent ease and cheapness of nuclear forces, tactical and strategic, and the fact that they seem to obviate the need for large-scale civilian armies and the petty annoyances of a prewar conventional military buildup in part explain their attraction for civilian-minded governments, particularly conservative governments. This was the case in the United States between 1953 and 1960, and the same tendency has been at work in the Soviet Union, where there have been sizable cutbacks in conventional forces since 1955. It is also at work in Western Europe—within NATO, where the goal of thirty divisions on the Central Front has always been unpopular, and particularly in France, which is now more or less attempting to get more "bang for the buck."

power into a small, highly portable, and instantaneous package, but rather on a shared unwillingness to risk fighting wars of extreme violence, whatever the weapons employed. Therefore, looking around for and staying with the most salient threshold, whatever it may be, is a reasonable course of action for two antagonists. In short, if the intention of the combatants, real and potential, is to *limit* war, then "illogical" constraining elements in the rules of the game are not simply an impediment, but, on the contrary, are likely to be essential to the process of war limitation. Limited war must, almost by definition, be artificial, and the higher the degree of artificiality, the clearer—and perhaps the more reliable—the inhibitions on raw violence.

Some Additional Arguments in Favor of a Breach of the Nuclear Threshold

We have examined the most common arguments in favor of a nuclear first use by the United States—the "illogic" of sanctioning the battlefield use of large chemical explosives while prohibiting even small nuclear weapons, and the desirability of a first use to match the alleged numerical advantage in ground forces of an adversary. Although these arguments are not persuasive, in fairness some other arguments favoring the use of nuclear weapons must be noted which, coldly considered, have greater force.

One of them is that a world in which nuclear weapons have been used, and used purposefully and effectively to punish an aggressor, is a stable world. The lesson that nuclear weapons exist to be *used* against an aggressor (say, China) would be a deterring one, and it would be a lesson that would gain force from repeated demonstration. This is an argument that does not deny that such a use would accelerate the process of the diffusion of nuclear weapons. It incorporates the objection. But its conclusion is that such an accelerated proliferation of weapons, far from provoking a catastrophe, is more likely to bring about a peaceful world, or at least one without major war. In such a world, clashes of national interest, if allowed to lead to violence, would nevertheless be fought out at a low level of violence, under an umbrella of strategic parity or at least a balance of terror.

This argument draws still greater force from the notion that in a world in which one or two dozen nations possess adequate stocks of nuclear weapons, no single nation, or even any reasonable combination, is likely to take up aggression. The process of weapon diffusion would enable any one of these nations to strike a painful and even anonymous blow against the aggressors. Such a world would clearly be discouraging for a Hitler. And it is not an improbable international political-strategic order for the future.

This is a strong argument for nuclear use, although I, nevertheless, am not convinced by it. In any event, in the present climate of opinion in the United States—which is bitterly hostile to the proliferation of nuclear weapons—the argument, however persuasive, is not likely to win much of a hearing.

A second argument in favor of the United States breaching, or at least being more willing to breach, the nuclear threshold, is that not to do so increases the strains on our alliances. By failing to make a credible threat of controlled, small-scale nuclear response in actual or potential war situations in Western Europe, the Middle East, or Southeast Asia, the United States, it is argued, is, in effect, conceding these regions—or demanding of its allies (European or Asian) that they raise the troops to fight nonnuclear wars, whereas, in a nuclear world, these nations are, for a host of reasons, unwilling to raise sufficient conventional forces. But the American pressures on its allies to raise ground forces—"cannon fodder"—*have* strained the alliance system. This is, perhaps, part of the reason for the present strains on NATO.

One flaw in this argument is an empirical one: the United States has *not* had to concede Western Europe, the Middle East, or Southeast Asia. The failure by the United States or its allies to raise large nonnuclear forces, coupled with the "incredibility" of the United States nuclear threat, has not actually triggered major aggressive moves by Communist forces.

The empirical answer to the argument is not a decisive one. It must be added that while Communist aggressiveness has diminished in recent years, the Soviet Union has not had an invulnerable missile force. As Soviet strategic forces grow and become hardened and dispersed, thus achieving a rough strategic parity with American forces, the conditions would be created in which the Communists might attempt to advance their objectives by sublimited and limited war, under the shield of their deterrent.

There is, finally, a persuasive argument that has been advanced by Edward Teller, among others. It is, in effect, that no nation can fight "progress," and that in this context progress means weapons technology, the inevitable development of new and more efficient engines of war. The attempt to prohibit the use of weapons in being merely weakens the morale of the United States, without eliciting concessions from the Soviets and without fending off a supposed inevitable day of confrontation. We may be, at least for the present, in an era of relatively small—or no—wars. But it is impossible to predict the future. A nation that denies itself access to a whole spectrum of violence by adhering to restrained war conventions which may at any time be breached by a ruthless aggressor does, in fact, run a serious risk of defeat.

Thus, looking ahead, it may be possible to distinguish certain long-range effects of a continued ban against the use of nuclear weapons. A nation that habitually or conceptually denies itself a first use of nuclear weapons is likely to impair its psychological ability to use these weapons with determination, possibly even in self-defense. Yet, as a practical matter, these fears, for the present at least, seem overstated. The resolve of the United States is not yet so impaired that it could not credibly threaten nuclear retaliation, although Teller's argument may apply with greater force to the United Kingdom, where the threat of second use or nuclear retaliation is not, at the time of writing, entirely credible.

For the U.K., the assumptions underlying policy may be those of "pre-emptive" or "preventive accommodation." That is, deterrence would be maintained to the last possible moment by threatening a nuclear counterblow. But if deterrence failed, the victim could forestall disaster by accommodating in time. Deterrence is, in this formulation, maintained by bluff and the uncertainties surrounding the situation, of which one—a real one, in view of the historical record—is the possibility that the British would, in fact, back down if it came to the test. Pre-emptive accommodation (or surrender) thus describes a policy in which, consciously or implicitly, a nation intends to accommodate or surrender if a situation ever arises in which tactical information has been received that the other side has actually committed itself to launch an attack, or is actually launching an attack. The policy, then, is not to pre-empt by *attacking* in turn and trying to blunt the attack, a very difficult thing to do, but rather by holding back whatever forces one has and at the same time accommodating to whatever extent is necessary to induce the other side not to launch, continue, or augment. Such pre-emptive accommodation seems, to almost everybody who has considered it, a more reliable damage-limiting procedure for a European power attacked by the Soviet Union than any pre-emptive or blunting nuclear attack could possibly be.

The *preventive* accommodation tactic is an even more cautious policy designed to prevent an intense situation. It is less a military action than a political one. It covers those situations a nation considers too dangerous to risk waiting until an opponent is about to launch an attack. It seeks to prevent this by accommodating during severe crisis before the last possible moment has arrived.[17] All this

[17] It should be realized that, to a great extent, the above are the implicit and in some cases explicit tactics of the Europeans. Up to a few years ago, there were very few knowledgeable Europeans (if any) who could envisage their country's surviving a large nuclear war in which they were a major target; and if they were members of the NATO alliance, they could not imagine a large nuclear war in which they were not major targets. Both notions could be wrong, particularly if the war were conducted as a no-city war or as mostly a no-city war, as envisaged in the current U.S. controlled-response doctrine. But, at least until a few years ago, practically nobody in Europe had taken this possibility seriously, and, in fact, very few do now. Furthermore, very few Europeans believe that a nation can justifiably commit suicide or initiate actions that would lead to its total extinction, or even watch passively if events are occurring that have a high probability of leading to such a result. Thus, on a recent trip to Europe, I talked informally with a number of Europeans, and in each case conjectured that the strategy of their country was something between pre-emptive and preventive surrender. The word "surrender," not "accommodation," was deliberately used in order to make the choice starker. Actually, many Europeans who have thought about this possibility tend to believe either that some limited accommodation would work or advocate some form of passive or active civilian resistance as a last resort. The conjecture was not contradicted by any of these Europeans. However, most of them did not think that this was necessarily a serious matter. They do not believe that the Soviets feel any great desire to attack Europe; moreover, in their view, the Soviets could clearly not be certain that the pre-emptive or preventive surrender would be carried through in time, either because the U.S. would not allow it or because the opposing government would not, in fact, change its policy, or for any of hundreds of other reasons. They felt the fact that the Soviets could not be sure would,

may seem far-fetched; yet it is perfectly possible for all to agree that a nation's basic policy is, in fact, pre-emptive or preventive accommodation, and yet to have that policy succeed. The aggressor simply cannot be certain that a nation will continue with this policy in a real crisis. There are too many buttons, too many possibilities for accidental, unauthorized, or irrational behavior, too many new political and emotional factors that would come into play in a crisis for an aggressor to rely on the defender's carrying through the accommodation successfully. Thus, it may be that the only serious military requirement some countries need in some situations is a force that "looks" as if it might be used in some way—if only to trigger off a larger war. At the very least, the defender needs to be able to assert that no one can absolutely guarantee that the force will *not* be used.

I should note that I am not arguing that deterrence by uncertainty, particularly in the form of pre-emptive or preventive accommodation or surrender, is necessarily a satisfactory strategy. There are at least three circumstances in which such tactics would tend to work out badly:

1. *If there were a very intense crisis in which stark choices might be presented.* The assurance of the Europeans would be likely at that point to vanish.
2. *If there were a systematic debate on national-security policy.* Of course, the Europeans do not expect any such debate, but

---

in itself, be sufficient deterrent to prevent them from trying any probes serious enough to make pre-emptive or preventive accommodation, much less surrender, a plausible possibility. I tend to agree with this analysis by my European friends. However, as discussed above, the policy can still be undesirable even if it is likely to work.

That is why I believe that it is important to raise these unpleasant problems now, during an era of relative calm and an atmosphere of *détente*—raise them, perhaps, as dramatically and seriously as one can (which, given the likely apathy, is not going to be very dramatically or seriously). In this atmosphere, there is likely to be very little disutility in raising these questions. If one is afraid to talk about them, one is certainly not equipped to be very firm in a crisis. This is now the time also to think about and institute corrective actions. In particular, I would like to see some variation of the "proportionate nuclear reprisal" strategy (discussed in Chapter XIII) considered for its possible worth in fulfilling European political-military objectives.

if there were one, then the policies thus expounded would not be likely to prove politically palatable. Actually, so many realize this truth that few are anxious to rock a seemingly leaky and unstable boat; there is an implicit agreement not to debate. This itself could be a serious source of later problems.

3. *If deterrence actually failed.* The policies could then lead to excessive accommodation, to surrender, or to an extremely or unnecessarily destructive war.

A final point must be made about a nation's emphasizing nuclear avoidance and concentrating on conventional forces and doctrine. It could eventually result in lowered morale and adverse career choices by talented officers and, in time, in antiquated or defective hardware, nuclear postures, and training. The process might not be a deliberate one. It might be masked, and not necessarily consciously masked, by a continued theoretical doctrine of use under extreme provocation.

If this should happen, it could parallel the situation in 1940, when the French and English found themselves helpless before the Germans' blitzkrieg tactics. A decade or so that saw major advances in the design, procurement, training, operation, and doctrine governing the use of such weapons made by one side only might provide that side with a crushing battlefield superiority. Yet, so far as the United States is concerned, if we retained an adequate strategic force in being, and particularly if the Europeans obtained an "adequate" deterrent of their own, it is difficult to see how a local tactical battlefield advantage could be translated by even a determined enemy into a crushing political-strategic defeat for the United States. A too-great ambition in Soviet war aims would tend to trigger an American or European strategic strike, at least one of a controlled punitive or even symbolic character. More limited aims would allow time for emergency and mobilization measures—particularly if the recommendations discussed later (in Chapter VIII) were implemented. My own strong belief, though, is that a U.S. policy of minimum prudency, even if this country continues to observe and reinforce the nuclear threshold, would be to continue with theoretical studies and an ambitious research-and-development effort, as well as to maintain some form of dual capability.

Nevertheless, the "ban" on first use has in some sense been in effect for eighteen years. It gains force, real and symbolic, with each additional year. This suggests that with another decade or so of nonuse, a breach might be so unfamiliar an act, so fraught with danger, that an aggressor would make only tentative or gingerly use of nuclear weapons, feeling his way. Or he might seek his advantage in the psychological significance of the act—in its demonstration of commitment, even of recklessness or ruthlessness.

But while this is plausible, it is not certain: an aggressor also might judge that there was no advantage in incurring the odium of the act as well as the strategic risks unless he pressed home the advantage of surprise. Thus, when Napoleon broke the conventions of war in his Italian campaigns, his break was a savage one, driven home with determination. So was the German violation of Belgian neutrality in 1914, and so were the Japanese attacks—without formal declarations of war—at Port Arthur in 1904 and at Pearl Harbor in 1941. In every case, the breach, once made, was exploited with vigor.

One important effect of the convention of nonuse thus far, and one that might be expected to be accelerated in the years to come, has been increased emphasis on sublimited war (propaganda, political warfare, terrorism, and subversion) and limited conventional war—that is, on conflict at the lowest levels of violence. Whether this trend is seen as desirable or not depends on the estimate of American and Western ability to meet the challenge. Some observers have felt that the Soviet Union and its proxies have demonstrated an overwhelming superiority at this game. But the record of successful or moderately successful anti-Communist action in Greece, Malaya, the Philippines, Burma, Korea, and much of Latin America (where large-scale civil violence has been contained), as well as in the reconstruction or development of Western Europe, India, and Japan, suggests that the reverse may be true. In fact, almost all of the large-scale territorial gains achieved by the Communists since World War II came directly in the aftermath of that war and had generally been achieved by 1949, when the Soviets first tested their nuclear weapons. Even today, whatever increases the Communists seem to be achieving are not associated directly with an increase in their nuclear power. The Korean War marks the high tide of Communist post–World War II conventional aggression. Since the early 1950's, the level of Communist-inspired war and violence has diminished, not increased.

Recapitulation and Concluding Remarks on Preserving the Nuclear Threshold

Under current conditions, the major determinant of whether a number of nations get nuclear weapons will be whether they *want* them. And whether other nations want nuclear weapons will depend partly upon the political and emotional environment of the world. Specific local factors will influence the environment for a particular state. But the decision may depend more on general influences and upon world-wide patterns and attitudes.

On the one hand, there could be a situation in which France and England continued to maintain their independent nuclear forces, in which no pan-European nuclear force was established, in which there was no test-ban agreement, in which NATO forces were extensively armed with tactical weapons integrated into the force structure at the division level, and, finally, in which other European countries developed independent national nuclear deterrent forces. In this situation, nuclear weapons would be likely to appear to be an inevitable (an "ordinary") part of a nation's armament, and necessary to an important nation's safety, self-respect, position, and international status.

On the other hand, there might be a situation in which first England and then France merged their national nuclear forces in a European nuclear deterrent force independent of U.S. control, and in which tactical nuclear weapons were a relatively small part of the NATO ground-force structure. Here, it would seem reasonable to think that European countries other than France and England would not seek their own nuclear forces. If the other European countries did not feel a need for their own nuclear weapons, if they indicated that any fighting on the Continent was likely to be limited to nonnuclear weapons, it seems somewhat likely that no other nation would feel a strong incentive to get such weapons.

In other words, there is a psychological effect involved, and one that can work in either direction. Either there can be an atmosphere and a set of understandings in the international community that make it seem only natural for nations to seek nuclear weapons as they achieve the technical and financial capacity, or there can be an atmosphere, a pattern of thinking that reduces the incentives for nations to achieve nuclear status. It should be remembered that, outside Europe, most of the countries concerned are not used to playing the role of innovator in international politics; they are likely to adopt much of their attitudes and ideas from the United States and European countries. Thus, if the point is made credible that these nuclear systems are relatively unusable weapons and may represent a useless financial sacrifice—that the same investment put into nonnuclear capabilities is far more likely to further the nation's policy than nuclear weapons—one would expect diffusion to be discouraged. Even military defeats suffered by the United States at Communist hands might thus have one good effect in showing that the mere possession of nuclear weapons is far from solving a nation's problems.

With this in mind, we can gain a clearer understanding of the objections made to the use of nuclear weapons in such wars as those in Korea and Indochina. Assume that the United States had, in fact, used nuclear weapons in Korea in 1950–51 and had, as a result, won the war easily, pushing the Chinese back to the Yalu, or possibly stopping short at the narrow waist of Korea, near the 39th Parallel. Let us also imagine that in 1954 the U.S. had used nuclear weapons reasonably successfully in Indochina, and thus preserved the French from defeat at Dien Bien Phu. The argument could be made that in neither case would these victories by themselves have made the world very different from what it is today. It is most unlikely that the French could have maintained their rule in Indochina indefinitely; nor could the fact that the North Korean–South Korean border lay some 100 miles farther north change the balance of world power very much (although there might be further beneficial ramifications of such victories). On the other hand, all the nations in the world would have seen that nuclear weapons were going to be used in wars. One would suppose that the Swedes and the Swiss would have achieved nuclear weapons by 1965; that the Germans, instead of having an atomic-energy program that virtually discriminates against the conversion of research and capacity to a weapons program now would possess a nuclear-weapons program or, at the very least, a basic nuclear-energy program that could easily be changed to weapons development and production. The Indians might have acquired nuclear weapons. The Japanese would have a program. And so on.

The power structure of this alternative world in the year 1965 would not be much different from what it is today. After all, we are not particularly concerned about Swedish or Swiss aggressions. But one could confidently predict that before 1975 there would be twenty, perhaps thirty, nations with nuclear weapons, and not all of them stable democracies; that the manufacture of missiles for export would either be a thriving business in some countries, or would be a seriously considered line of action. The prospect would be that by the 1980's and 1990's almost every nation would have missile forces of one type or another. Finally, the use of nuclear weapons and the accelerating arms race might have acted as a spur to various kinds of ban-the-bomb movements, some wholly irresponsible, thus increasing the pressures of these groups upon democratic governments. Such groups could impair Western morale, leading to diffidence and uncertainty in the pursuit of national objectives.

This obviously is not the only possible interpretation of what could have occurred as a result of a U.S. first use of nuclear weapons. It also is possible that their use could have marked a decisive turning point in Communist–non-Communist relations. Communist leaders, particularly the Chinese Communists, might have given up their grander designs and pushed more softly in the years after 1954. But the value of this gamble had to be seen at the time in terms of the equal probability of our first use leading to greater Communist efforts and deeper antagonisms.

One can, of course, emphasize the fact that it may be impossible to defer indefinitely the diffusion of nuclear weapons. One can argue that the picture I first presented is in fact a desirable world —one in which there is a *gradual* increase in the number of nations owning nuclear weapons and therefore in the instances of occasional use. In this fashion, reliable conventions might be established and information transmitted, nations might learn the utility and disutility of the weapons, thus becoming skillful, and perhaps prudent, in their threat and use.

It is perfectly true that as a result of the seeming unusability of nuclear weapons and the revulsion against them, only a small number of nations may actually acquire nuclear weapons in the next decade or two, possibly only an additional European nation or two. But this will not prevent the technology from improving and the theoretical availability from increasing. As a result, sometime in the 1980's or the 1990's, an incident might occur that would result in a number of nations *suddenly* procuring the then easily available weapons within a very short period of time, possibly only a year or two. We might thus experience an explosive diffusion of nuclear weapons to fifty or sixty inexperienced and "uneducated" nations. Such a diffusion could present a far greater danger, a far greater potential for disaster, than the gradual adaptation of international and national societies to these devices. We cannot close our eyes, such an argument would run, to the fact that these weapons exist: they will be diffused, nations will possess them, and in spite of all our attempts, humanity will have to come to terms with their existence. It is far better, then, that society be allowed to adjust to these weapons in a series of small steps. There might then be no violent and explosive impact of nuclear diffusion, as could result from "successful" but temporary attempts to restrict the diffusion of these weapons.

Which of the two views one takes is partly determined by assumptions and values. From the first viewpoint, a U.S. policymaker, contemplating the use of nuclear weapons on a moderately important issue, faces several possible aftermaths, among them: (1) no genuine restoration of the *status quo ante,* but such a great revulsion against both nuclear weapons and the user of them that a potential loss of political influence may more than cancel out narrow military gains achieved by the use of the weapons; (2) an international acceptance of nuclear weapons as "conventional" and the rapid diffusion of them; or (3) both—a revulsion and animosity against the United States, plus a rapid diffusion. Facing this prospect, almost all the *civilian* strategists—such people as Brennan, Brody, Buchan, Kaufman, King, Kissinger, Knorr, Schelling, Strachey, Wohlstetter, and so on—seem to be in agreement that it is better for the West to defer as much as possible the diffusion of these weapons.

It is difficult for some in the United States, which possesses a high-grade nuclear arsenal (and sophisticated means of delivery and putative defense), to believe today in the threat of small-nation strike forces or in the power of future Nth countries. This is shortsighted in the extreme. The ultimate effect of the proliferation of nuclear weapons, if it were coupled with a tradition of nuclear use, would be, unless the Soviets and the Americans made major efforts, to reduce the United States and the Soviet Union from the rank of superpowers to that of chiefs among "equals" in a multisided game of gingerly diplomacy and strategic war. While *present* Nth-country arsenals and delivery systems may be crude, they are not likely to remain so: cheap, small fusion weapons—the "poor man's bombs" of the future—are only a single case in point, very likely attainable within a decade or two. The long-range effects of nuclear weapons are almost certain to be to "equalize" states—to neutralize the importance of conventional wealth, population, or geographical advantage. Thus, in a world where nuclear weapons are used, the United States will have surrendered its traditional advantages and will face the prospect of fighting wars according to the rules of a game which a dozen powers or more can learn to play with roughly equal effect and skill.

Thus, if fears for the arms race are legitimate, a U.S. decision to breach the nuclear threshold for some strategic or even tactical convenience would seem extremely shortsighted and imprudent. If there is no way to prevent the eventual spread of nuclear-weapons technology and the technology of cheap missile systems, there is a hope at least that a reasonably effective tradition of nonuse may be established in the world.

Application of the "No Nuclear Use" Discussion to the Other Basic Thresholds

Implicitly, our discussion has covered the six basic thresholds: don't rock the boat, nuclear war is unthinkable, no nuclear use, central sanctuary, central war, and city targeting. Much of what I have said about the nuclear threshold would apply to all these. There are, of course, important differences. None of the thresholds is completely objective and unambiguous; and I have already noted that we can, if we wish, confuse the difference between nuclear weapons and conventional weapons. We can also violate the central sanctuary by degrees. But the nuclear threshold and the central sanctuary are probably the two most salient and objective of the thresholds.

There is no intention in this discussion to argue that sharp and precise distinctions between the different groups of rungs can be maintained or defined, but only that something like the distinctions discussed are likely to—and should—be observed or noted in many situations. Indeed, there are many more thresholds possible than the six basic ones, and they can be defined in sophisticated and subtle ways. An awareness of the significance of the thresholds, both small and large, and an adaptation of one's tactics to their existence seem to be central requirements for any reasonable policy. Furthermore, if one wishes to violate thresholds, one must be conscious of the negative effects and act in a manner that minimizes them, as well as exploits the gains that are sought. More important, in a world in which there is no legislature to set new rules, and the only method of changing rules is through a complex and unreliable systems-bargaining process, each side should—other things being equal—be anxious to preserve whatever thresholds there are. This is a counsel of prudence, but a serious one: it is not often possible to restore traditions, customs, or conventions that have been shattered. Once they are gone, or weakened, the world may be "permanently" worse off.

VII

Bizarre Crises and Exemplary Central Attacks

Basic Description and Definition

It is convenient now to discuss in one chapter the next two sets of rungs on the escalation ladder. Assuming that one side or the other has decided to cross the nuclear threshold, I will discuss the very restrained and limited use of nuclear weapons (or the very intense and credible threat of such use). For our purposes we can divide such situations into two classes: Rungs 21–25, which lie between the "no nuclear use" and "central sanctuary" thresholds; and Rungs 26–31, the kinds of "small" and discriminating attacks that can occur between the "central sanctuary" and "central war" thresholds. (See Figure 3, p. 39.)

Despite the fact that nuclear weapons have already been used twice, and the nuclear sword has been rattled many times, one can argue that for all practical purposes nuclear war is still (and hopefully will remain) so far from our experience that it is difficult to reason from, or illustrate arguments by, analogies from history. Thus, many of our concepts and doctrines must be based on abstract and analytical considerations. If, in discussing intense crises (Chapter V), we entered relatively uncharted ground, the ground is so uncharted here that it seems to many positively bizarre. In fact, some argue that any public discussion of these possibilities, or even any examination or discussion of them at all, is not only bizarre, but is at best an academic and useless exercise, and at worst immoral if not psychopathic.

I would argue that the fact that these issues are hypothetical and analytical does not mean that they should not be taken seriously. So far as the threat of a nuclear central war is concerned, this chapter may be more important than the chapters on central war itself, since the options discussed here could be both an alternative to central war and one of the most credible routes to such war. They actually seem more probable routes to central war than direct eruption from the low rungs precisely (and paradoxically) because some decision-makers are likely, in a desperate crisis, to prefer them to the alternative of central war. Thus, these options can provide the basic outbreak scenarios for discussing all-out wars.

To some extent, the options of this chapter should be thought of not as ways to get into central war but as ways to avoid it. And many analysts do believe that as the balance of terror grows more stable, the possibility becomes more remote that any country would be willing to initiate a central war with all its inevitable extreme destruction and its risks, if not reality, of total annihilation of great nations. These analysts argue that whatever the motivation or pressure may be for a nation to resort to central war, one of these "bizarre" options is the more likely to be chosen. The alternative, after all, is likely to be a very stark and immediate form of national suicide.

Others, of course, will argue that it is exactly this kind of reasoning that makes discussion of these problems so dangerous. They will point out that if decision-makers are deterred from erupting in a grave crisis, they ordinarily would be deterred from choosing one of these bizarre or exemplary options; but the discussion of such thresholds as central sanctuary, central war, and city targeting can give a false expectation of the possibility of limiting the forms of nuclear war, and indeed, if the thresholds between bizarre crises and exemplary central attacks or military central wars are really more fantasy than reality, then it may be that a nation should make concessions, compromise, or even surrender rather than resort to one of these options.

But it is also possible that if a nation is given only the choice between holocaust and surrender, it may choose holocaust. In any case, the possibilities discussed here can not only be invented at the last moment, but some of them are being prepared for in terms of government procurement, deployment, and planning; and thus they must be studied. One wishes, too, to guard against their possible use by an enemy. Finally, I would argue that we must have such options as these available because we might need them in some desperate but conceivable circumstances. Moreover, I would argue that the thresholds at these escalation levels are more stable than they seem to many, even if they are less so than they seem to some others (i.e., there are people on both sides of this argument).

Let me examine, however, why it is that many believe that these thresholds can be maintained. To make the argument very clear, I will consider first a simple and stark example, and then go on to a more reasonable situation. Let the reader assume for the moment that both the Soviet Union and the United States have 10,000 hard and dispersed missiles on each side. (While this would be very expensive, it might not be preposterously expensive—even in the medium run. It might then cost substantially less than $10 billion a year to maintain a posture of 10,000 ready missiles.) Let us also assume (very plausibly) that whatever active or passive defenses each side has are negligible compared to this threat. It would then be almost inconceivable that any circumstance could arise, other than a very large central attack by one side, in which either side would press very many of these 10,000 buttons—for it would thus ensure that the other side would launch a large, perhaps annihilating, attack in retaliation. Some buttons might be pressed in various situations, but neither of the opponents is likely to press all the buttons, even under extreme strain—such as the limited exemplary use of weapons by the opponent against one's homeland.

While I do not expect the kind of balance of terror envisaged above actually to occur, I do expect a much firmer balance of terror than has existed in the past. It should also be realized that even if one side has a large and "usable" advantage over the other, it may not want to use this advantage by actually making a large first strike against the other side's military forces, even if it felt it could achieve an important degree of force reduction by such a strike: it might believe that the risks of such an action were too great and that it should use its first-strike advantage to achieve some kind of escalation dominance. In other words, with its advantages, it could threaten much more persuasively than its opponent to escalate or erupt to a large war if a situation became desperate enough. Its argument would be that it was the other side that had to back down in confrontations.

One can imagine negotiations in which the "stronger" side said more or less explicitly to the other side: "Neither of us expects this crisis to escalate to a large missile exchange; but you must have noticed that if you strike first, even with a large or all-out salvo, we can and presumably will annihilate you, whereas the opposite is not true. If we strike you first, we can make a large strike and we can do so much damage to your forces that it would be difficult for you to cause profound damage to us in return, though, of course, we know that the damage might be great. Further, we would expect our postattack blackmail, or intrawar deterrence, to work. We really expect to be able to intimidate you from seriously retaliating against us. Now both of us realize that the crisis will never escalate to the point where these matters will actually come up, but you must notice the facts of the situation and realize that if this crisis continues too long, the unthinkable may in fact occur."

Thus, even if a conflict did not escalate to the bizarre-crises or exemplary-central-attack rungs, the effect of the disparity in the strategic balance could have an important effect on negotiations conducted at a lower level of escalation.

In other words, the chief effect of some degree of "credible first-strike capability" (plus an invulnerable and large second-strike force) may be tacit. It is less likely to be used, or its use even explicitly threatened, than it is to provide an extra degree of pressure in dealings in an intense crisis and even farther up the rungs of the ladder. The side with strategic superiority may still prefer to use the dangerous and eruption-prone measures discussed in this chapter, rather than go to central war directly, because it believes that while the options of bizarre crises or exemplary central attacks are dangerous, central war would be even more dangerous. The stronger side may also feel that once it has shattered its opponent's nuclear incredulity, the escalation dominance available to it may be so much strengthened that it will have its own way relatively easily.

The Rungs of Bizarre Crises

RUNG 21. LOCAL NUCLEAR WAR—EXEMPLARY: As I have pointed out, most U.S. analysts who have seriously studied these problems firmly oppose initiation by the U.S. of the use of nuclear weapons under almost any circumstances. They believe that since the weapons exist, we should procure, deploy, and maintain adequate systems unless and until better arrangements prevail in the world. But these analysts do not believe that these nuclear systems should be used, except as a last resort in a vital situation or to retaliate against use by others. However, it is important to ask how these nuclear weapons might be used in the event it became necessary; or even more important, how we might react to someone else's use of nuclear weapons. Almost every analyst is now agreed that the first use of nuclear weapons—even if against military targets— is likely to be less for the purpose of destroying the other side's military forces or handicapping its operations than for redress, warning, bargaining, punitive, fining, or deterrence purposes. For example, one side could drop a nuclear bomb or two in order to show the other side that, unless it backed down or accepted a reasonable compromise, more bombs would be likely to follow. Such a use could easily occur in the following limited-war situation:

One side is losing conventionally and decides to use nuclear weapons. It doesn't use them to damage the other side in a way that really hurts, because that could easily cause escalation to get out of control. But it might drop a bomb or two on some logistical target, such as a supply dump or a railroad yard. This might not kill a large number of soldiers; it might not even hamper logistical operations very much; but it would unmistakably tell the enemy something like the following: "I have dropped two bombs. Having dropped two, I may be willing to drop twenty. In other words, I'm either crazy or determined, or both. I've demonstrated it. Don't you want to listen to reason?" Such an act might cause escalation. It might produce the desired results. Or the other side might reply in a tit-for-tat fashion to show that it had not been deterred, and then (since it actually is deterred) consider ending or compromising the conventional war rather than fully exploit its initial advantage.

The use of nuclear weapons would probably be more escalatory —and therefore more frightening—if, instead of being launched locally, the weapons were launched strategically, though against local targets. By using the same weapons systems that would be used in a general war, one would communicate to the enemy a willingness to disregard precedents and a likely willingness to go either to the limit or at least very high on the escalation ladder. It would also make it more difficult for the local conflict to be terminated or stalemated by purely local military actions. Thus, it would make either negotiation—or escalation—almost inevitable. Conversely, if one wished to diminish somewhat the possibility of large escalations, possibly making a more sustained but more limited escalation more likely, one might use only locally available launchers of nuclear weapons, such as the relatively short-range missiles of the U.S. Army.

RUNG 22. DECLARATION OF LIMITED NUCLEAR WAR: In accompaniment to actions at either the previous or the next rung, or as an act in its own right, a government might choose to make a formal declaration of limited nuclear war. Such a step might have several advantages. The declaration itself could set exact limits on the type of nuclear action that the declarer intended to initiate and that he was prepared to countenance from the enemy without escalating further himself. In this way, eruption to all-out war might be made less likely and the escalation itself made more explicit—which might increase the pressure to compromise.

Such a declaration would also give some legal form and sanction to acts of war that are regarded with abhorrence by many people at home, in the enemy country, and (perhaps even more) in neutral and allied countries. The declaration could include a formal announcement of the conditions under which the declarer would be prepared to de-escalate.

In addition, the declaration would have the ten characteristics and results enumerated in the discussion of Rung 32 (formal declaration of war).

RUNG 23. LOCAL NUCLEAR WAR—MILITARY: Past NATO planning has envisaged the immediate use of hundreds of nuclear weapons in reply to even a conventional attack in Europe by the Soviets.

As opposed to the exemplary purposes of Rung 21, NATO planned to use nuclear weapons for traditional military purposes—for defense, denial, destruction of opponent's capability, and so on—and the scale of the action and the targeting was to be dictated by these military considerations. Such a war, whether in Europe or elsewhere, seems to many military strategists to be a worse alternative than compromise, massive conventional war, or immediate escalation to a higher rung of the ladder. I think, however, that among analysts (as well as the lay public), an almost dogmatic unwillingness to consider this possibility seriously can be detected. Some of the reasons for this were noted in the last chapter, and while I will follow the current fashion and not discuss the possibilities of local military nuclear wars at any length, I think that we must not forget that this option always exists, even if only to the opponent, and a challenged nation should be prepared to deal with it. The increasing actual or potential availability of a varied inventory of small, inexpensive nuclear weapons (including such esoteric devices as the Davy Crockett and the neutron bomb), and the growth of the French nuclear capability (and France's seeming adoption of a "no pause" strategy), are both likely to renew discussion of this possibility. In any case, it is, and will likely continue to be, an important objective of U.S. military forces to be able to wage such a war—at least in Europe, even if a "no bomb use policy" is explicitly adopted by all nations.

RUNG 24. UNUSUAL, PROVOCATIVE, AND SIGNIFICANT COUNTER-MEASURES: It is possible for one side to carry out threatening maneuvers or military preparations that have the effect of shifting the balance of power by, for example, sharply increasing the other side's vulnerability to surprise attack. Thus, our warning system has not been built to deal adequately with peacetime spoofing and jamming, and it would be possible for the Soviets to institute these practices on a scale so large that we could no longer tell the difference between small training missions and actual attacks (and presumably, the reverse circumstances also hold). By thus making the possibility of a successful surprise attack much greater, one might succeed in looking much more threatening; one would, in fact, be more threatening. It is quite possible that if one side has a secure second-strike capability and its opponent is vulnerable to spoofing and jamming, these actions could take the place of the classic ultimatum or quasi ultimatum. However, one can make spoofing and jamming even more frightening by actually delivering a quasi or full-fledged ultimatum. What can be done about these tactics? If the Soviets used aerial jamming against our early warning lines or BMEWS system, there probably would be little we could do directly, since it is currently almost impossible for us actively to defend these lines. Moreover, the Soviets might even use shipboard jammers, since this would be somewhat less expensive and in some ways more satisfactory than airborne equipment. A half-dozen ships stationed 50 to 100 miles off our shores could aggressively jam our contiguous radar cover, and in this case even our hard missile bases might become vulnerable to surprise attack, since it might put our radars out of commission and Soviet bombers could sneak through. If they were really provocatively inclined, the Soviets could increase pressure on us by simultaneously stationing missile-launching submarines or ships off our coasts, by sabotaging communications, command and control, or other warning systems, and by carrying out still other threatening or confusing maneuvers.

Of course, none of the above would be overwhelmingly threatening if we had confidence in the adequacy of our Minuteman and Polaris forces, but the mere use of such tactics would cause a searching examination for, and re-evaluation of, our potential vulnerabilities.

Under current conditions, it seems plausible that, from the narrow military point of view, the Soviets and Nth countries would in fact be more vulnerable to such tactics as these than we. But these tactics might be used to attack the morale and will of the opponent as well as his physical capabilities. Because of the ever-present fear of eruption, both sides are likely to be sensitive to such indications of "seriousness," whether or not they are militarily effective.

RUNG 25. EVACUATION (APPROXIMATELY 70 PER CENT): At this point, a situation would seem dangerously near large-scale war. It might seem advisable to evacuate the maximum convenient number of people from cities—probably between two-thirds and three-fourths of the population. If only very helpful working adults were left behind, perhaps one-quarter to one-third of the population, all the important industries, communications, transportation facilities, and other activities the government might want to continue could be operated. There would be, of course, an enormous loss of GNP, but most of it would be in industries or businesses that are ultimately expendable. In other words, there would be a loss in the rate of accumulation of wealth and in current standards of living, but an evacuation such as this might not affect national defense preparations very severely. Actually, evacuation is just one of a series of emergency-readiness and tension-mobilization measures available to the modern state (and which are generally ignored in current discussions because of their emphasis on sudden and devastating attacks). I will leave discussion of these possibilities to the next chapter.

The "Central Sanctuary" Threshold

I have already pointed out (in Chapter VI) that the chosen firebreak for the present administration has been, in our terms, relatively low on the escalation ladder—the nuclear threshold. I quoted a Department of Defense spokesman, who said that beyond the nuclear threshold, there was "no other obvious 'firebreak.' "[1] The key word in this argument is "obvious." Attacks that avoid the zone of interior of the enemy also have a salient threshold, one that may reasonably be considered at least one of the most important of the transnuclear thresholds. Almost any state unequivocally divides into categories of "homeland" and "not-homeland."[2] To recognize this distinction does not mean a denial of the important relations that may exist between a major power and its allies and dependencies, still more its overseas forces. But the dis-

[1] See pp. 94–95.

[2] The reason for my qualification, "almost," has to do with such divided states as East and West Germany, the curious situation in the Soviet Union where Belorussia and the Ukraine are treated as separate states with separate U.N. representation, the possibility of the creation of a quasi-political community such as a European Political Community or even a European Defense Community with an "automatic" tit-for-tat controlled-response firing doctrine, and so on.

tinction between the homeland of a nation and the territory of its allies, or even its overseas bases and forces, is perhaps as salient as "nuclear"-"nonnuclear."

Indeed, the line between the external world and the nation may even be stronger as a firebreak than the threshold between conventional and nuclear war, since it is an older distinction, invested with far more emotion and prestige. Of course, as in the case of nuclear-nonnuclear, it is possible to blur the difference. Thus, many in the West want to obliterate the distinction between "Natonians" (Donald G. Brennan's term) and Americans. Yet, the very awkwardness of the word "Natonian" implies how far the Atlantic Alliance's peoples are from a common nationality. (But if the word were used more, it might go far toward creating a new "H" and "not-H" line. In these matters, the word is often to a surprising extent, the thing—or the use of the word might simply blur or confuse the important differences in national interests.)

Under current conditions, it is reasonably clear that in the next decade the credibility of a nation inviting certain annihilation for the sake of its allies is going to tend to diminish to the vanishing point, however repugnant or dishonorable this development may now seem. But the credibility of a nation risking the kind of restrained attacks I am discussing in this chapter may or may not diminish so sharply, depending in part on the decision-makers' expectations of the rules being observed. All these remarks apply with equal force to the Soviet Union and its guarantees to its allies.

At least two important thresholds remain. The first is that between very discriminating, very controlled, and very small attacks in which the objectives are also very limited, and large attacks in which the objectives may or may not be so limited. The second threshold is the distinction between large attacks directed at military forces and large attacks directed at civilians (as discussed in Chapter IX).

The Rungs of Exemplary Central Attacks

RUNG 26. DEMONSTRATION ATTACK ON ZONE OF INTERIOR: I have discussed the very limited use of nuclear weapons in a local war or in a demonstration of force to warn the enemy to consider backing down. The same kind of warning might be delivered even more effectively—and dangerously—by a "harmless" attack on the other side's country which, however, did do recognizable and unmistakable physical damage. For example, the Soviets could explode a small weapon in an uninhabited part of the Rocky Mountains or in the great American desert. Or they could explode a weapon over one or more American cities high enough to break windows, but not to do much real damage. Or they could do a relatively small amount of damage to military, industrial, or agrarian targets ("small" as compared to all-out war, or to the three attacks considered below). Similar possibilities are open to the U.S.

RUNG 27. EXEMPLARY ATTACK ON MILITARY: The next step might be to begin actually destroying portions of the other side's weapons systems, but in a relatively careful way so as not to cause much collateral damage. The simplest thing, of course, is to attack airplanes, ships, or submarines outside the opponent's territory. One can imagine this going on without actually touching off an eruption, but it might start a limited escalation. One could also attack warning stations much more openly or intensely than was considered in previous rungs, or even destroy isolated SAC bomber bases or missile bases. These attacks could be made purely to exert psychological pressure or to reduce the defender's military capability significantly by finding leverage targets. We could, for example, attack the Soviet staging bases in the Far North. This would seriously degrade their ability to use medium bombers against the U.S., although it would be a small attack as compared with other possibilities. Whether or not we could get away with this would depend a great deal upon the strategic equation, but there are circumstances when this kind of attack might appear less undesirable than either all-out war or compromise and accommodation.

RUNG 28. EXEMPLARY ATTACKS AGAINST PROPERTY: It is hard to decide at this point what the next rung really should be. One possibility is a limited attack on cities, presumably after warning has been delivered and the cities evacuated. The purpose would be to destroy property, not people. But a controlled reprisal could also involve the destruction of relatively "sanitary-looking" targets, expensive industrial installations—particularly ones that have a semi-military character, such as gaseous-diffusion plants, and that could be considered legitimate military objectives. Alternatively, there could be attacks with bacteriological or chemical weapons against food or crops. There could even be incapacitating, but not overwhelming, attacks against population.

In a modern, wealthy industrial society, reprisals taking the form of destruction of material wealth are probably a more satisfactory method of using force than exemplary attacks against people or important cultural or symbolic targets. The destruction of moderate amounts of property does not jeopardize the survival of the community. If no one is killed, it's "only money." In fact, it is conceivable, if implausible, that the controlled-reprisal concept could reach a point where, rather than actually launching missiles, one simply insisted that the other side pay a "fine" or ransom—perhaps to the U.N. In controlled reprisal, the objective is less to gain advantage than to punish the side being coerced. If there were a series of such incidents, the precedent could become institutionalized (in a manifestation of systems bargaining) as one means for coping with intense conflicts. The ultimate development might be the creation of a system of customary (agonistic?) resorts to arbitration or legal judgment to set the fines.

RUNG 29. EXEMPLARY ATTACKS ON POPULATION: It is difficult to believe that population attacks can occur without touching off some kind of all-out war. But if the balance of terror were sufficiently stable, and if fearful governments retained self-control, even these attacks might occur without eruption to spasm or other central war. Once this rung was considered the highest rung short of all-out war on the escalation ladder, and in any crisis of the mid-1960's it would probably be placed much higher than it is here. But as the balance of terror becomes more stable, the possibility that this kind of attack could occur without an eruption becomes more plausible. Such an attack could take the much-discussed form of city-trading, fallout attacks on population, or even biological or bacteriological attacks (possibly partially disguised or anonymous in order partially to limit the explicit or public provocation).

RUNG 30. COMPLETE EVACUATION (APPROXIMATELY 95 PER CENT): At this point, the world is on the verge of, or actually in, a large war. If at all possible, each side is likely to evacuate its cities almost completely, leaving at most 5 or 10 per cent of the population behind to operate essential facilities. Such measures would, of course, cause enormous political, social, economic, and psychological problems, and it is possible that in the United States some form of martial law would be declared and some rights under the Constitution suspended.

A great risk in complete evacuation is that it might touch off an attack by the other side. Before carrying through such an operation, one would need to be confident of one's capabilities to deter such attacks and of the prudence of the opponent. However, with all its dangers, evacuation might be a safer measure than an all-out attack on the enemy and the almost certain reprisal that such an attack would bring. The main advantage of having an evacuation option as a deterrent move (threat) is that it is more credible than the mere threat of attack without evacuation, and, at the same time, if deterrence fails and evacuation takes place, the pressure on the opponent is increased while the pressure on the evacuating side may be lessened as the evacuation mitigates the effects of the war which has now become likely.

I am talking about an extreme (95 per cent or so) evacuation. Although there might have been a relatively large-scale evacuation before this (see Rung 25), in which the majority of the people would have been moved, even with only 30 per cent of the population left in large cities the United States would still present in the neighborhood of 20 million obvious hostages to an enemy. If these were reduced to 2–4 million, then the potential casualties, if the evacuated population were safe, would approximate those of World Wars I and II. This might indicate convincingly that war was considered "tolerable" by the threatened country.

RUNG 31. RECIPROCAL REPRISALS: If there should come about more or less continual tit-for-tat exchanges—whether of the symbolic, exemplary, or more destructive kind—the result would be a war of almost pure resolve. As I have remarked, such a situation has analogies with the labor strike or the game of "chicken." Many strategists believe that reciprocal-reprisal wars of resolve may be a standard tactic of the future when the balance of terror has become firm and absolute. Such wars, depending on their length and targets, could be at, or across, the next threshold (see Rungs 33, 34, and 39).

Some Comments on the Relative Technical Simplicity of Exemplary Central Attacks

I said at the beginning of this chapter that this area of discussion is relatively uncharted territory. This would be true even if there had been one or two uses of nuclear weapons, since each use would have been so special that it might not be possible to reason about the future from the precedent that had been set.

Many analysts and laymen thus feel that any possibility of control or rationality in nuclear war is eliminated simply out of technical considerations. They feel that uncertainties and surprises—both technical and human—are so inevitable that the only plausible picture of nuclear war is that conveyed by the words "spasm" and "insensate" (our Rung 34). Moreover, while technical assessments and calculations of interest and advantage can be made for situations of tit-for-tat exchanges or reprisals—for "slow-motion warfare"—there can be no reliable prediction of the changes that would take place in the public and political environments once the exchanges had begun. Unlike the quickly consummated nuclear wars of popular conception, slow-motion exchanges would allow time for extensive and crucial public reactions within the contesting countries and in the world as a whole. The issues are not only those of losses or gains in assurance or morale, war fever or panic, but the chance of profound changes in public confidence in governments, of radical changes in the perception or estimate of world issues and questions concerning the competence or character of the social structure's functioning once nuclear blows are struck.

Yet, at the technical level alone, exemplary central nuclear attacks offer significant advantages. The problems of command, control, and communications, which are very great in sustained high-intensity nuclear wars, are much reduced in slow-motion exchanges that are limited and deliberate. This has led some analysts to argue that this increased possibility for control will, under most conditions, make almost any of the central-war options a much less desirable alternative to exemplary central attack. There is no technical military reason (as distinct from psychological or political factors) for immediate reaction to "slow-motion" attack. The attacking country can fully inform the defending country on what it is doing and intends to do. Indeed, to the extent that an attacker might attempt to use the nineteenth-century legal concept of "reprisal" as justification in international law for an attack, it would be obligated to announce ahead of time what it intended to do and what its demands for redress, if any, were.[3]

[3] In the nineteenth century and earlier, under the principles of international law, a reprisal, which by strict definition is an illegal act, could sometimes be legal if it met certain conditions and was justified by a prior illegal act by the state against which the reprisal was directed. Some hold that today reprisals can no longer be considered since Article II of the United Nations Charter requires states to "settle their international disputes by peaceful means." The rules limiting reprisals were these: (1) occasion for the reprisal must be a previous act illegal in international law; (2) the reprisal must be preceded by an explicit unsatisfied demand; (3) if initial demand for redress is satisfied, no further demands may be made (this is an important difference between reprisal and war; in war, A is not legally obliged to lay down its arms if B is ready to comply with A's request made before the war began); and (4) reprisal must be proportionate to the offense.

VIII

The Importance of Crises Concepts

A Serious Gap in Much Military Planning and Discussion

It seems proper here to interrupt the discussion of escalation rungs and thresholds to talk briefly about some of the special issues raised at the intense-crisis levels of escalation and to make some recommendations covering a gap that seems to exist in American planning for crises. There has been a curious dichotomy in American military thinking during most of the postwar years. On the one hand, we find that almost all the attention has been concentrated on the deterring or waging of central or general wars that started out of the blue, either as a result of a surprise attack on the United States or because of accident or miscalculation. On the other hand, several polls have revealed that most research analysts believe that any thermonuclear war is likely to be preceded by a very tense crisis (such as those which correspond to the middle rungs of the escalation ladder). These analysts consider it unlikely that any country today would start an all-out general war unless it was so desperate that it regarded war as less undesirable than any alternative. Such desperation is likely to occur only in a very tense crisis, and the decision-makers are more likely to be motivated by the conviction that the peaceful alternatives are bleak than by a hope that the war will turn out well. Similarly, during a tense crisis, the possibilities for inadvertent war increase, possibly to the danger point. By contrast, in a noncrisis period, the preliminary safety precautions and the unwillingness to take precipitate action that might cause irreversible steps are likely to prevent a war, even if there is an incident that, in the absence of safety precautions and "conservative" attitudes, might cause war.

Nevertheless, until quite recently, very little effort and attention had been paid by U.S. military planners to the deterring and waging of wars that could arise out of crisis situations, and to the range of other military and political actions these crises might necessitate. Probably one important reason for this is that a tense crisis is intrinsically unpleasant and bizarre, and many believe there is something sinister about planning to cope with such a contingency. Others fear that special preparations for or during a crisis may increase the probability of war. In some cases, people wish to bind the hands of the Executive Office by giving it no choices except "holocaust or surrender" (in President Kennedy's phrase), hoping thus, paradoxically, to avoid both. The notion is that if a decision-maker is given too large and flexible a capability to "use" crises, the danger of intransigence and war is increased. Yet the contrary may be more true. It would be irresponsible to be so unprepared to cope with crisis options as to have no choices other than holocaust or surrender. In any case, it would be indefensible to try to tie the President's hands without both having some discussion of the matter and giving him a choice in the decision.

The concept that a central nuclear war is most likely to arise out of the middle rungs of the ladder has great significance for the kinds of studies that should be done in evaluating the performance of various kinds of central-war postures. Thus, if one were to try to judge today the most likely outbreak scenario for a U.S.-Soviet central war, the order of the list that follows probably would represent a fair consensus of both expert and lay opinion:

1. Very tense crisis—some kind of unintended, accidental, or miscalculation war.
2. Very tense crisis—U.S. calculated strike.
3. Very tense crisis—Soviet calculated strike.
4. Normal situation—some kind of accidental war.
5. Normal situation—Soviet calculated strike.

Most of the experts tend to agree that all of the above are unlikely, even if there is a very tense crisis of the kind exemplified by the middle rungs of the ladder. The second and third possibilities could occur if the Soviets, relying on the balance of terror, chose to invade Europe either because they wanted to or because they felt compelled to by events (as in the scenario given in Chapter I). As discussed later, a U.S. calculated strike could occur if we "lived up to our NATO obligations" and struck the Soviets; the reverse would most likely occur if the Soviets became desperate, perhaps because we had escalated to some rung between 15 and 31 and retaliated with a strike designed (as described later) to equalize or degrade U.S. striking strength.[1] They might also strike because they had found some weakness in the U.S. system which they would then try to exploit or even because they thought some kind of post-attack blackmail or the shock of the attack would intimidate or degrade our response; or they might strike simply out of anger, stupidity, or tradition. Nor can we dismiss the fourth possibility on the list, even though it seems most unlikely, particularly as a result of the enormous increase in stability that has occurred in the last three or four years. Finally, there is the extremely remote possibility of a Soviet calculated strike out of the blue. It seems almost ridiculously remote if there is no weakness in the U.S. system or if the Soviets do not have important covert or secret capabilities of which we know nothing. Even then it would seem most unlikely that the Soviets would rely on such a capability. And if they did, it seems unlikely that they would accompany such a strike at U.S. strategic forces with a large attack on cities. They would presumably launch an attack corresponding to Rungs 33–38 and hope to intimidate our response by holding our cities as hostages. Even if they felt almost certain they could disarm us completely, they would likely do this as a hedge against being wrong—and they could hardly feel certain of a successful disarming strike.

Almost all current U.S. analysts would more or less agree with

---

[1] Under current conditions, if statements by public officials are at all accurate, it is not possible for the Soviets to disarm the U.S. by a first strike; but if they restricted their attack to leverage targets, they could improve the strategic balance.

the order of likelihood given above. If this point of view is correct (and has been correct for some years), then one can argue that there has been a startling misallocation of official emphasis in the past. It is probably a fair estimate that about 90 per cent of professional attention in the 1950's was directed to the fifth possibility and about 10 per cent to the fourth. By and large, the first three were almost completely ignored.

This example of past misemphasis is now widely known and is often cited by analysts. The change in emphasis to the first three scenarios can be attributed in part to the deliberate use of such methodological devices as scenarios and war games, as well as to the increasing seriousness and maturity of analysts. The idea now has grown that wars which escalate out of a crisis should be considered as the "design case," and the surprise attack out of the blue as the "off design" case which must be hedged against but which one should avoid overemphasizing. But it still is probably useful to remind ourselves that for many years senior analysts, policymakers, and decision-makers and their staffs, who had some degree of—or even complete—authority to decide their own ground rules, spent most of their time on problems which, in their own opinion, were relatively unimportant, as compared with the problems they could have been studying in the same area of responsibility. In this never-never land of preparing for hypothetical and unreal situations, to spend one's time on the less important areas of one's responsibility not only could happen—it did, and of course it is still happening.

It is also most likely that as a result of having passed through some rather tense crises, senior decision-makers on both sides have received an intense and concentrated education on military problems and strategic options—i.e., on what they can and cannot or should and should not do with their military forces. It is sometimes argued by psychologists that in such moments of stress there is a narrowing of alternatives and a concentration on small numbers of familiar options. This can clearly happen, and I shall discuss some aspects of this possibility in connection with "conservative strategies" (in Chapter XIII); but let me note here my belief that if the customary alternatives are bleak enough, decision-makers are very likely to look around for new ones and thus find their horizons widened rather than narrowed. In government, and in committees, a moment of truth is likely to sober all who are looking—or have looked—into the chasm; they are less likely to be satisfied with the familiar options when these familiar options are transparently and starkly inadequate. As Ben Jonson once said, "Depend upon it, when a man knows he's going to be hanged in a fortnight, it concentrates his mind wonderfully."

Crisis and Damage Limitation[2]

There is now widespread agreement in the United States on the need for maintaining adequate second-strike forces, but few argue that our currently programed second-strike forces need substantial increase. There is an almost equally widespread, but much less explicit, consensus that once the United States has procured adequate second-strike forces, it has accomplished its major strategic task. This implicit consensus results from several attitudes, including disbelief in the possibility of nuclear war and in the possibility of survival if deterrence fails.

While we can agree that deterrence of major war is the highest priority task of the strategic forces, the country still needs much more from its strategic forces than an adequate second-strike capability. Among other things, it needs some capability for limiting damage if, despite this second-strike capability, war occurs. There is a reasonably widespread agreement among analysts that this is true, at least to some degree; and today the decisions on marginal changes in our strategic forces are much more influenced by damage-limiting criteria than by customary second-strike requirements. With more or less adequate second-strike forces believed to be either in being or programed, relatively little additional deterrence is to be seen as gained by adding equipment that merely improves the second-strike characteristics. At the same time, studies have shown that a country like the United States can buy a very important increment in damage-limiting capability.

---

2 "Damage limitation" is current jargon for capabilities and tactics that attempt to limit damage if deterrence fails and war breaks out. It is almost, but not quite, synonymous with the concept of "war fighting" forces as discussed in Chapter X.

While increasing attention has been devoted to damage limitation, almost all present studies are inadequate because they still
evaluate what is, for all practical purposes, the normal "peacetime"
(though perhaps alerted) posture of the country when suddenly
subjected to attack. Yet it can be argued, for the reasons given
in the last section, that the most important characteristics of currently programed damage-limiting capabilities are less their performance under sudden-attack conditions than performance after
short- or long-term crisis and/or mobilization programs have been
actuated. Therefore, in the current situation (for purposes of
damage limitation, as distinguished from deterrence only), it may be
better—in several ways—to acquire additional capability for rapidly
improving the posture rather than to acquire additional capability
in being. That is, if studies are done in terms of fixed peacetime
budgets, impact on the arms race, political feasibility, consistency
with current *détente* policy, or flexibility to meet uncertain future
conditions (including increased availability of resources in crisis
or tension situations), a greater degree of effectiveness can be
achieved by increasing the emergency-readiness and mobilization
characteristics of systems than by increasing their capability in
being.

The lack of emergency-readiness and mobilization capability
seems to be the largest single defect in the currently programed
damage-limitation systems; and what is even more serious, the absence of such emphasis in both studies and discussion means that
it is likely that this lag will continue. One purpose of this chapter
is to indicate some of the characteristics that such programs might
have.

Seven Basic Options[3]

To illustrate the argument, I will distinguish five levels of crisis
tactics appropriate at various levels of international tension. The
levels seem sufficiently distinct and important to justify planning

[3] The next three sections are largely taken from published and unpublished work by W. Brown, M. Zlotnick, and R. Gastil, respectively.

for all of them, and for programs that provide options at every level. They are:

Programs	Estimated Time Available
A. Emergency-readiness programs[4]	0–6 months
1. Desperate	1 hour–7 days
2. Crash	2 days–2 weeks
3. Emergency	1 week–6 months
B. Tension-mobilization programs	3 months–2 years
1. Wartime	3 months–1 year
2. Peacetime	6 months–2 years

Both of the above classes of programs should be compared with normal (3–7 years) and moderately accelerated (1–4 years) programs. The principal distinction between emergency-readiness and mobilization actions is the estimate made of the imminence of a possible nuclear attack. In practice, a variety of modular plans might be designed—for each of the crisis programs separately and for situations in which they occur in various sequences.

Emergency-readiness programs would differ from mobilization programs in tending to disregard post-emergency values, emphasizing short-term capability at the cost of normal procedures, and being willing to risk waste and inefficiency. A mobilization program is more sensitive to questions of cost and efficiency and to the needs of competing programs, especially military programs. The mobilization program prepares for prolonged tension, siege, or low-level war. It is prudential in the sense that it tries to prepare for the future, possibly even at the risk of some short-run increase in danger, by adopting protective measures appropriate to the degree of international tension.

[4] Two years ago, a Hudson Institute study estimated that with appropriate plans, proper motivation, and good leadership, American resources were sufficient so that in two days' time it should be possible "to develop more civil defense capability during this time than has been obtained during the fifteen years following World War II." (See William Brown *et al.*, *Strategic and Tactical Aspects of Civil Defense, With Special Emphasis on Crisis Programs* [HI-160-RR, January 7, 1964], p. 7.) That estimate does not seem to need revision because of the civil-defense capability that has been added in the last two years.

Of the three emergency-readiness programs, the desperate program may respond to a state of national anxiety equivalent to that which might be found on a battlefield—such as might occur during an exemplary central attack or possibly in the early stages of a bizarre crisis. Thus, either bombs have already exploded in this country or the possibility is believed to be a matter of hours away. The program is termed desperate in the belief that U.S. decision-makers would be willing to take large risks in human lives and pay little or no attention to immediate material costs in order to achieve the highest degree of protection possible for the threatened citizens. Thus, in this kind of crisis, authorities (if an evacuation plan is being implemented) might overcrowd railroad boxcars to transport evacuees to safer areas, even risking some casualties. Large amounts of property would be destroyed to provide protective construction. Doors, fences, garages, barns, and interior walls of buildings would be torn down readily for building material. The government might attempt to evacuate perhaps 90–95 per cent of the population of potential target areas. (See the earlier discussion of Rung 30.)

The "crash" program differs from the "desperate" one in being less associated with terror, although sacrifices in procedure and cost are again accepted. But actions that would involve unusual human risks or extremely high economic costs would be avoided where possible. Evacuations, if part of the plan, would be less desperate, industries would shut down properly, and consideration would be given to the problems of assisting post-attack recovery efforts.

Finally, the "emergency" program assumes that sufficient time is available to create a large degree of short-run protection without unusual destruction of property or risk to life or health.

It is also important to consider the possibility of mobilization taking place after a declaration of war. This possibility has not been seriously studied in the nuclear age, with its emphasis on sudden and decisive strikes. But it is worth recalling that World War II began with a "phony war," which gave the French and British eight months of intense mobilization before their forces were seriously engaged. (I pointed out in Chapter I that this came as a distinct surprise to their military and civilian decision-makers, who had feared a knockout blow, perhaps by poison gas.) The declaration of war in 1939 was used by the Allies as a substitute for intervention in Poland, which was beyond their capabilities. And even the surprise Japanese attack on Pearl Harbor was preceded by two years of tension and partial U.S. mobilization. Similar symbolic or inconclusive confrontations are not impossible in future conflicts. In such a situation, particularly if it involved a formal declaration of war, we might, as in World War II, devote up to half our GNP (or more than $300 billion a year) to defense purposes. Thus, if advance preparations had been made, one could imagine tens of billions of dollars put into a nonmilitary defense program in less than a year.

Such a program would tap the readily deployable U.S. construction industry (with a theoretical capacity of about $100 billion) and other industry and agriculture (for survival and recuperation stockpiles). If extensive, and modestly expensive, preliminary preparations (which might take two or three years and cost in the neighborhood of $1 billion or so) had been made to take advantage of this tension period, a nonmilitary defense program could be phased so as not to compete excessively with military mobilization, much of which is necessarily slower—even with a tension-mobilization base for the rest of the military mobilization. And preparations could, with somewhat more difficulty, be made for a one- or two-year crash antiballistic missile program, as discussed below. (See discussion of Rung 32, formal declaration of war, in the following chapter.)

Thus, the effectiveness of crisis programs could be increased considerably to appropriate peacetime planning to reduce the long lead times that would otherwise be necessary. Such programs should be tailored to the local needs and capabilities of the various communities or regions involved. In this regard, the more detailed regional and local planning might be performed by planners with local or regional responsibility.

A Proposal for ABM Deployment

It seems implausible that the government would start a large antiballistic missile (ABM) program during the current *détente*. On the other hand, it also seems clear that the problem of active defense cannot responsibly be ignored. A useful preparatory low-level program which Congress might accept, and which deserves serious study, could probably be carried out for about $1–2 billion a year over and above the R&D and T&E costs. The primary objective would not be to provide a low-level coverage over a large part of the United States, although one might expect this to be attained. Rather, it would be to reach a position from which it would be practical in an emergency to spend an extra $20–$30 billion a year on ABM—in short, to buy a capability for rapid defense preparations.

However, the low-level ABM coverage, probably made up mostly of low-priced radars, relatively small computers, and small numbers of defensive missiles per target point (but staffed and laid out so as to allow for rapid expansion), would serve a number of important purposes. It would be:

1. A low-confidence measure that might work against badly designed or otherwise "easy" Soviet attacks.
2. A defense against accidentally fired missiles.
3. A defense against small and technologically unsophisticated Nth-country attacks.
4. A "façade" for psychological and political warfare or defense.
5. A factor forcing the Soviets to carry countermeasures in their missiles and thus making for reduced-yield warheads.
6. A useful change in threshold against exemplary attacks.
7. Probably close (with likely programs) to an "optimal" ratio of active to passive defense from the viewpoint of cost-effectiveness.

Perhaps the most significant value of such a program would be that it would give the U.S. the kind of capabilities and understanding of ABM that can come only from actually being in the ABM business. An organization would exist, manufacturers would be making equipment, there would be healthy activity in R&D because engineers, scientists, and even management would be more highly motivated, operators would be trained, reliability problems would be worked out, various techniques and standard operating procedures would be devised and tested, marginal efficiency would be noted, data would be collected, the understanding of many problems would be improved, a basis would be created for further improvements and innovations in the system, and a capability for rapid expansion would exist.

One should, however, be sensitive to the problems that would arise in creating an ABM tension-mobilization base. These problems are somewhat different, and in some ways substantially greater than the simple deployment of a low-level ABM cover. Thus, certain items, such as much of the real estate and long-lead-time buildings, would have to be compatible with an expanded program. In addition, maintenance of current information on the status of system development would be a major requirement, so that the best product would be obtained in the event of a rapid shift to a production and deployment program.

A Proposal for Evacuation Preparations

Crisis civil-defense preparations should include some mixture of paper plans for evacuation, training of relevant persons (for example, those concerned with emergency control of food and transportation and the development or improvement of fallout shelters, especially outside major urban areas). Evacuated citizenry, if well directed and supplied, could construct most of the new shelters they required. The fact that public fallout shelters are an accepted, if not fully budgeted, part of national policy should facilitate the development of a program of shelters and shelter managers.

A critical hurdle for the development in peacetime of crisis programs involving evacuation is the requirement for top officials to understand that: (1) currently discussed evacuation concepts are not based on the idea of "outrunning the missile," but rather on the likelihood that the development of crises and wars could give usable warning; (2) prevention of evacuee "panic" is largely possible, as studies of various natural disasters such as hurricanes and other situations with comparable warning times have indicated (and even with some panic or confusion, the over-all gains are likely to outweigh the losses); (3) for many reasons, the Russians are unlikely to have, or be able to use, enough weapons effectively to blanket great rural areas with blast, fire, or sufficient fallout to overcome the improvised shelters; (4) for most of the central-war possibilities that can be termed likely in the next decade, analyses, based on current studies of the American economy and of comparable historical situations, indicate that the country would be able to recover in a meaningful way from the damage; and (5) public cooperation with emergency evacuation measures can be understood as prudent, humane, and patriotic.

A particularly feasible evacuation measure that might save as many as 20–30 million Americans has been described as "medium-city evacuation."[5] Leaving aside 12 of the largest metropolitan areas and those areas (9) without an adequate close-in reception area, many cities (112 urbanized areas with a total population of 31 million) might be evacuated in a few hours to a close "ring" area containing reception fallout shelters (including, in the cheaper programs, crisis-prepared shelters). These rings might include communities 15 to 50 miles from the urban center. For many persons, these distances would be short enough to permit commuting back to city jobs during part of an intrawar or crisis period. Medium-city evacuation also falls easily into a program initially providing blast or ABM protection for the largest cities. It could be a tension measure that was part of a military strategy of avoiding population attacks and encouraging bilateral evacuations, as described below.

Such preparations for evacuation need not accelerate the arms race. From the viewpoint of the Soviets, it would seem likely that the property at risk in the empty cities would provide an adequate deterrent for most purposes. (Assuming the Soviets make the kinds of improvements in their forces that are generally expected, this city property would in fact provide the Soviet Union with a materially more valuable and psychologically more persuasive hostage than the fraction of the U.S. population they "held hostage" in the late 1950's and early 1960's.) The United States, moreover, might make clear, as a matter of national policy, that it would assume that all nations would allow their opponents to try to evacuate their cities as a moral, humanitarian measure, and that it would itself do the same. There seem to be no serious technical or strictly military difficulties with this approach to nuclear war, since civilians are not high-priority *military* targets, whatever the present importance of city attacks in deterrence. The nation that strikes first is likely—

[5] See Max Singer, *Phasing of Crisis Civil Defense Programs* (HI-330-D, February 14, 1964).

initially at least—to wish to preserve its opponent's civilians, both in order not to provoke retaliation and to preserve hostages.

Some may object that failure to retaliate "instantly" or "promptly" could cause U.S. assurance to weaken, or even that a delay in retaliation would, by itself, demonstrate a lack of assurance that could tempt opponents to greater provocations. Others may argue that if large numbers of American citizens have been killed, leaders or citizens will demand instant retaliation against populations. Still others may object to evacuation on the grounds that it would prompt an opponent to strike first, to pre-empt, or at least to make a countervalue first strike. An evacuation program for the largest cities might also prompt an opponent to try to stop an evacuation through "tie-down" tactics (such as a fallout attack) or by threatening to strike people while they are evacuating. A nation might also counter an opponent's reprisal strategy by forcing its own people to stay in the threatened cities.

These objections cannot be entirely dismissed. But the problem of assurance exists for both friend and enemy; indeed, the fact that one is not directly targeting millions of civilians may strengthen the will of many leaders to make reprisals. And this proposal does not preclude adroit and effective attacks capable of winning wars. Moreover, the objections have greatly diminished force as long as the U.S. has strategic superiority, a secure second-strike capability, and its will bolstered by the fact that it can put its civilians in a place of relative safety.

The approach described here has definite advantages over the usual massive-retaliation doctrines, limited countervalue attack, or even current controlled-response doctrine. It does not expect Americans or opponent peoples to sit still while their cities are "exchanged." Furthermore, it avoids as much as possible the moral problems attendant on the direct targeting of civilians. That civilians are not to be targeted is an old, very salient rule, and can be crucial to the kind of peace that follows a war. I think that targeting civilians is not necessary, even for wars with a large countervalue element, and this "evacuation as arms control" policy places evacuation preparations in a new context in which they should be more acceptable and their prudential and moral values more apparent. This argument is based as much on agonistic and familial principles as on instrumental considerations, and I believe that the U.S. should be willing to lock itself in—to accept, if the strategic situation changes, substantial disadvantages without considering changing this policy.

There are also particular strategic problems that this approach answers or helps to answer. It places an announced policy between the detonation of a weapon, apparently countervalue, and a U.S. reprisal. It thus inhibits and slows down the action, reduces time pressures, and gives more time for new information to come in. That is, if delay in retaliation is the announced policy, then such delay would be much less a sign of weakness or likely cause of demoralization than it would otherwise be. Such possibilities as anonymous attack, catalytic war, unauthorized action, or accidental war are reduced in likelihood. The policy is also likely to gain more time for successful U.S. evacuations.

This approach may also change the character of the exchange. For there is not the artificiality of the "first, second, third strike" analysis of the war games or the "fog of war" analysis of the realist. Rather, there is an inexorable and slowly developing plan of attack which the opponent can do little about—no matter how much he threatens or attacks. War would still be a test of nerves, of course, but within a moral framework, and a framework within which the U.S. expects to survive. Eventually, this approach could be adapted to the Nth-country problem.

Some Pros and Cons

Whether one argues for emergency-readiness and tension-mobilization programs on purely prudential grounds, or out of some more general military and foreign-policy considerations, it is not a decisive objection to these programs that we may not experience prewar tensions that trigger the programs or that a war might come without actuating them. As in deterrence programs, the justification includes a hope that the program will not be used, together with an inability to guarantee that this hope will be realized.

In some ways, emergency-readiness and tension-mobilization programs play the same role in relation to the distinction between usual international relations and crisis situations as the normal military establishment plays in the distinction between peace and war. A major purpose of the military establishment is to deter war and, if deterrence fails, to limit damage and achieve as satisfactory a political result as is practical. The purpose of the emergency-readiness and tension-mobilization programs is to help deter crises and tension situations—and, if this crisis deterrence fails, to alleviate the consequences. While, as with normal defense programs, some crisis programs can be inconsistent with or antagonistic to the current *détente* and arms-control atmosphere, not all are. Properly designed programs need not upset the *détente;* on the contrary, they could both reassure those in the United States and the West who fear the *détente* (because it could lead to an erosion of Western capability) and increase Soviet incentives to maintain the *détente.*

Because emergency-readiness and tension-mobilization programs are also useful if deterrence of crisis and tension fails, they have much the same prudential character as some war-survival programs. Without such programs, one can imagine a crisis touching off precipitate, thoughtless, counterproductive or dangerous actions. Shock, spontaneous evacuations from cities, contradictory news and advice from different levels of government, a perceptible confusion in national leadership—all could gravely affect public confidence, interfere with the President's policy, and hurt the morale and assurance of our allies or increase those of the enemy. On the other hand, prepared contingency plans could enormously increase the strength and ability of a U.S. President in a crisis or tension situation.

Elaborate emergency-readiness and tension-mobilization capabilities complement and support the current deliberate and selective controlled-response strategy. Technically, they could make such controlled response more feasible and desirable because of the preparatory measures that would have been carried out. In turn, the slower rate of escalation (both pre- and post-outbreak of war) that is likely to result from a successful controlled-response strategy would probably enable crisis programs to be implemented with some measure of deliberation and reliability. To the extent that many U.S. cities might be avoided in the early stages of a war, there would be more time available to carry through the emergency-readiness measures. And in an extreme situation, having the kind of control by which a war might be fought and terminated at a very low level could enable the U.S. to carry out a holding operation that would permit tension-mobilization programs to be actuated.

One great fear that many analysts have expressed with regard to emergency-readiness programs (particularly evacuation), and even to tension-mobilization programs, is that these might cause the Soviets to pre-empt in a crisis. This fear is to some degree legitimate, since the purpose of such programs, prudential as they are, may be as much for bargaining—in other words, to put pressure on the Soviet Union. On the other hand, it is one purpose of strategic forces to deter such a pre-emptive strike. It seems reasonable to believe that in a desperate situation, the American President, relatively secure in his reliance on the deterrent capability of U.S. second-strike forces,[6] would prefer the escalatory risk of this kind of increased pressure on the Soviets to letting the crisis continue without such pressure for settlement or concessions.

It seems fair to say that if emergency preparations were at least moderately expensive, and very explicit so that the Soviets found them credible, the Soviets could be presented with the following alternatives if they allowed a very tense crisis or other situation to develop which in turn touched off an emergency-readiness program or a tension-mobilization base:

1. They could strike the United States before the buildup got very far. This might look very unattractive, especially since the buildup would almost certainly be accompanied by an increased alert and other measures to reduce the vulnerability of SAC.

2. They could continue or even intensify the crisis in the hope of making the U.S. back down. This would accelerate the crisis program and subject them to real dangers. Also, they would probably find it difficult to match the U.S. program, but to the extent that they did, they would be committed to huge economic and other costs. An arms competition or mobilization would have been provoked that was to the ad-

---

[6] As indicated in the discussion in the following chapter, it seems quite likely that a U.S. President would, indeed, feel secure.

vantage of neither side (except to the degree that it had contributed to preventing a more serious contest). To the extent that they did not match the U.S., they could experience a serious worsening of their strategic position.

3. They could back down, even though this too might be very unpleasant. In each case, the costs and risks of the Soviet provocation would have been very high. It is likely that the Soviets would take these extra costs and risks into account before attempting any provocation. And if they were not deterred, the American posture would have been greatly improved as a result of the emergency-readiness program or the tension-mobilization base having been actuated. Such improvement might be great enough to enable us to correct or negate the results of their provocation or at least to deter them from exploiting these results.

In the current and developing strategic balance, these emergency-readiness and tension-mobilization capabilities might, in fact, affect the degree and frequency of "provocation" more effectively than a naked military threat or very limited military reactions. This is so because the use of these preparations is wholly credible. For example, the Soviets will scarcely have forgotten (and if they have, we can remind them) that once before the United States increased its defense authorization fourfold as a reaction to their provocation.[7] No matter what successes the Communist cause had in Korea, the increased U.S. authorization that followed hard upon the North Korean invasion represented an enormous military defeat for the Soviets, with enduring consequences. If Korea had not been invaded, the U.S. military establishment might well have been scarcely a housekeeping establishment by the mid-1950's. What result this lack of power would have had is difficult to say, but it could have been decisive in the Cold War. In addition, many analysts believe that many of the Soviets' difficulties in the satellites in 1953 and 1956 were directly due to the economic aftereffects of their

[7] For the fiscal year 1951, Congress had debated whether the defense budget should be $14 billion, $15 billion, or $16 billion. In June, 1950, North Korea marched into South Korea. Before 1950 was over, Congress had authorized $60 billion.

trying to meet this U.S. mobilization. If this is true, the Soviets are not likely to have forgotten the lesson.

It was, however, almost three years before the increased U.S. budget authorization was fully translated into increased expenditures and corresponding military power. As valuable as it is to be able to increase defense expenditures, this ability becomes many times more valuable if authorizations can be translated into operational capability in a year or so. If an opponent knows that deterioration in international relations will provoke a pre-programed crash defense program, he may be much less willing to let international relations deteriorate.

Conclusion

Surprise attack has weighed so heavily in American planning in part because it was the easiest case to study and in part because it seemed to be the most dangerous threat, in terms of the damage it could do to American society. Many have felt that it was essential to plan for the worst—that to do anything else would be to indulge in wishful thinking. But they have found, in fact, they are unable to defend against this "worst" situation—can only deter it at best. Yet this concentration on the "worst" has led to the neglect of defensive measures that might work quite well in more plausible situations, even though they are of little value in the "worst" situation. Moreover, there are some conceivable cases in which a surprise attack may not be the "worst" situation. As described in the previous and following chapters, a war situation that had been preceded by ultimatums and tensions could put strange and unexpected strains on existing and programed strategic systems.

IX

Military and Civilian Central Wars

Basic Description and Definition

In this chapter I will discuss the final section of the escalation ladder, comprising Rungs 32–44, which deal with central wars. (See Figure 3, p. 39.) Here we consider some new aspects of the traditional threshold between war and peace, but these new aspects are not as unprecedented as much current discussion would suggest. The fact that the war-peace dividing line seems smudged by the many "new" thresholds that lie both below and above it, each marking a point where violence could be limited, does not really change the classic situation as much as may be supposed. These new thresholds have been created by the new conditions of the balance of nuclear terror, but analogous thresholds have existed in the past—as we have noted in the bombing campaigns of World War II. In any case, a threshold between all-out war and peace remains, the term "all-out" being understood as characterizing the effort put into the war, the resources committed, and not necessarily reflecting indiscriminate or unrestrained attacks on cities and non-military targets.

There are, of course, many different kinds of "central" wars, with thresholds between the kinds. There is, for example, an important threshold between city-sparing and city-destroying campaigns which quite possibly would be very hard for a nation to cross—provided it had understood from the start that war was possible that was not a total assault on the population of the enemy, or that it had learned of this possibility during the crisis or enemy hostilities. Secretary of Defense Robert McNamara has said that the "principal military objectives, in the event of a nuclear war stemming from a major attack on the Alliance, should be the destruction of the enemy's military forces, not of his civilian population."[1] In practice, of course, this distinction may be difficult to establish—for example, as in a situation where major counterforce targets are practically inseparable from the cities. Nevertheless, particularly if the escalation proceeded slowly, without skipping too many of the central-war rungs, it would require a great and momentous decision to begin attacks on a large number of cities. In particular, to quote a recent study, "Nations are far more likely to back into a nuclear war than plunge into it; it is more probable that they will find themselves in a nuclear exchange than enter it with full foresight, and they are most likely to enter it gingerly with small attacks, than with precipitous large attacks."[2] But the possibility and importance of observing this threshold are not widely understood today, and even when understood conceptually are not usually accepted. The example of strategic-city bombing in World War II is so firmly held in many people's minds as what a modern war is that they cannot visualize a large strategic war in which cities are not priority objectives.

Yet, thermonuclear wars are likely to be short—lasting a few hours to a couple of months at most. As I have said, in such a war it is unlikely that cities would in themselves be targets of any great military consequence: factories would not have time to turn out weapons; millions of soldiers would not be needed; there probably would not even be elections in which the morale of the civilian population could bring about changes in national policy. Cities might be destroyed in a strategic war, but there would be no urgent reason for an attacker to do so, or at least to do so quickly. Cities are immovable: populations, of course, may run away, but buildings and property cannot, and it seems unlikely that one side or the other in a new war would feel so strongly motivated to destroy

[1] In a speech at Ann Arbor, Mich., on June 16, 1962.

[2] William R. Davey *et al., Strategic Considerations for Increased Readiness* (HI-477-D, January, 1964).

civilians that it would attempt attacks to pre-empt the movement of civilians early in the war.

None of this is necessarily very clearly understood by the governments and war planners of either side. In a new war, it is perfectly possible that a nation might, simply out of a failure to have thought about what it was doing, attack cities. The United States has more or less formally enunciated a "no cities except in reprisal" strategy, but the strategy is neither clearly understood nor firmly held even here. In any case, if intrawar deterrence broke down, or "bargaining" seemed to require it, cities might get hit. Soviet strategists and political leaders have declared that Soviet forces would not recognize any such "artificial" distinctions in a nuclear war. This position of theirs could be an accurate reflection of current Soviet strategic doctrine, but it could also be a posture publicly adopted to discourage disarming attacks on the Soviet Union and to decrease the credibility of U.S. threats by indicating that our counter-counterthreats do not intimidate their counterthreat. Most likely is that it is a mixture of all these beliefs and attitudes, and that it is a very unreliable indicator of actual Soviet behavior in a "moment of truth"—or of Soviet beliefs about U.S. conduct at such a time.

Secretary McNamara modified his 1962 statement on city avoidance when he subsequently gave evidence before the Senate Armed Services Committee on the defense budget for the fiscal year 1964:

In talking about global nuclear war, the Soviet leaders always say that they would strike at the entire complex of our military power including government and production centers, meaning our cities. If they were to do so, we would, of course, have no alternative but to retaliate in kind. But we have no way of knowing whether they would actually do so. It would certainly be in their interest as well as ours to try to limit the terrible consequences of a nuclear exchange. By building into our forces a flexible capability, we at least eliminate the prospect that we could strike back in only one way, namely, against the entire Soviet target system including their cities. Such a prospect would give the Soviet Union no incentive to withhold attack against our cities in a first strike. We want to give them a better alternative. Whether they would accept it in the crisis of a global nuclear war, no one can say. Considering what is at stake, we believe it is worth the additional effort on our part to have this option.

> In planning our second-strike force, we have provided a capability to destroy virtually all of the "soft" and "semi-hard" military targets in the Soviet Union and a large number of their fully hardened missile sites, with an additional capability in the form of a protected force to be employed or held in reserve for use against urban and industrial areas.

Thus, he strongly implied that this reserve force would be used against urban and industrial areas only if the Soviet Union initiated attacks of this type.

Let me assume then, for the moment, that this threshold between military and civilian central attacks can be maintained in an actual war, and consider the possibility of waging a very large, "all-out," but very closely controlled central war, in which there is a deliberate attempt to avoid civilians and their property. One or both of the warring nations may be assumed to be acting out of religious, ethical, or other agonistic inhibitions in not targeting civilians, or they may hope to make intrawar deterrence work by practicing some version, complete or partial, of a "no cities except in reprisal" doctrine.

The Rungs of Military Central Wars

I will assume that the first large attack is *mainly* (though not necessarily completely) on military targets. There may be forces withheld specifically for the possibility of later city attacks, but most or all enemy cities are spared initially—perhaps for use as hostages or pawns for bargaining in the later stages of the war.

RUNG 32. FORMAL DECLARATION OF "GENERAL" WAR: As I have noted, a major possibility, almost completely overlooked in modern defense planning despite the fact that it seems less implausible than many possibilities that are considered, is that a nation might respond to a provocation with a formal declaration of war but without major acts of war. Or there might be an explicit (rather than implicit or quasi) ultimatum that amounted to a conditional declaration of war. Such an ultimatum or declaration of war might, as happened in World War II, be followed by a "phony war" period, perhaps with some limited tactical or strategic harassment, but without large attacks. One reason for this is that during the period of crisis that developed through the medium rungs on the ladder, both sides presumably would have put their forces into a state of superpreparation for defense and reprisal. The United States and the Soviet Union, for example, might have deployed their missile-carrying submarines, dispersed their strategic bomber forces, and placed their ground-based missiles on alert status. An effective disarming attack would thus be very difficult or impossible. Just how difficult depends on details that cannot be discussed here. But, given the strength of the balance of terror and the general fear on both sides, it is not at all unlikely that both nations would at such a point be so cautious that, whatever the provocations, neither would really want to make a large attack.

The formal declaration of war could cause either escalation or de-escalation. In either case, it could indicate that the side issuing the declaration had no immediate intention of attacking (since if it had such an intention, there would be strong reasons to ignore prenuclear convention and simply attack, without alerting the opponent[3]). Such a declaration would have the following character-istics and results:

1. It would be a solemn, formal announcement that would seem very significant.
2. The declaration would give information—both symbolically and through content and interpretation.
3. It would tend to prevent de-escalation to an ordinary crisis, and would threaten further (eventual) escalation, thus keeping the issue that was the *casus belli* open. It would thus tend to prevent even implicit "ratification" or accept-ance of any *fait accompli*.
4. It might, however, appear to be temporizing—i.e., it could have some de-escalatory aspects, but not many in most situations (depending on whether the alternative was talk and threats or missile launchings).

[3] Unless it is a double double-cross, as in the Minsk-Pinsk joke.

5. It would remove some inhibitions against the use of force and coercion (controlled reprisals and ultimatums), such as described at later (and also earlier) rungs of the ladder.
6. It would put pressures on allies and some neutrals to cooperate.
7. It would have many legal effects (blockade, internment, confiscation, control of travel, etc.).
8. It would release energy: one can easily envisage the United States increasing its defense budget to $300 billion a year in such a situation.
9. It would mobilize people and tend to suppress internal opposition.
10. It would force the other side to recognize explicitly that a formal peace treaty will have to be written before the issue is settled; delaying tactics will not settle the matter.

Actually, the declaration of war is just one of a series of legal and quasi-legal measures (such as Congressional resolutions) which have a role in escalation situations. The precise escalatory character of these measures, including that of the declaration of war, would depend on specific conditions and tactics.

RUNG 33. SLOW-MOTION COUNTER-"PROPERTY" WAR: In this attack (which could accompany or follow a slow-motion counterforce war, as well as precede it), each side destroys property on the other side in a more or less tit-for-tat fashion. This is one of a number of types of possible wars of resolve. In such wars, each side attempts to force the other side to back down by means of an almost naked matching of "resolve" against "resolve." In this case, the matching takes the form of an attrition of property rather than lives—although some lives would be lost.

This kind of war might become a substitute (either through agonistic or instrumental considerations) for the war of attrition in which people or weapons are the major targets. An ultimate, if fantastic, form of this line of development could conceivably be the payment of fines (blood money?), as a form of war, or the symmetrical destruction of the victor's property as in a "potlatch" war, perhaps with the emergence of quasi-legal methods to set rules and amounts. While this seems almost unbelievable today, such institutions are not implausible eventualities if there are several slow-motion counter-"property" wars.

If the number of exchanges was relatively low, we would tend to call this kind of war one of "reciprocal reprisals," as described in Rung 31.

RUNG 34. SLOW-MOTION COUNTERFORCE WAR: In this campaign (which might follow a force-reduction salvo), each side attempts attrition of the other side's weapons systems over a period of time. Conceivably, a slow-motion counterforce war could last for weeks or months, with Polaris submarines being hunted down, hidden missiles found, hardened fixed installations dug up, and so on. While this possibility now is almost unstudied, as forces become less vulnerable it would seem to become most important. A not unlikely war might start with a series of force-reduction salvos that might or might not include attempts to avoid collateral damage to civilians and then be followed by a slow-motion counterforce war, with the losing side always threatening to escalate into some form of countervalue attack if the winning side did not desist or negotiate.

RUNG 35. CONSTRAINED FORCE-REDUCTION SALVO: This is an attack in which the attacker attempts to destroy a significant but relatively small portion of an enemy's forces in a single strike. The usual reason for the limitation would probably be the difficulty of operating within certain assigned constraints when attempting to destroy a large part of the defender's forces. It is especially likely to be used against weak links or high-leverage targets.

This option is the first of a series in which there is increasing collateral damage to civilian populations, yet the primary effort is to attack the other side's strategic forces. The word "constrained" indicates that there is an attempt made to set a definite limit to the amount of collateral damage, and all operations are conducted within those limits even if this results in major reductions in military efficiency. (The constrained attack is to be distinguished from the "avoidance" attack, in which strategic forces try to avoid collateral damage whenever this avoidance does not entail important military disadvantages. In the constrained attack, large military disadvantages may be accepted in order to keep down collateral damage.)

RUNG 36. CONSTRAINED DISARMING ATTACK: One of the most important options (under current conditions) may be called a constrained disarming attack. A major argument for the next rung, the counterforce-with-avoidance attack, is that not much is lost with it in narrow military calculations, yet it increases enormously the possibility that postattack coercion and deterrence would work. In the constrained disarming attack, the same argument is made with even greater force. Tremendous military disadvantages might be accepted in order to improve the prospects of negotiations to terminate the war on an acceptable basis. In this attack, the attacker would try to destroy a significant portion of the defender's first-strike forces and even some of his second-strike forces, but would avoid, as much as possible, civilian targets. This would make it disadvantageous for the defender to launch a counterstrike since the defender's damaged forces might be able to do only a limited amount of damage even with a countervalue strike, while the attacker might be able to deliver an annihilating blow in reprisal with his withheld and regrouped forces. The defender is also under pressure to negotiate since it is now probable that the attacker could threaten another attack, this one an all-out strike against the rest of the second- and first-strike forces.

If one side had the kind of strategic superiority some today claim for the United States, it might make its case for negotiations more convincing by giving the other side very detailed calculations about what could happen in the war at the same time that it made its initial attack. These calculations would emphasize to the opponent what would happen if he did not "obey the rules." If these calculations were given before the actual attack, this kind of *counter-counterthreat* would make the *counterthreat* of spasm retaliation less plausible, which in turn would make the *threat* of first strike more credible. It is difficult to believe that the opposing side would not be willing to look at these calculations, or not be influenced by them if the alternatives were sufficiently stark. Of course, the defending side might launch some retaliatory missiles out of reflex or anger, or because this was what its war plans called for; and it might then ask for a cease-fire. The attacking side might accept this cease-fire to terminate hostilities or to prevent further escalation. Since such a retaliatory attack is not likely to be as careful or well coordinated as the initial attack, it might turn out that if things were settled at this point the initiating side would have suffered more casualties than the defending side, even though the initiating side had seized and kept a military advantage and used this advantage in the subsequent negotiations to "win" the war. It is also possible that the initiating side would insist on a final counter-reprisal before agreeing to a cease-fire. In fact, the "tit-tat-tit" sequence may be about as likely as a "tit-tat" sequence.

A scenario for such a constrained disarming attack might go as follows: Because of some incident or crisis, or as part of a planned aggression, the Soviets threaten a massive attack on Europe and refuse to back down, even though the U.S. goes through the temporizing measures of evacuating its cities, alerting SAC, and augmenting its air defense. The Soviets might still consider the U.S. deterred from attacking them. They might have calculated that even if the U.S. launched an all-out attack against their strategic forces, they could still destroy 50 to 100 partially emptied American cities in a retaliatory blow. The Soviets then launch a large conventional attack on Europe, and NATO fights back with augmented conventional forces. There would then be two basic possibilities: NATO forces hold (or even push the Soviets back), or NATO impedes the Soviet advance but does not halt it.

Assume the latter possibility, and assume that a conventional military defeat for the United States and its allies seems imminent. At this point, the U.S. would have a number of choices: it could accept defeat, or it could use nuclear weapons in the combat zone and hope that the resulting bomb damage to civilians (either from the enemy's weapons or our own) would not be too great and that such use of nuclear weapons would not escalate into all-out war or strategic bombing in Europe or cause its allies to initiate preemptive or preventive accommodation and surrender. Or it could attack the Soviet Union.

Suppose that the U.S. was not deterred by the Soviet threat to destroy 50 to 100 of our empty cities. U.S. decision-makers might believe the various studies indicating that the U.S. could "recover" from such a blow in about ten years or less. Perhaps the American decision-makers would argue that the Soviets must be stopped before they have added Europe's resources to their own—that delay will only allow the Soviets to become decisively stronger. Or perhaps the U.S. President would not read studies or make calculations, but would simply act out of a sense of obligation and outrage. Whatever the reason, assume that he decides to attack the Soviet Union.

While he would then be forced to risk those "empty" cities, he would not be eager to lose them. In such circumstances, he might most sensibly limit U.S. actions in a very careful and controlled fashion. SAC might strike missile bases in Siberia, Soviet bomber bases away from cities, identified submarines at sea, and in general any target that does not involve the destruction of important non-military assets. SAC could take particular care to avoid civilian targets. It could postpone the destruction of air defense, command and control, and logistic targets that entailed excessive collateral damage until absolutely necessary. If the Soviets happened to have an important target such as a bomber base near a city such as Leningrad or Moscow, SAC might deliberately refrain from attacking it, even though this self-restraint might result in the U.S. suffering more eventual damage. Alternatively, if SAC did attack such a base, it might use low-yield kiloton bombs rather than multimegaton bombs, and thus greatly limit the collateral damage to the adjoining city. The President might simultaneously point out to the Soviets[4] that since their strategic forces have been damaged in the U.S. strike, there are no possible ways in which they can win the war. The President could then reiterate that his only war aim is the ending of their threat against Europe. He would ask: "Do you really prefer to start a city exchange rather than accept our peace terms? Is it the right time for you to start trading cities when we have such a large military superiority?"

Finally, if the President had (or pretended to have) great con-

---

[4] As already indicated, it is more likely that this would have been pointed out as part of an ultimatum lower on the ladder, or "unofficially" in inspired reports on U.S. strategy, or by deliberate private "leaks" and conversations.

fidence in the intimidating character of this counter-counterthreat, he would use this confidence to make more credible his deterrent to Soviet attack on Europe.

Under the conditions of the mid-1960's, even if a U.S. first strike were only moderately successful, it would very likely be successful enough in these hypothetical circumstances to leave the Soviets with little rational alternative to de-escalation, since if they were to continue at this rung, they would be beaten. Thus, the only rational thing for them to do at this point would be to negotiate for at least a cease-fire or to de-escalate to exemplary attacks and controlled reprisals. It is, of course, implausible that human beings would be this rational, even in the case of the relatively self-controlled (two steps forward, one step back) Soviets. But even if they struck back with a relatively large attack and hostilities continued at this level for a short time, they might prove willing to limit their counterblow to counterforce targets. They might do this because it would be clear that if the war ended in stalemate, it would be much less costly to both sides if each had been careful about how it had used its strategic forces. Care on the Soviet part would have been made more probable by care by the U.S. and the limited objectives it had proclaimed. Moreover, even if things went wrong and the war degenerated into "city-busting" after ten or twenty hours, the reluctant attacker might have gone a considerable way toward achieving his "limited-damage" objective. After ten or twenty hours of war, much of the defender's forces would have been destroyed, used up in the controlled phase of the war, or degraded in effectiveness because of impairment of important parts of his system.

As discussed earlier (in Chapter VI), the pressures upon our European allies to limit a general war would be even stronger than the pressures upon the U.S. Because of proximity, concentration, and the odd Soviet preoccupation with IRBM's and the "medium-range mission," as opposed to ICBM's and the intercontinental mission, it would be easier for the Soviets to destroy Europe than to destroy the United States. Thus it might be sensible in some cases for the U.S. to encourage Europe to declare some degree of armed or even unarmed neutrality, depending on U.S. tactics and strategy and Europe's capabilities. Because of the development of the ICBM and the Polaris submarine, and because of vulnerability and warning considerations and the difficulty of maintaining secrecy in operations, European-based forces will not be as valuable military assets to the NATO alliance as they were in the past. A European declaration of neutrality or military disengagement on the open-city[5] model thus might in some circumstances be militarily acceptable even though costly. There is also a possible bonus in some degree of European "abstention": to the extent that Europe can preserve some independent military or political bargaining power in a Soviet-American war, it might provide a third force which, after United States and Soviet attacks on one another's military forces, could exert pressure on both sides to be reasonable in their negotiations. An armed China might be able to do the same thing; and neither the Soviet Union nor the United States is likely to relish the thought that, if they knocked each other out, the Chinese Communists would reap the benefits.

European neutrality could bring another important bonus. Europe's undestroyed economy could help rebuild the destroyed areas elsewhere. I will mention below a type of independent European strategic deterrent based on a proportionate-nuclear-reprisal concept which is consistent—politically and militarily—with these considerations.

RUNG 37. COUNTERFORCE-WITH-AVOIDANCE ATTACK: This attack differs from the constrained disarming attack by being less scrupulous in avoiding collateral damage to cities, and by ignoring the possibility of sparing a certain amount of the enemy's second-strike force. Here there is a counterforce attack that tries to pick up every target that does not involve *major* collateral damage to civilian targets. In the case of a Soviet attack of this type on the United States, a city such as Tucson (250,000 population), which is completely ringed with Titans, would probably be hit, but the San Diego Naval Base, Norfolk Navy Yard, and the Pentagon in Washington would probably be avoided as involving too great a number of collateral civilian casualties. If the Soviets did hit these targets, or any SAC bases near very large cities, they perhaps would

---

[5] In international law, it is not legal to attack a city that is not being defended locally and not being used to aid the military forces directly.

use 20-kiloton (rather than 20-megaton) weapons in order to keep down the collateral destruction. After such an attack, one must assume an almost certain counterattack, but one can still try to use threats of a further escalation into countervalue wars to limit the defender's response.

One possible attraction of such counterforce warfare is that it looks like traditional warfare. It is the military fighting against the military, rather than the military destroying helpless civilians. But, of course, a "military" victory would not necessarily mean that the defeated side would allow itself to be occupied by the enemy, or even that the victor would have the military forces to occupy the defeated country. The victor might have to threaten, or actually destroy, some of the defeated side's cities in order to force acknowledgment of defeat. In a sense, then, counterforce attack is a preliminary to the bombardment of cities, and the possibility of controlled reprisal attacks against cities would always be present. However, the fact remains that, as in the past, the defeated side might be expected to surrender when it could no longer protect itself or, even if it still had some ability to inflict damage on the superior side, that it might nevertheless accept a compromise peace.

RUNG 38. UNMODIFIED COUNTERFORCE ATTACK: Unlike constrained or avoidance attacks, in an unmodified counterforce attack no inhibitions on the counterforce operations are accepted in order to avoid collateral damage; the military plans are formulated and the operation is carried out with general disregard as to whether enemy civilians are killed or nonmilitary property destroyed (though there may be disadvantages accepted to avoid fallout or other dangers to allies or neutrals). No attempt would be made either to lessen or to increase collateral damage to the enemy, except perhaps the most minor adjustments. This attack might be described as the classic form of all-out or total war, with only lip service paid to avoiding civilian destruction.

The Rungs of Civilian Central Wars

We turn now to wars in which there is a deliberate attempt to hurt civilians and their property, particularly large cities. At this point, the warring nations are at another threshold. Under current U.S.

"controlled response" doctrine, not only do we intend to observe the city threshold, but an enormous incentive is given to the Soviets, in a war against the United States, to do so as well and to avoid attacking U.S. cities in their first wave—whether this wave is the first or second strike of the war. Even if the Soviets thought they could take out much or all of U.S. strategic forces, they could not be certain of this, and it would make sense for them to think of American cities as hostages to be used to protect their own cities from retaliatory strikes and to improve their bargaining position in terminating the war. If their first wave in any way went astray, or if a war ended in negotiation, their avoidance of U.S. cities would have paid off. If, on the other hand, they hit U.S. cities early in the attack, the U.S. would be likely to make a "spasm response" in reply. Then, unless their strike had been extraordinarily successful, they would be likely simply to disappear as a nation—or at least to be set back 25 to 100 years in industrial and material wealth. This means that they would lose little by sparing cities on their first wave, and they might gain a great deal.

This reasoning is inconsistent with current, or at least announced, Soviet doctrine. Many Soviet planners and writers seem to feel that one of the best ways to defeat an enemy, presumably without suffering defeat oneself, is to attack the opponent's society. It is difficult to believe that this would be true of a short war, and it also is difficult to believe that any nation—including the Soviets— would resort to nuclear war unless they thought the war would be short (and, in some reasonable terms, victorious). Long wars are too uncertain a quantity to be begun except in desperation. Thus, no matter what their current doctrine may be, these arguments are likely to look persuasive to Soviet decision-makers at a time when they come to think seriously about launching a first strike.

It is important to note that even if population is not the target for the first wave, it could be the target of the second or later waves. In any case, it would always be threatened. The residual vulnerability of the civilian hostages and cities could then affect, to a great extent, the kind of peace treaty the Soviets could force on us, or that we could force on the Soviets. For this reason, it makes sense to try to protect people from being threatened by second- and later-wave attacks, even though they may not have been adequately protected on the first wave. And it is easier to do this than to protect them from a first-wave strike, particularly one that to some degree comes "out of the blue." (All of the enemy's large vulnerable ICBM's and many of his protected ones will, after a first strike, either be destroyed or already launched, and all the emergency-readiness programs fully activated. The forces that the Soviets have withheld for bargaining and intrawar deterrence purposes are likely to carry relatively small warheads.) If the U.S. population is not adequately protected against second- and later-wave attacks, and it becomes necessary to make unwise or dangerous concessions in negotiations in order to protect them, then something will have been lost.

Controlled response is official U.S. strategic doctrine today (already taken more or less seriously in various quarters, it will probably be taken increasingly seriously as time goes on). It seems to me that in accordance with the presuppositions of such a doctrine, the United States should, at the minimum, undertake a civil-defense program that is compatible with what this doctrine foresees in a time of war. Part of such a program would be fallout protection for the entire population and blast protection for the 5–10 million people who live within about 10 miles of priority strategic targets. Such a program might require $5–$10 billion spread over five years or so. In a very large range of types of wars (both counterforce and countervalue), these measures could save the lives of 30–50 million people, and in addition make it more likely that a war, if it came, would in fact be a war of controlled response. In particular, this program would clearly announce to the Soviets (and our own people and allies) that the U.S. takes controlled response seriously. Action rather than talk should be very educational, improving discussion and understanding of these issues generally—a rather important by-product.

Thus, I would suggest that a careful reading of current controlled-response doctrine indicates: (1) that the strategy of the "pause" in Europe implies the desirability of considering seriously a program for emergency readiness; (2) that the strategy of "no cities" implies that civilians near SAC bases are less than adequately protected by deterrence and therefore are entitled to blast and thermal—in addition to fallout—protection (one might argue that the city of Tucson deserves an independent nuclear deterrent —or at least shelters—since it clearly is not protected by the same deterrent threat that protects New York; (3) that fallout protection at least should be supplied for all who might be collateral targets (which is just about everybody); and (4) that there be some stockpiling and other preparations for economic recuperation as a prudential hedge against a "city-busting" campaign or to improve the U.S. bargaining capability.

In conclusion, let me emphasize the difference between being threatened on the first wave and the later waves of a nuclear attack, since I have found widespread misunderstanding of this point. Some people are not really familiar with the strong reasons the Soviets might have to avoid U.S. cities on their first-wave attack, and other people seem not to understand why it is important to be able to protect the cities from later-wave attacks. Protecting against later waves is likely to be much easier than against the initial attack, and failing to do so could decrease U.S. capability to resist post-attack blackmail and thus reduce both our deterrence of deliberate Soviet attack and our ability to achieve a "satisfactory" political and military outcome if deterrence failed. Our ability to do the last would depend on our capability to fight and terminate a war. (That almost undiscussed subject is considered in the next chapter.)

RUNG 39. SLOW-MOTION COUNTERCITY WAR: This again is a war of resolution, but one that takes the ultimate form—"city trading." It is, of course, the most bizarre of all the options that are discussed in modern strategic analysis. The possibility of city trading arises because of today's unprecedented situation, in which both sides may have almost invulnerable forces while both sides' civilians may be completely and irrevocably vulnerable to these invulnerable forces. There has hardly been such a situation in the history of mankind: the only limited correspondence is with those occasions in ancient and medieval times in which kings, emperors, and others exchanged important members of their families as hostages. The particular hostages that are being traded here are, of course, major elements of the societies themselves. This kind of war would be the extreme and ultimate form of deliberative, selective, and controlled response—but one not necessarily or even likely to be beyond the psychological capabilities of decision-makers to make if the only alternatives are told distribution and complete capitulation.

RUNG 40. COUNTERVALUE SALVO: As part of some other kind of slow-motion war, it is always possible that one side or the other will, as a deliberate or inadvertent tactic, launch a large salvo of missiles or bombers at the other side's cities. This need not be an indiscriminate salvo covering the entire target system and using all forces. It might be carefully (or inadvertently) chosen to cover a portion of the system. The attack might be delivered for the same kind of symbolic communications reasons that I already discussed in connection with exemplary central wars, though now it would be done in the context of an ongoing war. Whether this partial eruption were inadvertent or deliberate, it presumably would increase sharply the possibility of a "total" eruption. I am not considering a single city's inadvertent or unavoidable collateral destruction as a countervalue salvo.

RUNG 41. AUGMENTED DISARMING ATTACK: This is the kind of counterforce attack that was much discussed in the late 1940's and early 1950's, when both sides had a very small number of weapons but still could think in terms of destroying or damaging the other side's society as well as his forces while attempting to pay at least lip service to the concept of avoiding civilians as deliberate targets. Such a counterforce attack is deliberately modified to obtain as much collateral countervalue damage as a "bonus" as can be achieved without diverting significant resources from the military targets or deliberately focusing on an entirely civilian target. Thus, in the 1940's and 1950's, it was possible to find discussions of targets chosen supposedly because they were military in nature, but actually because they maximized collateral damage. If carried very far, this policy quickly becomes a complete and obvious subterfuge and in fact constitutes the kind of attack considered under the next rungs.

RUNG 42. CIVILIAN DEVASTATION ATTACK: This attack corresponds to the usual popular picture of nuclear war in which there is a deliberate effort to destroy or greatly damage the enemy's society.

It may or may not be accompanied by a counterforce attack. It is distinguished from spasm or insensate war only by having some element of calculation and by the fact that there may be some withholding or control. The objective may be revenge, a deliberate attempt to prevent the other society from ever recovering from the war (or at least to degrade its recovery), or a theory that the other side would surrender once its major cities were destroyed, because of despair, a recognition of the futility of the protected military forces of the destroyed society continuing the "senseless" destruction, and an awareness of the inhumanity of destroying "innocent" civilians. While it seems to me almost incredible that a Soviet decision-maker would give this possibility much weight, a number of Western thinkers and planners take it seriously as a potential Soviet tactic.

RUNG 43. SOME OTHER KINDS OF CONTROLLED GENERAL WAR: The reader should now be quite clear that, at least conceptually, there are many kinds of general wars possible, corresponding to different outbreak scenarios, objectives, tactics, and postures. He may gain further perspective on the matter by examining Figure 4, which lists a number of different attacks that could start or occur in a general war.

FIGURE 4

ATTACK OPTIONS IN A GENERAL WAR

CLASSIC	1.	Countervalue Devastation
	2.	Mixed Counterforce-Countervalue
	3.	Augmented Counterforce
NO-CITIES DOCTRINE	4.	Unmodified Counterforce
	5.	Counterforce with Avoidance
CONTROLLED-RESPONSE TACTICS	6.	Constrained Disarming
	7.	Countervalue Salvo
	8.	Slow-Motion Countervalue
	9.	Slow-Motion Counterforce
	10.	Force-Reduction Salvo
	11.	Exemplary or Reprisal
	12.	Show of Force or Demonstration
ALSO-TO-BE-CONSIDERED	13.	Environmental Counterforce
	14.	Environmental Countervalue
	15.	Anti-Recuperation
	16.	Special Instrumental
NEVER-TO-BE-FORGOTTEN	17.	Weak Link

The list of options contains many that have already been discussed; only options 13–17 are new. The arrangement of options indicates how doctrine evolved in the postwar period until the early 1960's. In the 1950's, only the first three attacks were considered seriously by decision-makers or their influential advisers. McNamara's "no-cities" doctrine made options 4 and 5 "respectable." Outside the esoteric literature of strategy, there has been little or no discussion of options 6–12, but such discussion is now beginning. In the past, I have referred to these options as *avant-garde,* but there is now so much implicit understanding and conceptual acceptance of these possibilities, even among laymen, that it is no longer correct to so consider them (whether or not they are judged to be realistic).[6]

[6] I have found, in recent briefings and lectures, that almost any audience in the United States is at least implicitly familiar with the concepts that are the basis of options 6–12. Thus, the following question can be asked by many American audiences (such as college students, businessmen, members of the League of Women Voters, etc.):
"Just to illustrate how much understanding is possessed by this audience of modern strategic doctrine, let me ask members of the audience to volunteer what they think would happen if President Johnson were suddenly notified that a large bomb, say something between 5 and 20 megatons, had just exploded over New York City." Almost nobody in the audience now (as opposed to five years ago) will reply that Johnson would go ahead and launch a large all-out attack on the Soviet Union. The overwhelming majority always suggests that he get on the Hot Line to find out such things as: Why is there only one bomb? Where are the others? Why was New York City chosen? If the Soviets wanted to launch an exemplary attack, why had they not made some preliminary demands or sent us a message so that we could understand what was going on? The attack is clearly not part of an overwhelming surprise attack that is going according to plan. Was it a case of somebody beating the gun; a true mechanical accident; unauthorized behavior, possibly by somebody trying to get the Soviet Union into trouble? Could it be the Chinese trying to touch off a U.S.-Soviet war? In any case, the overwhelming majority of the audience agrees that President Johnson should get in touch with the Soviets.
The more sophisticated members of the audience will often ask whether or not there is any pressure on Johnson to act rapidly because of concern about the vulnerability of our strategic forces. An equally large number of people understand that our forces are not vulnerable (or at least that Johnson presumably so thinks) and that as far as this concern is important, there is time to wait. Some even ask how vulnerable the Soviet forces are. Almost no one suggests attacking these forces without raising this question. A few suggest that Moscow should be destroyed in retaliation.
In order to pursue the example even further, I have suggested an elaborate scenario outlining why the Soviets had in fact launched the attack

It may be worth while to discuss briefly the last five attacks on the list.

Environmental counterforce attacks exploit the fact that megaton weapons are comparable to such gross forces of nature as earthquakes and hurricanes and, paradoxically, that the effects of the use of such weapons, besides being extremely violent and widespread, can also be very subtle and hard to predict. The effects of nuclear weapons include blast, thermal and electromagnetic radia-

---

deliberately and so informed the U.S. What, then, should we do? Again, almost nobody suggests a spasm response. A large percentage of the audience now are very interested in the degree of vulnerability of the Soviet forces to a U.S. blow and the adequacy of our defenses vis-à-vis their retaliatory blow, and in what would happen to the U.S. as a result of the damage done by this Soviet strike. When I suggest that just for the sake of example, we assume that the Soviet forces are invulnerable and could destroy the United States totally, even in a second strike, almost all agree that there should be retaliation but that it should be limited. Most suggest that Moscow be destroyed, but many object to this on the grounds that this city is much more important to the Soviet Union than New York is to the United States. These usually suggest that the destruction of some smaller city, such as Leningrad or Kiev, would be an appropriate counterescalation.

I have asked those who did want to destroy Moscow if they would want the U.S. to continue the escalation if the Soviets, pointing out that Moscow was more important to them than New York City was to the U.S., then destroyed Philadelphia. Most of the audiences are willing to quit at this point, feeling that the U.S. had made its point and one side or the other had to desist first; and moreover, that the Soviet argument had some justice because by destroying Moscow, the U.S. had in part overescalated.

I do not imply that any of the above is a plausible or correct view of what would or should happen. I am pointing out that if the same questions had been asked five years ago of quite technical and skilled audiences, to say nothing of lay audiences, the overwhelming majorities would have opted for some kind of large or spasm response without any further communication with the Soviets or indeed any investigation at all.

In the past five years, almost everyone in the U.S. who has any interest in these problems or is even modestly well informed has, as a result of both serious and fictionalized discussions, learned that there are possibilities for control in such bizarre situations. Audiences in Canada and Europe seem to be distinctly less aware of these possibilities, and when aware of them take them much less seriously. But it seems quite clear that this is more due to the absence of discussion and thought rather than to greater soundness of judgment, because if they are pressed to serious discussion and argument they very often eventually reach the same positions taken by the American audiences. I should probably repeat that I do not take the agreement as validating the theory, but only as validating that most citizens, at least of NATO countries, will accept the theory if presented as a hypothetical "if . . . then" question.

tion, ground shock, debris, dust, and ionization—any one of which may affect people and equipment. Indeed, the effects of multi-megaton weapons are so powerful and complex that even if they do not destroy a system by blast, they may damage it by more subtle effects or change the environment in such fashion that the system will be temporarily or permanently inoperable.

For the first time in the history of war, we face what might be called the problem of the post-attack environment—the real danger that both the short- and long-range environment in which we live and must conduct our recuperation and operate our weapons systems will be adversely affected in both expected and unexpected ways.

An example of how an effect that has not been predicted and thus not adequately prepared for can cause an unexpected operational failure is the blackout of high-frequency communications that occurred once during the testing of some high-altitude weapons over the Pacific Ocean. News stories mentioned that about 3,000 square miles were blacked out. Any system that depended on high-frequency communication, and was not corrected for this effect, might well run into serious and possibly disabling trouble in the first few minutes of war.[7] Actually, of course, the environmental counterforce attack could come under the classification of unmodified or augmented disarming attack, but it is potentially important enough to deserve a special classification of its own.

---

[7] In *On Thermonuclear War,* pp. 428–33, I gave other examples and further discussion of such possibly unexpected weapons effects. Because of these possibilities, it would not surprise any sophisticated observer too much if even a seemingly well-designed system manned by adequately trained and indoctrinated personnel failed to operate because of some unexpected human or physical failure.

There are many known examples of systems which almost everybody had agreed should be quite workable when they were designed but which subsequently revealed vulnerability to subtle effects that had been overlooked. Such effects are now taken seriously, as was made clear in a speech President Kennedy made: "We are spending great sums of money on radar to alert our defenses and to develop possible antimissile systems—on the communications which enable our command and control centers to direct a response—on hardening our missile sites, shielding our missiles and their warheads from defensive action, and providing them with electronic guidance systems to find their targets. But we cannot be useless—blacked out, paralyzed, or destroyed by the complex effects of a nuclear explosion."

Environmental countervalue attacks against people are also worth study. Such attacks could be made to enhance such effects as long-term radiation (cobalt bombs), short-term radiation, area fires, tidal waves, the covering of large areas by blast by a pattern bombing technique, and so on. There has been much discussion of such attacks in popular and semipopular literature, and many people think of them as either the most likely or the only forms of attack.

At first sight, such attacks do not seem to make too much sense. It is expensive to be prepared to deliver them; furthermore, they typically use very large weapons, and the missiles that are required are also large and therefore difficult to protect. In other words, such preparations tend to go in a direction exactly opposite to that followed by the United States (toward smaller weapons, for a reason—they are easier to protect). This means that a force designed for an environmental countervalue attack may not be a very reliable second-strike force. On the other hand, an environmental countervalue attack is a very poor first-strike tactic; even though it can destroy an enemy's civilians and property, it is not likely to harm his properly protected strategic force very much. Even when combined with an environmental counterforce attack, the countervalue portion of the attack would represent a large and needless diversion of resources.

However, further examination indicates that there also are arguments in favor of being prepared to deliver an environmental countervalue attack. Such attacks are so horrible and destructive that even a very small probability of such an attack—either first or second strike—may indeed contribute either to the balance of terror or to nuclear blackmail. For example, if the Soviet Union possessed 20 or 30 ICBM's, each carrying 100-megaton warheads, even though these ICBM's might be vulnerable, the United States could not be certain of destroying them—indeed, it might not even know exactly where they were. Under such circumstances, the Soviets would have a pretty good deterrent to attacks by the United States, and many in the United States—particularly those who were willing to believe in the possible irrationality of Soviet decision-makers—might be fearful of provoking the possessor of such fearful weapons into a first strike against countervalue targets.

Environmental countervalue attacks could be carried out for either retaliation or instrumental reasons.

Antirecuperation attacks are also possible. There are many reasons why a country might wish to be able to deliver such an attack. First, its opponent might have been able to put his civilians under fairly effective protection. Indeed, studies have shown that it is relatively inexpensive, particularly if there is one or two weeks' notice, to defend civilians (by a combination of movement and improvised shelters). However, it is much more difficult to protect concentrated wealth in the cities, or such natural resources as forests or the fertility of the soil, if an attacker has the capability to destroy them. Therefore, to maintain its deterrent in the face of countermeasures, a country might wish to be able to concentrate on destroying its opponent's ability to recuperate.

There is another reason why a nation might be interested in an attack on recuperation. To the extent that there is no conflict with other war aims (particularly the possibility of having a controlled war and an early peace treaty), a nation might be concerned about the long-term competition between the two societies, and, to the degree that one side could handicap the other, it might wish to attack the other side's ability to recuperate.

Special instrumental attacks include the many other "rational" or goal-seeking attacks which can be devised in addition to those we have discussed. We can think of at least four such attacks that are worth noting. They are labeled "problem-solving," "blackmail-enhancing," "regime subversion," and "covert or anonymous." Very briefly, these attacks can be described as follows:

a) *Problem-solving:* This category denotes a situation in which some special problem is presented to the potential attacker and he feels that he can solve this problem by destroying people or objects with strategic weapons—or at least that this "solution" is his best or least undesirable alternative. One far-fetched but simple example would be the extinction of a mad leader who had access to strategic capabilities and whom one wanted to kill before he could do irrevocable harm. (This example also might be included in regime subversion, discussed below.)

A similar situation could result if some blackmailer got control of a small number of missiles. Whether or not this blackmailer was a member of any government, one might desperately want to destroy him or his missiles or both. Or, warned that some nation was about to launch an exemplary attack, one might judge it desirable to forestall the attack by destroying or damaging launching sites even before or simultaneously with the transmittal of an ultimatum or threat to the would-be attacker. Or some nation might have begun to build a "doomsday machine" or something similar, and a prudential government might decide to destroy the work in progress, and yet be unwilling to launch a large attack for fear of an unacceptable response or because it did not wish to cause excessive destruction. Or, some of the potential defender's forces might be indulging in extremely annoying or threatening but still legal operations; for example, an opponent might be jamming radar from ships at sea, and in order to prevent the jamming one might wish to destroy the ships or the ports from which they came. The attack might be carried out covertly in order to minimize the pressures for reprisal that would be generated. (If, instead, the attack were intended to give warning or to cause pain or fear, it would come under the exemplary category rather than the special instrumental.) Or a would-be aggressor might destroy some important or critical defensive installations of his intended victim—perhaps under the guise (or partial reality) of an exemplary attack.

A final, even more bizarre, example could arise in a situation in which a nation was shipping arms to a potential enemy of the attacker. An attack could then be directed against the storehouses or ships that were being used.

b) *Blackmail-enhancing:* We have already mentioned that one of the chief purposes of any instrumental attack is the facilitation of negotiations, whether open or tacit. Sometimes this can be achieved by an attack on a special target system other than those which fall into the usual counterforce and countervalue categories. For example, one might imagine the U.S., in some desperate situation, destroying the crops of the Soviet Union or China, then pointing out that the only way these nations could hope to survive would be to get food from the U.S. or another Western nation, and that such food would not be forthcoming except on our terms. An even more violent example of a blackmail-enhancing attack would be an attacker destroying in descending order of size cities 11 to 200 of the defender nation. The attacker would then point out to the defending nation that it could still survive the war since its remaining 10 largest cities contained all the essentials needed for recuperation, but that national survival now depended on these few extremely vulnerable targets. In a war or crisis, one can also imagine an attack to kill decision-makers particularly likely to be intransigent, in the hope that the new decision-makers would be more reasonable. (The last attack could also be included in the next category, regime subversion.)

c) *Regime subversion:* I have already referred (in two previous examples of instrumental attacks) to the killing of individuals in order to change the character of the regime. One can imagine other attacks whose special purpose would be to change the character of a regime or to overthrow it. For example, one could attack the administrative centers, troops and police used to keep order, key decision-makers, warehouses, communications, transportation, and so on.

Some of the symbolic attacks already described could also be used to create pressures that might change a regime, and these pressures might be enhanced by the destruction of selected targets. Or one can imagine the existence of a political opposition to a regime (perhaps created or strengthened by the pressures resulting from previous escalations or even by the current escalation) and a very limited attack being launched to help this opposition group carry through a *coup d'état* by eliminating or weakening selected parts of the existing regime and its organs of government and by internal coercion. This could be done with or without the cooperation of the rebels. It might be done to influence the outcome of an ongoing rebellion or civil war.

d) *Covert or anonymous attacks:* There are many reasons why a nation might want to launch covert or anonymous attacks. I have already referred to one possibility in the discussion of symbolic attacks. Another reason would be that anonymity might provide a relatively safe way of carrying out any of the first three special instrumental attacks. In addition, the known possessor of a covert capability is likely to find his ability to deter provocation enhanced since it is obvious that he can be more reckless with his symbolic attacks. Indeed, the possessor of a covert-attack capability potentially has a rather effective reprisal against being covertly attacked himself. If he is willing to risk punishing an innocent group, he can launch a covert reprisal attack on mere suspicion. If he is right in his choice of victims, the original attacker will have been punished. If the victim is innocent, in many circumstances he is as likely as not to assume that he is simply the second victim of the first attacker.

Weak-link attacks, as suggested on the chart, should be a "never-to-be-forgotten" possibility. I have already mentioned that our forces might unexpectedly be vulnerable to some environmental effects. There are other kinds of weak links that could exist, some of which we might not be aware of since nuclear forces are invulnerable by analysis rather than by test.[8] (On the whole, they have not even been proof-tested in peacetime, much less by experience in an actual war.) The weak-link attack is important because of the present Soviet relationship to U.S. strategic forces. There is today a good deal of analysis (most of it classified) which argues that U.S. forces, at least, are invulnerable. In fact, if published estimates of the Soviet missile inventory are correct (a few hundred or so), then the Soviets do not have enough missiles even to target more than a small part of the total silos in the U.S. Minuteman force. The Soviets would have to find some new physical effect that would increase the lethal radius of their weapons so that they could get a better than one-for-one exchange, or exploit the vulnerability of some part of the system (such as command, control, or communication), if they wished to make an effective disarming attack.

In addition, at least so far as the published literature is concerned, our Polaris system does not seem to have any serious vulnerabilities. Thus the Soviets, in trying to prevent or reduce retaliation, are likely to find that their available "rational" targets are very limited. They can withhold most of their forces, attacking such lucrative targets as bomber bases, the more vulnerable or more im-

[8] However, this is a much improved situation over the 1950's, when forces were invulnerable by assumption rather than by analysis. (See Albert J. Wohlstetter, "The Delicate Balance of Terror," *Foreign Affairs,* January, 1959; or *On Thermonuclear War.* pp. 423–26.)

portant missiles, such as some of the Titans and Atlases, or command, control, and communication facilities, and possibly a small number of cities to induce terror; but they apparently would have to leave the bulk of U.S. strategic forces unattacked.[9]

There are, of course, at least two remaining questions. The first is, "Is this analysis correct?" The system, after all, has never been tested, and much of it is classified. Indeed, because of various bureaucratic problems, "obvious" defects may exist and not even be known to the authorities. The second question is, "Will this condition remain as satisfactory in the future?" And the fact is that a weak link need not be in the United States. For example, if the Soviets worked out some method of intercepting our missiles so that they could not get to their targets, this would constitute just as weak a link in the U.S. system as if our missiles were destroyed on the ground (though possibly less reliable).

Because of the importance and gravity of the issue, it is worth emphasizing that degrees of vulnerability are estimated quantities, and that history is filled with examples of elaborate and impressive-appearing military organizations that were destroyed by a smaller but more competent or ingenious opponent. The day of brilliant stratagems and tactics may not be over.

The vulnerability issue, of course, cuts two ways. There are reasons to believe that the Soviet system may have substantially greater vulnerabilities than that of the United States. This leaves open such questions as, "Are these known to the United States?" or "Are they so reliably known and reliably exploitable that U.S. decision-makers would be willing to take any additional risks or be able to make more credible threats?"[10] Despite such uncertainties, it is

---

[9] This is one of the main reasons why so many U.S. analysts feel confident that the Soviets will not launch an attack against the United States, even if greatly provoked or desperate. Any adviser trying to persuade a Soviet decision-maker that he should strike would have to have effective advice on what to do about the Minuteman and Polaris weapon systems. It is widely believed that he could not—even with a fertile imagination—devise a story that would satisfy even an imprudent or reckless Soviet decision-maker. If the major part of the U.S. military installations actually go untargeted, there hardly is much room for wishful thinking among Soviet decision-makers.

[10] See *On Thermonuclear War*, pp. 196–99, for a discussion of the extreme difficulty of proving reliability.

possible that the resolve of the Soviets (or the United States) could be greatly eroded in a crisis either by sudden discovery (perhaps because of sudden interest) of certain vulnerabilities or by a belief that the other side, whether accurately or not, thought it had discovered such vulnerabilities. (For these purposes, the belief by an opponent that the other side's system is vulnerable could create a war by miscalculation. There would be little or no satisfaction if this unwanted war were mutually, rather than unilaterally, disastrous.)

RUNG 44. SPASM[11] OR INSENSATE WAR: My use of the terms "spasm" and "insensate" does not necessarily denote blind, overwhelming fury (though it may often carry such connotations), but might only mean that a response is automatic, unthinking, and uncontrolled—a function of the central nervous system, so to speak, rather than of the brain. Spasm or insensate action is, of course, the usual picture of central war. Thus, John Foster Dulles once remarked that if war ever broke out, the State Department would be closed down. Presumably, he felt its functions would thereafter be superfluous.

Actually, the United States has never, I believe, had an official policy of uncontrolled destruction employing all available means, or even war plans directed to civilian devastation. At all times, it has been considered appropriate to exercise discrimination and to target only military installations or installations rationally useful to a war effort (although this sometimes has been done more in the spirit of Rung 41, augmented disarming attack, than in that of the military central wars). Thus, to use such invidious terms as "spasm" and "insensate" in connection with some tactics and targeting pro-

[11] The term "spasm war" is now almost standard jargon in military and government circles and, to some degree, in journalism as well. I believe the expression originated in briefings I gave some years ago in which some war-plan proposals were referred to as "orgastic spasms of destruction." During one of these briefings, I said to the audience, "You people do not have a war plan. You have a 'war-gasm.'" These expressions were put forward with no particular reference to their sexual implications, but some of my colleagues, more conversant with Freudian concepts and literature than I, argue that the term "spasm war" is more accurate and descriptive than one might like to think. The point is, in any event, outside the scope of this discussion.

posals has aroused hostility, and my use of them clearly is a debating tactic; but in the present case it is a useful and reasonable one, since it must be said with reference to some widely held positions or proposals that it is not entirely unfair to apply these terms.

It has come as a distinct shock to me that many people not only accept, in effect, the concept of spasm or insensate war, but assign a humanitarian value to it, arguing that if this is the only conception of war a country has (or discusses), war becomes "unthinkable" or "impossible"—or that deterrence is improved. Thus, there is a curious area of agreement between some extreme "militarists," some arms-controllers, and some members of the peace movement, although they arrive at their agreement from quite different assumptions and moral positions. Some moralists and some finite-deterrence advocates are against studying limitations and restraint in central wars for fear that it might lead the government to put too great a faith in limitations and cause it to be too ready to resort to war. Some militarists (and many Europeans) are against the study of limitation and restraint in central war because they feel that by appearing to reduce the consequences of deterrence-failing, such studies also decrease the reliability of deterrence; and they may fear, too, that these studies might simultaneously erode U.S. or Allied determination and will.

Thus, there are those who believe that this ultimate escalation option should not only be available, but that it should, either by default or deliberately, be the only option—no others being planned for. Hence the rung is included in the escalation ladder; although the original purpose for its inclusion, to dramatize—perhaps unfairly—a lack in official thinking, has been fulfilled.

X

Some Comments on "War-Fighting"

The Current Neglect of Strategy and Tactics

The term "war-fighting" is now much used as an antonym of "spasm" or "deterrence only" in describing tactics and forces concerned with how a strategic nuclear war might start, be waged, and be terminated, and how postwar survival and recuperation problems can be handled. Many find such concern strange, if not offensive. Probably never in the history of the world has there been so widespread a conviction that "war is unthinkable" or "impossible," and so extensive a belief that a serious concern with the problems in fighting and surviving a war—as opposed to deterring it—is misguided and perhaps even immoral. Today tactics are not merely considered—as they often were in the past—as a matter of relatively narrow professional concern; instead, there is a fundamental and almost self-righteous disavowal of interest in the whole topic.

Strategy is not treated with quite the same hostility as tactics, since it does have an important, apparent, and "felt" relationship to such other national concerns as deterrence and foreign policy. There is even an interest in military capabilities since these have to be secured and maintained in peacetime. (Decisions must be made whose consequences will be seen and felt, so decision-makers and their staffs are necessarily concerned.) But the detailed requirements for the wartime use of capabilities, as reflected in the tactics to be chosen if war occurs, are not forcibly brought to anybody's attention. Decisions are made passively, perhaps by default or inattention, and are not fully understood; their consequences are neither necessarily fully grasped nor, indeed, very visible. Often these decisions are classified, which further decreases discussion of them, since, by and large, one does not know what they are.

In addition, since nuclear tactics are to be implemented only if deterrence fails, the attitude of mind illustrated by the term "nuclear incredulity" (an attitude that almost everybody shares so long as we stay below Rung 10 on the escalation ladder) makes it difficult to take seriously all the possible consequences of a failure of deterrence—or of the importance of thinking through to the bitter end at least some of those possibilities. Thus, there are many conscientious, responsible, intelligent individuals who would not tolerate an obvious (conceptual or actual) lack of understanding of any topic in an area in which they were working or for which they were responsible, but who are disturbed or annoyed by attempts to discuss central war tactics in a sophisticated or complex way. It does not seem to them worth while to master the various distinctions and cases, even when it is clear that these distinctions and cases may be relevant to an understanding of the alternatives. This lack of interest in tactics is unfortunate first of all because many major strategic issues are almost impossible to discuss seriously without analyzing tactics in a more detailed fashion than is customary (even though the discussion may still be relatively superficial).

Thus, despite the enormous current interest in national-security issues and the consequent expansion of scholarly and professional work, there is relatively little serious, sophisticated consideration of the military requirements, advantages, and weaknesses of various strategies and tactics for the middle and upper rungs of the escalation ladder. I am inclined to believe that the chief reason for this is a psychological obstacle, even among professionals and scholars. When the atom bomb was developed, many scholars, military professionals, and informed laymen believed that strategy and tactics, as they understod them, had come to an end. This feeling was reflected in the late 1940's in such phrases as "the absolute weapon," and in many aphorisms and analogies that made the point, more or less dramatically or ironically, that the inevitable result of a nuclear war would be mutual annihilation. Since this would happen no matter what tactics were used, tactical theory was irrelevant. Strategy was equally irrelevant, since it could not be an objective of strategy to bring about the destruction of the nation. Atomic war thus became unthinkable, both literally and figuratively. And, in fact, most of the strategists and technicians were so awed by the existence of this new weapon that they almost did stop thinking.

On the military side, this block against thinking about the problem sometimes resulted in a compensatory denial of the problem: atomic bombs were simply "bigger bombs" or "quality weapons." The initial nuclear strategic targeting and tactics of the Air Force were almost identical to those used for conventional bombing in World War II. Sometimes there was an attempt to correct the mistakes of World War II—as these were disclosed, for example, by the Strategic Bombing Survey—but these attempts again were conceived in terms of high-explosive war and merely made clearer the lack of serious creative thinking about nuclear war.

In the late 1940's and early 1950's, there was a partial reawakening, which led to some initial discussion of the various options open to a potential nuclear attacker. Particularly studied were the threats he might make and the appropriate tactics if threats failed. The counteroptions available to the defender were also examined. The discussion on such topics as rationality-of-irrationality, withholding tactics, various mixtures and levels of counterforce and countervalue targeting, and so on, reached a fairly high level of sophistication, but it came to an abrupt end with the development of the hydrogen bomb, which seemed so close to a "doomsday machine" that details seemed to become irrelevant. Multimegaton weapons appeared to be unusable for any rational, and even for many irrational, purposes. "War was obsolete." So once again there was a block in strategic thinking. In a widely read article, "Strategy Hits a Dead End,"[1] Bernard Brodie stated:

> One of the commonest slogans in strategic literature is the one inherited from Jomini, that "methods change but principles are unchanging." Until yesterday that thesis had much to justify it, since methods changed on the whole not too abruptly and always within

[1] *Harper's Magazine,* October, 1955.

definite limits. . . . There could therefore be a reasonable choice among methods of fighting a war or "strategies." If the time has not already arrived for saying good-bye to all that, it will inevitably come soon.

Brodie ended the article with the following exhortation:

In a world still unprepared to relinquish the use of military power, we must learn to effect that use through methods that are something other than self-destroying. The task will be bafflingly difficult at best, but it can only begin with the clear recognition that most of the military ideas and axioms of the past are now or soon will be inapplicable. The old concepts of strategy, including those of Douhet and of World War II, have come to a dead end. What we must now initiate is the comprehensive pursuit of the new ideas and procedures necessary to carry us through the next two or three dangerous decades.

Today we are beginning again the comprehensive pursuit of new ideas and procedures. We realize that, terrible as these weapons are, they exist, and therefore they may be used. In any case, their use will be threatened, and such threats are a kind of use.

Rather ironically, much of the strategic and tactical discussion that follows in this chapter would have been most relevant in the 1950's and early 1960's, when forces on both sides were vulnerable and the United States had an enormous strategic advantage. It would then have been reasonable to ask how the thermonuclear wars might be fought and terminated in such a way as to be advantageous to the United States. But the discussion of that question had just gotten started by the end of the period, and it had barely influenced policy until quite recently. Furthermore, discussion now seems again to be dying down with the growing belief that, as both sides develop relatively or absolutely invulnerable forces, strategy and tactics *really* do come to a dead end; war really is obsolete. There may be some justification for this feeling, in the sense that certain traditional tactics and strategies may become almost completely irrelevant, but it is nevertheless misleading, in part because new strategies and tactics may be invented and become more important than ever.

Thus, it is possible that we may now find a strategy or tactics competition complementing the technological competition, and partially substituting for it. In a balance-of-terror environment, technological changes may be relatively unimportant unless they upset the balance of terror or allow for new strategies or tactics. However, men are inventive, and so long as current weapons exist or can be made available, men are likely to search for new and ingenious methods of obtaining benefits from them.

In any case, even if the balance of terror becomes relatively stable, war can still occur. And particularly in a balance-of-terror situation, the difference between intelligent, sophisticated, and rational use of weapons, and stupid, thoughtless, or emotional use, would loom very large.

Regardless of whether there is a decreasing likelihood of nuclear-weapons use or greater difference between "good" and "bad" uses, good strategies and tactics will still be needed, even if the lessened probability of war makes them seem less important. And concern about escalation may still be expected to dominate or influence many peacetime relations and crises. The difference between good and bad tactical planning can thus be important in peace, particularly in preserving the peace.

The Need for Limited Objectives If Deterrence Fails, and the Consequent Central Role of "Negotiation"

The first and most important principle is likely to be that, if there is a war, neither side should attempt to force the other to unconditional surrender, not because it may not be desirable to do so (the reasons for wanting unconditional surrender seem increased in the thermonuclear war era rather than decreased), but because it is important to obtain a cease-fire before one's opponent has fired all of his weapons. One must negotiate for such a cease-fire, and, presumably, successful negotiations require some compromises even by the "winning" side. Even if one were sufficiently superior to be able to force an unconditional victory, such a victory might be prohibitively expensive.

In past wars, this principle has sometimes been learned at great human and material cost. In a jet-bomber and ballistic-missile age, events go so fast and improvisation is so difficult that to learn by experience is a very bad way to learn. If a war is to be terminated by negotiation before overwhelming damage has been done, it probably is necessary that the strategy of the war be clear to at least one of the decision-makers even before the war has started, or at least in the very early stages.

Furthermore, one cannot, as in World Wars I and II, plan to fight a war to a conclusion and then settle most of the details of the peace at a postwar conference. Since once there is a cease-fire, deterrence is likely to begin functioning again, as a two-way street, it is vital to have peace offers worked out so that the "prizes" can be delivered, practically or completely, together with the cease-fire; and it is important to start negotiations at the outset of war to coerce or persuade the opponent into an early cease-fire.

World Wars I and II were characterized by a totality of the war effort and consequent "democratization" of participation. As a result, war aims had to be such as to enlist the enthusiasm of the man in the street. This would hardly be the case in a World War III. There would probably not be any drafting, training, war mobilization, bond drives, or voting between the first and the last shots. Such a war most likely would be relatively technical, run by government authorities and technicians, with little or no attention paid to the immediate problems of support from, or the morale of, the civilian population. It would probably be fought relatively coolly, and be guided by considerations of national interest little affected by propaganda or popular emotion.

It would seem most unwise for a country that hoped to terminate such a war on a reasonably satisfactory basis to avoid consideration of these matters. If I were to pinpoint what I believe to be the single greatest lack in U.S. central war planning, it would be insufficient thought about how and under what conditions we would wish to terminate a war, and what kinds of offers and threats we could make to an enemy. Thus, calculations and map exercises on various thermonuclear war tactics often have an air of unreality: they start with the assumption of a strike by one side and a counterstrike by the other, and they possibly stop there or go through one or two more strikes. At this point, residual forces are calculated, and discussion stops. The roles of threat and counterthreat, and of these residual forces in such threats and counterthreats, at any point in the war (perhaps to induce a successful termination at that point, or to prepare for a successful termination at a later point) are rarely, if ever, discussed. There is thus no way to estimate or even seriously discuss the consequences of increasing one's own residual forces or decreasing the opponent's.

It is similarly difficult to make detailed plans for other aspects of war-fighting and postwar recuperation, since most people, including professional analysts, find it difficult to think of how a thermonuclear war could end and to visualize the subsequent transition to recuperation activities. The lack of discussion of these subjects has a circular effect, inhibiting people's abilities to visualize war as a real event with a beginning, a middle, and an end, followed then by recuperation. Therefore, in order to deal with these practical and psychological problems, it seems to me worth while to include here some comments on war termination.

In any war, each side could have one of the following basic options:

1. To surrender unconditionally.
2. To accept a conditional defeat and still ask for a cease-fire on terms under which it retains forces and obtains guarantees.
3. To try for some such inconclusive outcome as:
    a. The *status quo* as it exists at the moment.
    b. Some other compromise settlement that more or less reflects the current status of occupied and unoccupied territory or other accomplished facts, but includes some *quid pro quo* trades.
    c. The *status quo ante*.
    d. A disjunctive "solution" with little relation to current or past patterns.
4. To claim victory but be willing to accept a cease-fire with conditions and guarantees satisfactory to a defeated but still armed opponent.
5. To demand the unconditional surrender of the opponent.

In an age of increasing weapons invulnerability, the outcome of even a general war is likely to be inconclusive whether it is fought in a carefully controlled fashion with relatively little unintended collateral damage to civilians, or whether it is fought indiscriminately. I include mutual annihilation as an indecisive outcome, even if there is a technical "win" by one side or the other. Thus, the possibilities under the third option above seem to characterize the most likely forms of such an indecisive outcome.

The outcome does not, of course, have to be indecisive: one side may possess an obviously significant strategic superiority, or just have greater skill, luck, or resolution. It is also possible, if often overlooked, that unexpected tactics or weapons effects might bring a significant victory to one side or the other. These possibilities are indicated in the second and fourth options above, where one side is defeated but still has the ability to inflict great damage on the opponent. The victor, though, can threaten the defeated side with massive destruction, pointing out that such a threat is credible since, although he risks great damage, he believes that the damage will be tolerable; at the same time, he can point out that a peace treaty is possible that may reflect the huge disparity in threats beween the two sides, yet be far from unconditional. The losing side might be allowed to keep a significant deterrent force, which would increase its ability to rely on the promises of the victorious side being carried out. As far as a new surprise attack is concerned, the victorious side could risk the losing side's keeping a deterrent force since it possessed the larger deterrent force, and deterrence is likely to work again in the postwar period. There would always be a possibility of treachery by the superior side, but the situation would not be very different from a prewar situation in which deterrence could be reasonably stable even if asymmetric. The more likely difficulty is that, once the fighting has stopped, the superior side may not have a credible coercive threat.

Finally, one side may press for unconditional surrender. I have already suggested that normally this alternative should be rejected. That is, the strategy even of general war should call for some sort of limited objective. This seems incomprehensible to many experienced and informed people; they argue that if the passions of World Wars I and II forced or led us to proclaim unlimited objectives, even more will the passions of a World War III with its much greater destruction. Some argue that total victory should be sought: that the only possible justification for a World War III would be the establishment of an international authority with adequate arms control (e.g., a world empire or world government), and that it might be impossible to establish such an order if one side were allowed to retain independence of action.

The above arguments have force, yet probably are misleading, at least so far as the probable cases are concerned. First and most obviously, the immediate dangers in pressing for unconditional surrender can far outweigh the possible long-run advantages. Second, it is unlikely that there would be time for decision-makers to be much influenced by the reaction of the general public. As I have said, this kind of war is likely to be short; and the objective issues of risk and destruction are likely to outweigh emotional considerations. Finally, it is unnecessarily defeatist to believe that it would be impossible to organize the world if an opponent had any independence left; it is equally likely that as a result of the necessary compromises, such a negotiated order, whatever its form, would be more practical and viable than one that was imposed unilaterally by the victor.

What might the limited objectives be in the case of a war between the United States and the Soviet Union? In part, they would depend on how the war had started. If, for example, the Soviets launched a ground attack in Europe, our minimum objective might be to stop their advance or to get their troops removed from Western Europe. A more ambitious objective might be to ask that the East European satellite nations be freed from Soviet military domination and Soviet forces be restricted to current Soviet borders. An additional demand (that need not be part of wartime negotiations) could be that the satellites be allowed—or forced—to hold really free elections, possibly under our supervision.

Another possible objective would be the rollback of the Soviet Union itself to something like its pre–World War II borders. Or the partial disarmament of the Soviet Union might be sought, with some kind of inspection. If the U.S. felt sufficiently powerful and secure, it might demand that the Soviet Union not only be partially disarmed, but be subordinated to some kind of an international authority.

The most ambitious objective might be the total disarming and occupation of the Soviet Union. This would come very close to, or be equivalent to, an unconditional surrender, although there might be limits set to the occupation and qualifications to the terms of the final postwar settlement.

There are additional demands, which might or might not be realistic, which could supplement or complement the ones mentioned above. Thus, the elimination of the Communist Party might be sought, or free elections in the Soviet Union, or simply the removal of certain individuals.

The Soviets have a similar range of possibilities. They have an additional degree of freedom in that they can threaten, and negotiate with, various European authorities. The most successful result of Soviet negotiations might be a collapse of European resistance before or immediately at the onset of an attack. As discussed earlier (in Chapter VI), this is not wholly impossible, since many Europeans frankly believe that deterrence is supposed to deter, and that if it failed, the best tactic would be "pre-emptive surrender." There are many ways in which the Soviets might try to capitalize on this European view of their national interests, and possibly on similar attitudes in our own country. It should be a major purpose of our military policy to hold forth the possibility of less than total annihilation in any new war, or support for policies of pre-emptive (or preventive) surrender or accommodation will not only increase but will make sense.

Bargaining in a Central War

The list below summarizes some of the factors involved when a nation tries both to use or to threaten restrained or controlled nuclear attacks in an attempt to coerce an opponent into restraining and controlling his own attacks and to negotiate the termination of a war. The important points are:

1. How the war begins:
   a. The pre-attack scenario (degree of tension and mobilization).
   b. Direct cause of war (miscalculation, accident, inadvertence, or deliberate intention).
   c. Initial tactics (which of Rungs 32–34 are used).
   d. The war aims (e.g., resolution of a political conflict vs. permanently decreasing the other side's power).

206 • On Escalation

2. Each side's current and future threat against the other side's:
   a. Society (people, economic recuperation capability, environment, wealth, social system, etc.).
   b. Military forces (countervalue and counterforce capabilities).
3. The interplay of contractual, coercive, agonistic, stylistic, and familial elements:
   a. Utility of promises and disutility of threats.
   b. Credibility and reliability of threats and promises.
   c. Communications and tactics.
4. P's resolve vs. Q's resolve:
   a. Expectations, attitudes, and morale.
   b. Current emotional and objective state.
   c. Strategy, tactics, and technical capabilities.

How a war is fought and terminated will clearly depend in an important way on how and why the war began. There are at least the four broad classes of issues listed above (under 1) to be considered. The exact status of each side when the war broke out includes, of course, not only the condition of the military forces, but also the degree of immediate and future protection of the civilians. The initial tactics of the war and, to some degree, the strategy may well depend critically upon the degree of planning and deliberate intention that preceded the outbreak of war. Lastly, the war aims should influence the targeting, negotiations, and tempo of the war in a very basic way. In the past, this last-named factor in a thermonuclear war has been almost completely ignored, but much attention has been directed to it in the last two or three years.

A war that accidental and unintentional elements play a large part in triggering is probably the easiest case to consider abstractly, and it may also be the most important. If both sides' military forces have the kind of invulnerability that permits them to hold back for a significant period, even after they have been attacked, and the kind of command and control arrangements exist that enable decision-makers to recognize, perhaps by the lack of coordination of the initial attack, or perhaps by receiving a message from the other side, that the war is accidental, then there is a good possibility it may be stopped quickly. Yet, terminating such a war might still be difficult and would depend to some extent on whether the initial attack came "out of the blue" or whether it followed a period of tension. An accidental war in which an attack was launched "out of the blue" would very likely use only those strategic forces on routine alert, and probably only a portion of those. If the initial damage were small, and the attack were not highly coordinated, there might be some chance for terminating the war at a fairly low level of damage.

Of course, the side that is the victim, even though it might recognize that the opponent has miscalculated and did not wish to carry the war on, might nevertheless make a reprisal attack. The conflict might then end at this level. A war initiated by accident after a prolonged period of tension might be more difficult to terminate or at least to terminate at a fairly low level on the escalation ladder. In such a case, the initial attack might be fairly well coordinated and use a large part of the strategic forces brought up to alert status during the period of tension. And even in a war started accidentally or by miscalculation, one side or the other may decide to continue or intensify the conflict and attempt to win a decisive victory, at least in the military sense.

The problem of terminating a war in which explicit political objectives are being contested is still more difficult to consider in the abstract. In this case, there is not only the problem of war termination, but also of bargaining and negotiating. During the intrawar period, there might be extensive pauses in certain kinds of attacks in which the bargaining might take the form of verbal exchanges —of offer and counteroffer—while only very limited operations were being conducted. However, even then the bargaining and negotiation might also be punctuated by attempts to show resolve and commitment, and these would very likely involve an additional use of weapons. How each side fared would be affected not only by such factors as resolve and assurance and the estimates of these factors, but by the estimates each side had of the other side's estimates, and so on.

Let me consider the counterforce and countervalue capabilities available, since these would influence the capability and attitudes of each side in whatever post-attack bargaining and negotiation might occur. The classic cost-effectiveness analysis grades these forces by looking at the number of dollars invested in a particular system as compared with the number of targets the system would destroy in various circumstances. This analysis is important, but it should be extended to include a more complicated analysis of new types of dividends and costs.

Instead of defining effectiveness by counting the number of targets a missile force might destroy, we could now define effectiveness in terms of improvement in one's bargaining position. This improvement is measured before, during, and after an attack, and therefore includes one's ability to "manage" the Cold War conflict before the attack. The multiple "costs" that are now considered include such items as effect on the arms race, stability of the balance of terror, value of the force in solidifying an alliance or affecting the attitudes of neutrals, effects on values of being prepared to fight a war as well as deter it, and so on.

All these things are very difficult to analyze. I will concentrate here on how one measures the improvement in one's bargaining position. Let me consider briefly some of the dynamic factors that would have to go into substantive studies. In any particular instance, pre-attack or post-attack, each side has a certain threat capability. That is, it can do a certain amount of counterforce damage, a certain amount of countervalue damage, or varying combinations of these.

Furthermore, the notion of damage is complex. For example, a counterattack by the United States against the Soviet Union might have as its objective Soviet advance bases in the northern part of the U.S.S.R. so as temporarily to make it difficult or impossible for Soviet short-range medium bombers to use these bases for refueling. But the Soviet Air Force could probably regroup, improvise, use aerial refueling and otherwise recuperate its capability. Other attacks in the first strike or in subsequent waves, might hinder or permanently prevent such improvisation.

Damage to command, control, and communication is obviously a critical factor, and yet hard to evaluate. In so far as there were weapon carriers which were not destroyed in an attack (e.g., Polaris submarines, very hard missile sites, and mobile missiles), and which did not need operational coordination, the major effect of destroying or degrading command and control might be a delay of an eventual order to fire, elimination of some possible retargeting, and added opportunities to coerce or intimidate the enemy. But the threat of enemy attack would remain. Thus, the concept of damage is a dynamic rather than a static concept. It can increase or decrease over time, by deterioration or recuperation.

When it comes to countervalue damage, a nation's decision-makers and their bargaining position would be affected by the number of people killed, the amount of property destroyed, whether this property had cultural, sentimental, or other special values, and how badly the environment had been affected. Furthermore, in most circumstances, a nation's leaders would be even more concerned with the enemy threat that remained, the people who might yet be killed, and the further degradation possible in the capability to recuperate or in the speed with which this recuperation could be carried out.

Bargaining might also be affected if some portion of the country were considered to be relatively invulnerable. Decision-makers might be greatly affected by their estimate of what would be left in an extremity: what is the *ultimate* threat the enemy can pose at any particular point? There is, furthermore, a question as to the physical and political capabilities for command and control. And finally, actual bargaining would be much affected by the state of information about both sides, each side's estimate of the other side's estimate and vice versa, and estimates of the effect of attempts to bluff or otherwise to mislead.

Each side would be likely to attack the enemy's morale or resolve in addition to inflicting physical damage. In a bargaining situation, the enemy's resolution might be more vulnerable than his weapons systems. Attacks, using techniques of political warfare, against morale and resolve could be designed to frighten and deter while minimizing provocation that might lead to the "wrong" kind of emotional or irrational response. Or one might want so much to maximize apprehension that worries about provocation would be secondary.

One would not necessarily conduct negotiations with the prewar government, presuming that it survived the war. One might try to divide the enemy by attempting negotiations with military authorities or some other powerful group. Exactly what might be done would depend entirely on circumstances, but the possibility of an involuntary, or revolutionary, change or disintegration of governments involved in nuclear exchanges must be taken into account —and the possibility of influencing or exploiting these eventualities. The way in which the prewar crisis had begun and developed into a war could also make a great difference in the bargaining situation: in the process of escalation, war plans and political policies might be re-examined and changed; in any case, decision-makers would be likely to be exposed to considerable strategic education, while military leaders might have important and surprising constraints imposed on them.

All bargaining, at the upper as well as at the lower rungs of the escalation ladder, is bound to be complicated by the fact that each side's information would be different; each side might be attempting to bluff the other side, to give misleading information; there would be communication difficulties; there would be the pressure of time; there would be a play of emotions, irrationality, anger, miscalculation, bad doctrine, misapprehension, mistake, and shock. At the upper end of an escalation ladder, the effects of these are likely to be enormously intensified.

The thorough consideration of all variables in one country's threat against another is further complicated because a threat itself is a complex quantity. It is possible, for example, that if one side concentrates on the counterforce objective, its countervalue ability goes down, and vice versa. It is also clear that bargaining is affected by national resolve, which is itself a complex and dynamic concept. The contest of resolve will be affected by the expectations each side has of the outcome of the war. If one side feels that the other is very likely to back down, and the other side strongly doubts that the opponent will give ground, then the pressure on the second side to back down is indeed great.

The actual strategy, tactics, and technical capabilities expressed through communication, planning, and control are complicated, but may appear more complicated than they really are. Consider, for example, the case of two men bargaining over a house. The potential buyer's estimate of the seller's rock-bottom price can be crucial, and this is related to the seller's estimate of the buyer's estimate. This bargaining involves the buyer's estimate of the seller's estimate of the buyer's estimate, and so on. This seems complicated, but of course people actually in this situation intuitively estimate these variables and many others without much difficulty.

In a war situation, one would be interested not only in the opponent's current threat but in his future threat—in how his threat would change over time as his forces attacked and were attacked (for example, whether he had a minimum capability that could not be attacked or destroyed).

Finally, I should note that the analysis of bargaining, negotiation, and war termination can be made much more useful when the strategic and tactical capabilities of each side have been spelled out in sufficient detail to score them in different confrontations (or attacks). One can then evaluate performance in these confrontations and measure the extent to which the forces contribute to various political and military purposes and objectives.

The Problem of the "Fog of War"

As I pointed out earlier (in Chapter VII), the options of exemplary central attack are relatively simple from the points of view of administration and of command, control, and communications, whatever the political and psychological uncertainties. However, I also suggested that there has been a systematic overestimation of the importance of the so-called "fog of war"—the inevitable uncertainties, misinformation, disorganization, or even breakdown of organized units—that must be expected to influence central war operations. Clearly a total breakdown, a "fog" that made operations impossible, could happen, but I do not believe that this worst eventuality is inevitable. If proper preparations are made, it may not even be likely. One reason for this is that it may be possible to establish a certain capability to "run a war" for the first day or so with little dependence on gathering and evaluating information. One of the greatest misconceptions current in discussions of command and control is a failure to understand how well a central war might be run, at least initially, by "dead reckoning."[2]

---

[2] The term "dead reckoning" comes, of course, from navigation, where it is possible for a pilot or captain of a ship, by reading instruments internal to the ship and knowing his starting point and the environment, to deter-

The commander or decision-maker may know a good deal about how the war started and the basic conditions existing at the outbreak; or information may become available specifying these reasonably well, even though this information was not known before the war's outbreak. From this point forward, even though he is completely cut off from all information external to his own organization and forces, and perhaps even from much of that, he may still have enough of an idea of events and their timetable, at least in outline, and a sufficient judgment of what the other side is trying to accomplish (through knowledge of its logistics, forces, doctrine, and other constraints) to "play" both sides hypothetically by dead reckoning—adding and correcting with whatever information comes in. He could conceivably do reasonably well even with a minimum amount of information, and some of that confusing. One reason why it may be possible to do this is because there are many constraints on the possible modes of operation in a central war, and there is likely to be, as well, a certain simplicity and starkness about the operations.

It is clear that such a technique has serious limitations, but the point of importance here is that dead reckoning always takes place to some degree. Even in the best of situations, there will usually be some information missing or unable to be assimilated. What I am talking about really is one basic mode—perhaps *the basic mode*—of decision-making in any military headquarters. It should also be clear that decision-making by dead reckoning is even more dependent on the experience and good judgment of the decision-maker

---

mine where he is by mathematical calculation. He does this by considering the compass readings, the consumption of motor fuel, and the power that is exerted by the engines, and by knowing about winds and currents.

We should probably contrast dead reckoning with intuition, which is also a kind of dead reckoning but one that is done unconsciously and at least partly in response to subliminal stimuli. In other words, if someone makes a prediction by starting with initial conditions and looking at directions and estimating behavior, and does this reasonably explicitly (or can make it explicit with ease), we can refer to it as "dead reckoning." It is an "analytical" prediction. If he cannot make it explicit but simply depends upon his feelings, the prediction is an intuitive one. It may be wrong, a result of prejudice and bias, or it may be accurate, a consequence of the fact that the man is a very good analyst and "computer," but an unconscious one. Whether done well or badly, this type of prediction or judgment must be called "intuition."

and his staff when information is scarce than it is when late and processed information is available. Additional information that the command and control system gives may be used to improve this basic capability; clearly, it should not worsen it. The important point is that one key portion of the decision-making process can usually be defined; and the initial analysis of the command and control system, and in particular of the command post subsystem, should be carried out with a view toward both using and improving the dead-reckoning process. Lack of understanding of this aspect of the basic command and control mission often leads to attempts to do too much, or to discouragement at the magnitude of the total job. It is almost impossible to design a command and control system with a data-display capability that will enable a Martian—even an intelligent and technically well-trained, but substantively ignorant, Martian—to run a crisis. One judges, though, that many current systems are hopelessly trying to do this.

XI

Defects of the Escalation-Ladder Metaphor

I have laid much stress on the escalation-ladder metaphor, but now I want to discuss some of its defects as a model of a certain kind of international crisis. Some of these defects, of course, arise out of any view of crises from the aspect of narrow technical escalation. But the escalation ladder, like any metaphor or model, introduces additional simplifications and distortions into its study of a class of situations which are very complex in reality. Such simplification inevitably leads to gaps between real situations and the model employed to discuss them.

Discontinuities in and Importance of Distance Between Rungs

In the discussion of the escalation ladder, I treated all rungs as basically equivalent. There may have seemed an assumption that each rung was separated from the preceding and succeeding rung by the same "escalation distance." However, both the distinct quality of a rung and the distance between rungs can be blurred, particularly if a participant in the escalation wishes to blur them. Consider as an example the use of nuclear weapons to coerce an opponent by means of a spectacular show of force. In this case, it is clear that there is an almost continuous spectrum of alternatives available. They can be ranked as follows: (1) testing a large weapon for purely technical reasons almost as a part of a normal test program; (2) testing a very large weapon, or testing on a day that has particular political significance, or both; (3) testing a weapon off the coast of the antagonist so that the populace can observe it; (4) testing a weapon high in outer space near the antagonist's airspace; (5) testing lower in outer space, or directly over the opponent's country; and finally, (6) testing so low that the shock wave is heard by everybody, and perhaps a few windows are broken. Yet, despite this variety of options, from the very innocuous to the very provocative, we tend to think of a spectacular show of force as high on the escalation ladder because it would be so in most cases.

To take another example, it is possible to blur the distinction between the use and nonuse of nuclear weapons in tactical situations. One could, for example, simply increase the probability that nuclear weapons would be used by bringing them up to the front lines and decentralizing decision-making in such a way that the possibility of unauthorized or inadvertent use of nuclear weapons was increased. Or one side could use nuclear weapons that were equivalent to no more than a few tons of TNT, or even less. In such cases, it might be difficult for an opponent to know whether or not nuclear weapons had been used. At the extreme, it is hard to believe that upward escalation would be seriously considered simply because one side dropped a nuclear weapon equivalent to, say, 500 pounds of high explosives. This would be particularly true if the same side dropped 10,000 pounds of high explosives right next to it. If one could then move by degrees to larger and larger nuclear weapons, the process might become so automatic and gradual that the use of large nuclear weapons would not evoke discontinuous responses.

To the extent that the antagonists were anxious to maintain precedents, both might be very careful not to move into such twilight zones. From the viewpoint of bargaining, twilight zones may be the worst of all places in which to use nuclear weapons or other escalatory devices against which—in the optimum bargaining sense —one would prefer to maintain restraints. Indeed, the main purpose of indulging in twilight-zone behavior is less likely to be to increase bargaining strength than to break a precedent in order to make some technique more acceptable, to bring a rung on the escalation ladder lower deliberately so that it will be more usable in the future, or to gain an "unfair" tactical advantage (as in Rung 15, barely nuclear war).

Criteria for Evaluating the Position of Rungs

There are other objections to the escalation ladder as a model, as there must be to any attempt to describe a complicated sequence of acts on the international scene by a fixed linear progression. In general, even conceptually, such actions simply do not form a unique, one-dimensional array, unless both the criteria and the context are suitably limited and specified. In particular, depending on previous history and special circumstances, some rungs of the escalation ladder ought to have higher or lower positions.

I have suggested that there are different criteria for the ordering of rungs, such as degree of: (1) apparent closeness to all-out war, (2) likelihood of eruption, (3) provocation, (4) precedence-breaking, (5) committal demonstrated, (6) damage done, (7) effort, or (8) threat perceived. The correlation among these criteria can be quite low or even negative; thus, different escalation ladders could be drawn up for each criterion as well as for each context. Since I did not specify the criteria or context for the ladder used in this book, it must be looked upon as a very rough approximation to real structural relationships. Nevertheless, the structural relationships indicated, though both vague and occasionally misleading, seem valid enough to warrant display and discussion.

Dynamics of Escalation

Earlier (in Chapter II), I pointed out that the escalation ladder was particularly useful in describing and discussing the dynamics of escalation. This is certainly true as a metaphor, particularly as a propaedeutic and heuristic[1] metaphor, but much less so as a realistic model. In general, the arrangement of rungs and thresholds implicitly assumes that there is very little previous escalation history over the status of the world that exists at this writing. The thresholds are likely to be much less significant if they have already been transgressed. This is particularly likely to be true in a de-

[1] See the Preface for definitions.

escalation, when the rungs are traversed in the reverse direction. Also, many of the rungs are easier to climb down from than others, and these very important differences are not displayed in the ladder. More important, the escalation-ladder metaphor is not very good at illustrating the effects of two or more simultaneous moves. In some cases, these moves are additive and would increase the escalation enormously; in other cases, they are distinct acts that would not increase the level of escalation inordinately. The occupation of multiple rungs could also affect de-escalation. If, for example, there were local nuclear war—exemplary (Rung 21) and a formal declaration of "general" war (Rung 32), it is not clear whether the cessation of the use of nuclear weapons in the local war or the repeal of the declaration would be more de-escalatory.

The Question of Style

I have only occasionally referred to national characteristics and idiosyncrasies. At the minimum, one must recognize that if there are two opponents there are in effect two escalation ladders, with all that this means in terms of confusion and ambiguities as to where each participant believes he and his opponent are on the ladder and each side's estimates of the other's estimate. In addition, despite the rather intensive East-West dialogue on strategic matters that currently is going on, there is no certainty that the Soviet and the U.S. escalation ladders are very similar, or that the two opponents share very many understandings. I have referred several times to the Soviets' claim that they neither understand nor will accept U.S. notions of thresholds or of limited nuclear wars as they have been enunciated in current U.S. doctrine.

Whether or not we accept this particular Soviet claim, it seems plausible that the Soviet Union's military behavior in general is likely to differ extensively, in kind and degree, from the probable American style of war. Thus, Thomas C. Schelling has observed:

> I am struck with how customary it is to propose that advance warning be given to cities that are to be destroyed, so that the people can evacuate. That is going to extremes. . . . It seems to reflect a peculiar American penchant for warning rather than doing, for postponing decision, for anesthetizing the victim before striking the

blow, for risking wealth, rather than people, and for doing grand things that do not hurt rather than small things that do.[2]

Soviet doctrine is not as likely to have such concerns included in it. It is also likely to differ extensively from current "explicit" doctrine as reflected in Soviet professional literature. In part, this is true because this literature is published for public consumption, but more likely because it does not correspond to strategic realities (or, at least, so it seems to most U.S. analysts). The Soviets do not seem to have thought about these problems as intensively or systematically as they could have. Therefore, just as at times in the past we have changed our policies rather abruptly, we may find the Soviets changing theirs, too, particularly in the well-known "moment of truth." But in most of this book, I have committed the besetting sin of most U.S. analysts and have attributed to the Soviets a kind of military behavior that may in fact be appropriate only to U.S. analysts—and not at all relevant to Soviet conditions and attitudes. As part of a general Hudson Institute program, several theories of escalation are being developed that seem consistent with Soviet ideological and political assumptions and with Russian national and military traditions and conventions. These are, of course, designed primarily as theoretical tests of U.S. strategic assumptions and policies. They are not extensive formal analyses of contemporary Russian policy or military doctrine. They are exercises in strategic thought that attempt to reflect some assumptions and characteristics of Soviet thought and society in a way comparable to the way in which American strategic doctrine expresses American assumptions and rankings of value. This work is still in an early stage at the Institute, but I will comment briefly on some work done by Edmund Stillman because of its relevance to the problems considered in this chapter.

One part of this work is the construction of hypothetical "Soviet escalation ladders." (See Figure 5.) The ladder is constructed so as to be consistent with Marxist-Leninist assumptions concerning the subordination of military to political action, the primacy of political doctrine in international policy, and the general nature of

[2] In Klaus Knorr and Thornton Read (eds.), *Limited Strategic War* (New York: Frederick A. Praeger, 1962), p. 254.

FIGURE 5

A SOVIET ESCALATION LADDER

ATTACKS ON U.S. ZONE OF INTERIOR	25. Salvo 24. Restrained Population Attacks 23. City Annihilation Attacks (with Evacuation Warning) 22. Slow-Motion Property Attacks

—————————————————
—————————————————
—————————————————
—————————————————

SANCTUARY-AVOIDING NUCLEAR WAR	21. Devastation Attacks Against U.S. Allies 20. Force-Reduction Attacks Against Major U.S. Overseas Bases and Forces (e.g., Polaris Submarines, Surface Fleet) 19. Population Attacks Against U.S. Allies 18. Property Attacks Against U.S. Allies 17. Symbolic (Nonlethal but Provocative) Demonstration of Strategic Nuclear Weapons (e.g., Oceans, Space) 16. Tactical-Nuclear Central War

—————————————————
—————————————————
—————————————————
—————————————————

NONNUCLEAR CENTRAL CONFRONTATIONS	15. Conventional Central War 14. Semi-Confrontation Conventional War Involving Soviet Volunteer Forces

—————————————————
—————————————————
—————————————————
—————————————————

NONLETHAL CENTRAL CONFRONTATIONS	13. Nonlethal Act of Central Confrontation with U.S. (Berlin Blockade) 12. Symbolic Central Confrontation with U.S. (Cuba) 11. Semi-Confrontation Wars (Large)

—————————————————
—————————————————

VIOLENCE BY PROXY (SUB-LIMITED AND LIMITED WAR)	10. Semi-Confrontation Wars (Small) 9. Proxy Wars 8. Terrorist Acts Against Persons by Proxy 7. Terrorist Acts Against Property by Proxy

—————————————————
—————————————————

POLITICAL AND PSYCHOLOGICAL WARFARE	6. Vitriolic Propaganda Attacks and Diplomatic Harassment by U.S.S.R. 5. Vitriolic Propaganda Attacks and Internal Political Harassment by Proxy 4. Subversion 3. Adverse Propaganda and Diplomatic Noncooperation by U.S.S.R. 2. Adverse Propaganda and Noncooperation by Proxy (International Front or Local CP) 1. Espionage

the relationship between Communist and non-Communist societies (i.e., the existence of a historically determined and fundamental antithesis between the two forms of society). Thus, the ladder is not primarily concerned with the deterrence or control of violence by counterviolence. It is designed to cause political damage or breakdown within the enemy society or alliance. The progression of the ladder is from political warfare to violence by proxy; to nonviolent direct confrontations with the opponent; to direct confrontations that employ conventional, limited, or unattributed means of violence; to nuclear violence directed to psychological and political effect; to violence directed at the opponent's allies—and only then to nuclear attack upon the opponent nation itself. The goal of this form of escalation is the destruction of the political structure of the enemy; the separation, if possible, of his government from the population, of the "ruling classes" from the laboring and "progressive" classes or elements in the enemy society; and the demoralizing, discrediting, or overthrow of the enemy government or alliance.

I will not discuss this Soviet ladder further, but it should be clear that, as in the American case, many other ladders could be devised; this is only one example.

Objections to the Upper Rungs

In addition to the general limitations of the escalation-ladder concept, there are some specific objections that must be noted in connection with the upper rungs of the ladder. The four most significant ones, listed in increasing order of importance, are: (1) assumption of rationality; (2) failure to deal with ambiguities and uncertainties; (3) existence of acceptable alternatives; and (4) long-term instability.

The first objection is that the escalation ladder presents an excessively rational sequence of events. Can it be assumed that decision-makers will actually do this kind of thing, that they will think clearly or that they will be calm and collected? These worries are, in fact, based on an important phenomenon: in normal circumstances, as well as under stress, decision-makers may not behave in an entirely rational fashion. However, researchers who study these problems do not really assume that decision-makers are wholly rational, but rather that they are not totally irrational—which is quite different from the assumption of rationality.

There is also likely to be, at least in the American case, a premium on cool conduct, a pattern of expectations built up to influence decision-makers in times of nuclear crisis. As courageous behavior, whatever personal fears may be felt, is expected from an officer or soldier as part of his professional standard, so coolness and rationality already have been established as part of the expectations the public has of its crisis leaders in the nuclear age. There is now a widespread hostility to defiant or rashly "brave" counsels of nuclear conflict or bargaining. (See the passage from President Johnson's 1965 defense message to Congress quoted in Chapter XIII.)

This current emphasis on coolness and calculation sharply contrasts with much in the Western tradition, which has inclined to a romantic or quixotic attitude toward war. The Soviets, unlike Westerners, have almost no tradition of chivalry or of war as a romantic occupation. They are more influenced by the Byzantine tradition of a cynical and instrumental use of force, waging war so as to maximize the gains. In addition, Marxist military doctrine derives from Clausewitz, who compared war to a settlement or accounting day in which the payoff of the previous investments was calculated. Because of this tradition and caution in doctrine, it would seem that the Soviets are unlikely to behave emotionally in making crisis decisions, or even to follow a rigid, preconceived plan if it is obvious that this plan is leading to counterproductive results.

The next objection I have encountered is that escalation discussions often underestimate the effects of ambiguities and uncertainties. Consider the city-trading notion. Are any two cities equal for trading? Is a "trade" to be based on population, on wealth, or on percentage of GNP? This is a very real objection, and, in general, it is a valid one. Moreover, the ambiguity problem is actually more complicated than this example indicates. In addition to the question of what constitutes an equitable tit-for-tat exchange, there is also a question of whether or not each side understands the other's intentions in taking any particular step on the escalation ladder. For example, one side might mobilize simply to signal to the opposing side that it was tough, but the opposing side might read this move as a real intention to go to war and, therefore, be tempted to pre-empt. It might be so tempted, not because it thought that the first side would go to war in weeks, months, or years, but because it believed war would start immediately. The possibility that such misunderstandings would occur is great, and in certain circumstances this possibility might be useful in deterring escalation. For example, given the great size of the stakes in international crises, there will be a tendency for each side to act conservatively—to overestimate the resolve and rigidity of its opponent. In such cases, the pressure for compromise will increase. Moreover, the chances of deterring frivolous escalations will also increase.

The problems of communication of intent in escalating can be interestingly contrasted with the problems of diplomatic communications in the eighteenth and nineteenth centuries. In those days, there was a rather precise format for communication, which went more or less as follows:

1. His Majesty's Government is not uninterested in this problem. (There is a vague implication that the country might go to war—i.e., 0.01 probability.)
2. His Majesty's Government is interested in this problem. (There now exists 0.05 probability of recourse to war.)
3. His Majesty's Government is concerned. (0.1 probability of war.)
4. His Majesty's Government is vitally interested. (0.25 probability of war.)
5. His Majesty's Government will not be responsible for the consequences. (There is 0.5 probability of war—the statement may be regarded as an actual ultimatum.)

When such statements were made, all sides recognized that war was actually possible; such language had been followed by war in the past—there were precedents to make clear the implications of the language. The precedents today are less clear, although something of the same phenomenon may be seen in the methods modern governments may use to demonstrate concern over a given situation. That concern may be privately expressed to a newspaperman who will write of the situation, ostensibly on his own authority. Or a newspaperman may be invited to attribute concern to "official circles" or "government analysts." Or a diplomat may express "off-the-record" concern to another diplomat or to an intermediary who will convey the information to those for whom it is intended. Or an editorialist or commentator may be invited to express a strong view of the matter, again on his own authority, or with implied official information, or with indirect or direct attribution to officials. In some countries, concern may be conveyed through newspapers or writers who have semiofficial status or are "known to reflect Foreign Office views," or the unofficial or semiofficial propaganda agencies of a government may be used to publicize or influence a situation. Finally, there may be direct government representations that may increase in seriousness from a verbal communication by an embassy official to formal notes, protests, demands, and ultimatums. This hierarchy of "seriousness" in communication varies in each country, and provides not only a medium expressing government viewpoints but the opportunity to test new ideas and policy possibilities, to express opinions that may subsequently be abandoned, to intervene in situations, to deceive an opponent, or to manipulate world opinion.

Yet the imprecision of these methods in the day of nuclear deterrence and possible nuclear war prevents the meaning of given moves on the escalation ladder from being unequivocally clear. The probability of deliberate war is low, and the right precedents do not exist: no nation has taken such verbal steps and then followed through with the use of nuclear weapons.

There are other kinds of ambiguities and uncertainties. Consider this example: Assume that P has blown up a bridge on Q's territory. Q might interpret this in several ways: (1) it was simply an accidental firing; (2) P actually intended to hit something much more important, but the plan went astray; (3) it was the first missile of a large attack, but somebody did not obey firing discipline and fired early; (4) P really wanted to destroy the bridge because he was trying to degrade Q's logistics; (5) P really wanted to destroy the bridge to symbolize that he might do still more damage later.

Q's response will depend on the way in which he interprets the act. P may or may not wish Q to interpret it accurately. For example, P may intend the bombing partly as a symbol of resolve, but he may also want Q to interpret it as an indication of nervousness or irrationality. Thus P leaves it to Q to decide whether to pre-empt or to back down. In this context, it must always be remembered that one purpose of climbing the escalation ladder is often to be able to say to the opposing side: "You really don't want to escalate further because it's too dangerous; in fact, it is even dangerous to stay where we are; therefore, you'd better back down."

This brings me to the third important objection to the upper rungs of the ladder—that "there ought to be acceptable alternatives." Let me consider some alternatives to escalation. I have already noted that situations could occur in which appeasement, accommodation, or compromise might be desirable. There are many cases in history where accommodation and flexibility have not only prevented war, but have also led to *détente,* entente, and friendliness. On the other hand, there are also cases in which the exact opposite has occurred—when appeasement, by making weakness clear, has provoked the aggressive side to make greater demands. Appeasement may also cause the appeasing side eventually, in disillusionment or anger, to become unnecessarily rigid. Thus appeasement may provoke objections to further appeasement or even to compromise. This should not be surprising: extreme policies often evoke extreme reactions. However, the outcome in any specific case would depend on the nature and degree of the appeasement and the nature of the two opponents. The slogan "Appeasement never pays" is clearly a misleading summary of history, but it is an understandable legacy of the unsuccessful appeasements of Hitler and, to a lesser extent, Stalin.

The statement that "there is no alternative to peace" is also misleading. If it means anything, it must be a call for "peace at any price—no alternative to any kind of peace." However, a very undesirable peace might have consequences that were worse than those of many wars—even thermonuclear wars (if sufficiently limited). Moreover, an attempt to impose a very undesirable peace on a nation might stir reactions that would produce a major war because of popular revulsion or refusal to surrender under dishonorable conditions. A bad peace might be accepted to avoid a war that would be worse, but the choices might not always be so simple. In any case, mutual destruction cannot be avoided by slogans or even by good intentions. And as Thomas C. Schelling has pointed out[3] in considering some defects of the usual discussion of the "chicken" metaphor:

First, "chicken" is not a game that it takes two to play. It is usually a game that it takes two not to play. If you are challenged to get off the road or to show your nerve by driving dangerously, you can perfectly well choose to get off the road. But to "chicken out" early is not the same as evading the contest.

Second, what is in dispute is usually not just the momentary right of way, but everyone's expectations about how a participant will behave in the future. To yield is to signal that one can be expected to yield. To yield often or continually may communicate an acknowledgment that that is one's role. To yield readily up to some limit, and then to say "enough," may guarantee that the first show of obduracy loses the game for both sides.

Third, the particular version of the game described by Bertrand Russell is not the best analogy to international affairs. The better analogy is the version we play on the highway when we do not drive directly toward each other but try to edge each other over a little, to claim or to hog a little more of the road. It is not a case of certain death or certain safety but of degrees of risk.

Fourth, what often goes unnoticed is that "chicken" is partly a collaborative contest. If the performers die, they die together, and there may be rules of behavior that can help both players. In the clear-cut form described by Bertrand Russell it makes sense for both players to have in mind that, when and if they swerve aside, they both swerve to the right. And, the game can involve some bargaining. The two players may wish to signal to each other that they will settle for something like a tie, each pulling a little to one side if the other does, each watching to see whether the other responds. (This is a game in which it is usually better to be opposed to a good player than to a poor one!)

Finally, "chicken" is a game that is often thrust onto players.

[3] In a talk before the fifty-seventh annual meeting of the American Society of International Law, in Washington, D.C., on April 26, 1963.

How one plays it should depend on whether it arose in a deliberate challenge to a showdown, or both parties were pushed by events or bystanders into a contest. Not just schoolboys but sometimes nations are thrust into situations where both sides must show their mettle. One can't just ignore the challenge because one can't disassociate his present reaction from expectations about his future performance. But both may be able to collaborate in deflating the crisis, evading the issue, or tapering off together. The Cuban crisis had all the earmarks of a direct affront; the Hungarian uprising, to the extent that it challenged the West to show what could be expected of it in the circumstances, was not an event contrived by the Russians to assert their impunity to Western intervention.

It is not enough to say that nations should have the greatness to ignore loss of face, to disown their reputations, to turn away from a challenge. A main constraint on the use of force in the world today is the expectation of a violent response. To some extent the limits or rules on international behavior—the expectations about what may lead to violence—have evolved out of their own momentum. Preserving those rules, inhibitions, laws, or whatever you call them requires maintaining the deterrent expectations. Forgiveness has its limits if we want to preserve a set of expectations to constrain behavior, particularly in a world in which the main adversaries do not acknowledge each other's claims as rightful and in which each side may have strong defensive motives for exploiting offensive opportunities.

The last objection to the upper rungs of the ladder concerns the long-term instability of such a system of international relationships. It is argued that if nations try to settle their disputes by climbing the escalation ladder, they eventually will find that they have climbed once too often, and an eruption will occur. This seems to me less an objection to the model than a valid objection to a process that is a part of the real world.

Yet, it is true that in all our discussions of the ladder of escalation I have assumed that the ladder itself was not changed much by the impact of previous events (although I have made occasional reference to the fact that thresholds would have been weakened or strengthened, or some of the rungs possibly changed in order and significance). However, basic changes in the international order could easily occur as a result of escalation, and one of the reasons so many view the possibilities of escalation in the middle and upper rungs with disbelief is related to the reason people cannot cope realistically with the possibility of nuclear war-fighting—because they cannot conceive of the war's termination or the process of society's survival after such a war.

For example, the usual view, that it is inconceivable that two nations could exchange the destruction of cities in carefully measured reprisals and then go back to their pre-escalation relations, is perfectly reasonable. Almost certainly, as we will discuss in the chapter on de-escalation and aftermaths, the structure of world relations would have been changed as a result of such an escalation. Indeed, one's attitude toward the whole concept of bargaining at the upper rungs of the escalation ladder usually is sharply affected by whether one thinks of this bargaining as a repeated process that somehow serves as a more or less permanent substitute for central war in settling disputes that normally would produce wars, or whether one thinks of it as more likely a crisis climax that will so change the nature of the international system that new theories and attitudes will be required to discuss the same kind of problems again.

It seems reasonable to view the possibility of bargaining at the middle or upper rungs of the escalation ladder as a last resort that can be used only once, a resort preferable only to all-out nuclear war. The instability objections, then, seem objections less to the escalation ladder as a theory of international relations than to international relations themselves—an objection to the very nature of the twentieth century, in which some 120 national sovereignties are each the final judge and arbiter of their own cause, the determinant of how flexible or intransigent they wish to be in pursuing their objectives and pressing their quarrels. Certainly any simple model of such a world, in which there is large-scale access to weapons of mass destruction, is going to exhibit instabilities, and these instabilities may not be so much a fault of the model as a fault of the world.

To make the point very clear, let me consider the following far-fetched example. Assume that it were possible to manufacture a "doomsday machine" from approximately $10 worth of available materials. While it might be "unthinkable" that the world would be destroyed by such a "doomsday machine," it would also be almost inevitable. The only question would be: Is it a matter of minutes, hours, days, months, or years? About the only conceivable way of preventing such an outcome would be the imposition of a complete monopoly upon the relevant knowledge by some sort of disciplined absolutist power elite; and even then one doubts that the system would last.

If the price of the "doomsday machine" went up to a few thousand, or hundreds of thousands, of dollars, this estimate would not really be changed. There are still enough determined men in the world willing to play games of power blackmail, and enough psychopaths with access to substantial resources, to make the situation hopeless.

If, however, the cost of "doomsday machines" were several millions or tens of millions of dollars, the situation would change greatly. The number of people or organizations having access to such sums of money is presently relatively limited. But the world's prospects, while no longer measured by the hour hand of a clock, would still be very dark. The situation would improve by an order of magnitude if the cost went up by another factor of 10 to 100.

It has been estimated that "doomsday" devices could be built today for something between $10 billion and $100 billion.[4] At this price, there is a rather strong belief among many, and perhaps a reasonably well-founded one, that the technological possibility of "doomsday machines" is not likely to affect international relations directly. The lack of access to such resources by any but the largest nations, and the spectacular character of the project, make it unlikely that a "doomsday machine" would be built in advance of a crisis; and fortunately, even with a practical tension-mobilization base, such a device could not be improvised during a crisis. In addition, one conjectures that if there were ever a strong case made for preventive war, the reliable information that a potentially aggressive nation (or even a nonaggressive nation) was building such a device would constitute that case.

But one does not need the technology of the "doomsday machine" to introduce instability into international relations; current

---

[4] See *On Thermonuclear War*, p. 175.

weapons systems do that already. While the existence of modern weapons systems is not necessarily the most important or persuasive argument for dramatically reforming the international order, it seems, to me at least, to be close to a sufficient one. This may be too quick a judgment; but some of the possibilities for change are discussed in the next two chapters.

XII

De-escalation and Its Aftermath

De-escalation and Crisis Termination

Just as the study of war termination is vital to the study of war-fighting and, to a lesser but still very important extent, relevant to the deterrence of war, the study of de-escalation and its limits and of crisis termination—how to climb down and off the ladder— is vital to the management of crises and escalation. And, as with the study of war termination, the study of de-escalation and crisis termination and their aftermaths is largely neglected.

The study of de-escalation must, of course, include the study of its aftermath. The whole purpose of escalation and the risks it entails is to facilitate the bringing about of desirable aftermaths and the prevention of undesirable ones.

In de-escalation, concessions and conciliation play something of the same role that demands and coercion play in escalation. But while we can think of the process as one that combines elements of pressure, inducement, and changing expectations, and while a situation is made largely escalatory or de-escalatory by the net balance of these elements, there is no necessity for the escalatory or de-escalatory elements to be mirror images—or negatives—of each other.

Thus, while one is tempted, in studying de-escalation, to set up a de-escalation ladder, the metaphor does not seem as useful: de-escalatory moves can sometimes be described as descending the rungs of the escalation ladder, but equally often this metaphor could be misleading. In many ways, escalation is an irreversible process. Moreover, there are aspects of de-escalation that do not correspond in any way to "escalation in reverse." Thus, there are typical de-escalation gestures that do not have the simple character of a reversal of a previous escalation. This inadequacy in dealing with de-escalation is one of the defects not only of the escalation ladder but of the whole escalatory model of crises. Nevertheless, de-escalation and crisis termination are usually discussed as escalation in reverse.

De-escalation also differs from escalation in that it is harder to force a suitable response. It is not really true that it takes two to make a quarrel; only one side need be aggressive in order to generate some certainty of a quarrel. But it usually does take two to make an agreement (barring total surrender by one side). Thus, de-escalation is even more sensitive to accurate communication and shared understandings than escalation is. The opponent might have a different conception of escalation and still understand well enough the pressures being applied to him; but, typically, in order to coordinate de-escalation moves by easing pressure, both sides must have a shared understanding of what is happening. They might not have a sufficient shared understanding if one side's paradigm of the world differed in important ways from the author's.

However, if one side or the other had "de-escalation dominance," then it would not need as much or, possibly, any cooperation to de-escalate successfully, since "de-escalation dominance" consists, by definition, of being able to achieve an acceptable *status quo* post at one's unilateral choice, so that de-escalation can be undertaken without sacrificing one's wartime objectives. De-escalation dominance might also involve being in a good position to resume fighting if the other side forced further action. The latter property could also be called "re-escalation dominance" (R. Axelrod's phrase).

If one did not necessarily have escalation dominance, one might be anxious to use methods in the conflict that were most likely to result in situations allowing for unilateral de-escalation—i.e., to choose areas or techniques that provided de-escalation dominance. The Soviet Union and China often find themselves in this position.

The fact that they can successfully achieve unilateral de-escalation when necessary, largely because of their use of proxies and their established tradition or convention of provocative behavior, increases their effective ability to probe and test.

Unilateral initiatives are often suggested to facilitate de-escalation. Although such unilateral initiatives may not be reciprocated, this does not mean that they should not be tried. Such measures may relax tension to a point where it is easier to settle a dispute, or to leave it unresolved but less dangerous. Even small concessions can be significant as turning points in the escalation process. Thus, even if a move is more symbolic than meaningful in itself, its de-escalatory value may be large. Also, communications in crises might rely heavily on small moves rather than on statements at the negotiating table, since ordinary trust and faith would be strained and feeling would be high that "actions speak louder than words." A serious concern, however, might be to maintain the appearance of resolve while making conciliatory moves. For this reason, the side that was doing better might find that it should take the burden of the initial de-escalatory step.

Typical de-escalation gestures might include: a reversal of a previous escalation move, the settling of an extraneous dispute, the freeing of prisoners, conciliatory statements, the replacement of a "hard" key official by a "softer" or more flexible individual, or simply waiting for time to have its usual cooling effect.

Concessions need not be made explicitly. They may simply involve acceptance of a *fait accompli*. Nor need the matter under dispute be settled, so long as tension is decreased to the point where the dispute is no longer as high on the escalation ladder as it once was.

In general, one judges that in many situations de-escalation by several steps down the ladder would be as likely as one large step. For example, a provocation followed by a controlled reprisal might occur in such a way that, while neither side backed down completely, fear would overtake both sides and the situation de-escalate to a lower rung—to local war, for example. This possibility was also mentioned as a tactic at Rung 15 (barely nuclear war).

Approaches to De-escalation[1]

There are many aspects of or approaches to de-escalation. Thus, any of the following could be important in a typical de-escalation: (1) escape from current "costs"; (2) insurance against further escalation; (3) learning to cooperate (systems bargaining?); (4) setting precedents (more systems bargaining?); (5) war-fighting or hostile aspects; (6) an aspect of crisis management; and (7) a special kind of conflict management.

ESCAPE FROM CURRENT "COSTS": I have several times referred to escalation as a "competition in resolve." Resolve is often measured by a willingness to pay costs in pursuit of certain objectives. One side or the other might decide to de-escalate simply because it felt it had suffered enough.

It is sometimes difficult for dedicated and resolute military leaders to accept this notion. Either they are concerned about setting precedents that might encourage the enemy and demoralize their own side or, more often, they feel a moral imperative to have greater staying power. The World War I theory of the "last fifteen minutes" (in which it was asserted that the side that could hold out fifteen minutes longer would win) is still very widespread. This theory of conflict is often completely inappropriate for a high-level escalation, and may or may not be the most relevant aspect of a low-level conflict. In low-level conflicts, both sides typically have virtually unlimited resources that could be deployed into the local conflict. Both sides thus can, and usually will, insist on a compromise solution. The drain on resources is only one of many pressures for compromise. However, in a long, drawn-out conflict, the pressure to escape from current "costs" can be a central element in achieving settlement.

INSURANCE AGAINST FURTHER ESCALATION: Escalation also is referred to as a "competition in risk-taking." One side or the other might decide that it no longer was willing to endure these risks. In the nuclear age, this is likely to be the greatest factor in de-escalation. In any escalation that has reached the middle rungs, it

[1] This section is a revised and expanded discussion of some suggestions by R. Axelrod.

is almost certain that the risk of further escalation or eruption would dominate or overshadow the issues around which the conflict originally revolved, and unless the escalation itself had generated pressures toward continuance, both sides would find themselves motivated to agree to a pause or cease-fire—whether or not they could achieve this objective.

Of course, de-escalation cannot guarantee that re-escalation will not occur. In fact, case studies of postwar crises by R. Axelrod show re-escalation to be a common problem simply because one side or the other cannot resist a probing action to test if it has sold out too cheaply. In addition, de-escalation, if pursued too vigorously, could be dangerous because the opponent might conclude that one's resolve or assurance was weakening and that more pressure would yield useful results. Finally, if the de-escalation were simply to a lower level of crisis, it need not necessarily reduce further damage because extended conflict at a lower level might be as destructive as a briefer conflict at a higher level. For example, some believe that this happened in Korea after the Panmunjom talks started.

LEARNING TO COOPERATE (SYSTEMS BARGAINING?): Any crisis that reaches the upper rungs of the escalation ladder is likely to be regarded by both participants as a disaster, possibly even regardless of the political gains achieved. It is interesting to note in the Soviet escalation ladder (illustrated in the previous chapter) that the Soviets have once, and only once, in the postwar period reached Rungs 11, 12, and 13. The "nonlethal central confrontations" that occurred were not repeated. This is probably due not only to the fact that the experience was so unpleasant, but at least in part to the fact that once such a crisis is settled, the opponent is sensitive to its repetition and there is a special danger to a delayed re-escalation. Such re-escalation could prove substantially more escalatory than the original crisis, even though superficially only the same level was reached.

There is also usually some systems bargaining going on. As each side learns that the gains of these conflicts are small compared with the dangers and other costs, they are likely to be cautious about either starting or intensifying such conflicts. Khrushchev's speech of December 11, 1962 (quoted in part in Chapter IV) clearly displayed this learning process. Among other things, he said:

> Must international disputes necessarily be settled by war and not by negotiation? No, the preachment of settlement of disputes among states by means of war is madness that can only bring suffering and calamities to the peoples. It has nothing in common with the teaching of Marx and Lenin. It is tantamount to denying the value of international treaties and agreements, to denying the principle of peaceful coexistence. Sensible norms of international relations exist. And we should not undermine them but strengthen them. Vituperation does not help to settle disputed issues. . . .
>
> It is true, of course, that the nature of imperialism has not changed, but imperialism is now no longer what it used to be when it held undivided rule over the world. If it is a "paper tiger" now, those who say this know that this "paper tiger" has atomic teeth. It can put them to work; and it cannot be regarded frivolously. In relations with the imperialist states it is possible to agree to mutual compromises, but on the other hand one must possess all the means to crush aggressors if they start a war. (*Prolonged applause.*) . . .
>
> When the revolution triumphed, the first decree of the Soviet regime, drawn up by V. I. Lenin, was the decree on peace. And although the Germans then occupied quite a large part of the territory of Russia, V. I. Lenin and our whole country sought to put an end to the war and conclude a peace treaty with the Germans.
>
> A delegation headed by Trotsky, who at that time likewise called himself a Marxist, was sent to Brest to sign the treaty. But he went against the Party, provocationally wrecked the peace negotiations with the Germans, and left Brest. Vladimir Ilyich was then obliged to send Chicherin, and the peace treaty was signed. History has confirmed the correctness and geniuslike foresight of V. I. Lenin. It has shown that the path that V. I. Lenin set forth and defended in struggle against pseudorevolutionaries was the only sensible and true path. The Brest Peace was, of course, a temporary concession to German militarism.
>
> But what was the final outcome? Who surrendered to whom? The Marxist-Leninist banner now not only waves over the whole territory of the Soviet Union but has marched beyond its boundaries and has been established in other states, including the territory of the German Democratic Republic, while the German militarists who invaded our country lie in the earth. Now judge who was right. The

Leninist approach to the settlement of such a complicated problem triumphed. (*Prolonged applause.*)

It is certainly not a matter of some analogy between the Brest Peace and the settlement of the conflict in the Caribbean. The point is that each time it is necessary to take into account the specific situation and the specific conditions. A dogmatic approach, without taking sober stock of the actual situation, is harmful, since it is the source of the gravest mistakes. Marxist-Leninists should remember that there is no abstract truth; truth is always concrete.

Some dogmatists have taken to Trotskyite positions and are seeking to push the Soviet Union and other socialist countries onto the path of unleashing a world war. They would like to impose the same provocational policy that Trotsky pursued in his day. Evidently the Albanian leaders and those who are prodding them on have lost faith in the possibility of the victory of socialism without war among states, or perhaps they never understood this possibility at all but believed that Communism can be reached only through war, by destroying millions of lives. But this madness cannot attract the peoples of other countries to follow the Communist Parties. What is more, it can repel millions and millions of people from the Communist movement.

The Albanian dogmatists are disappointed that a compromise solution was reached and that the dangerous crisis on which the American imperialists embarked in the Caribbean was liquidated. They are apparently disappointed that a thermonuclear war was not unleashed and that the peoples, having avoided the dangerous crisis, are living and working in peace. And this is why they criticize our party, our government, and are pouring buckets of filth on the Soviet Union, on the Soviet people.

SETTING PRECEDENTS (MORE SYSTEMS BARGAINING?): The role of the "agreed battle" in escalation was mentioned in Chapter I. A de-escalation can be thought of as a further "agreement" that lowers the level of conflict. In this case, the agreement must often be more explicit and more shared than for the agreed battle, because, as I have argued, de-escalation usually requires the acquiescence of both sides. Because the mutual acceptance is so explicit, a de-escalation often tends to set an important precedent for any future crisis. To some extent, this can make de-escalation harder, since both sides may feel that they are settling not only the issue under dispute but setting precedents—that there is more at stake than just the issue itself.

There is a particularly important precedent that is set by the de-escalation agreement—even if it is only intended to be temporary and the basis for renewed bargaining. Such an agreement immediately takes on the character of what we might call an *ad hoc status quo,* and while its only purpose may have been to allow the de-escalation of a conflict, it is likely to become more or less permanent. As time passes, even though the agreement was regarded at the time as temporary, and even though neither side gives up hope that better terms can be won later, further bargaining is rarely successful unless the conflict is re-escalated. The temporary agreement becomes permanent.

Thus, the division of both Korea and Germany constitute "temporary" arrangements deriving from World War II. The present Israeli borders were meant to be temporary, as were the armistice line in Kashmir and the division of Vietnam. The tendency of temporary agreements to become permanent illustrates the difficulty of bargaining for political change without employing escalation.

WAR-FIGHTING OR HOSTILE ASPECTS: De-escalation is usually thought of as a "friendly" act, but it need not be so. Thus, after the Battle of France, Hitler deliberately avoided provoking the British in an attempt to decrease their willingness to continue the war. In general, de-escalation can be used to "relax" the enemy in ways that weaken him. The current *détente* has had weakening effects on both the Warsaw and NATO alliances. Indeed, neither alliance may survive for long if this de-escalation of the Cold War endures.

The pre–World War II period is especially rich in the use of de-escalation as a hostile tactic. Hitler, of course, was such a master of this technique that he caused the word "appeasement" to change from a respectable and neutral term to one that is now used only invidiously. He also succeeded in causing the de-escalatory phrases "My last demand" and "Peace in our time" to take on connotations of, respectively, total aggressiveness and defeatism.

A hostile de-escalation today could be used to mislead or force (e.g., via propaganda pressure) the enemy to lower the alert status of its aircraft or reserves, promote a less complete evacuation or an earlier return from evacuation, hinder an emergency budget request, or strengthen a "soft" faction in his government. Such study of de-escalation as a war-fighting or hostile tactic is presumably as important and legitimate an area of investigation as the more usual emphasis on conciliation and compromise.

AN ASPECT OF CRISIS MANAGEMENT: De-escalation is, of course, as much an aspect of crisis management as of escalation. Thus, one can consider de-escalation from the viewpoints of administrative arrangements, human factors, or problems in command, control, communications, etc.

A SPECIAL KIND OF CONFLICT MANAGEMENT: There has been much interest recently in the general use of de-escalatory tactics or moves as part of a systematic attempt to bring about better international relations and even to cause structural changes in the international system. A carefully hedged and limited "turning the other cheek" is argued not (or not only) out of moral or agonistic motivations but for instrumental reasons: it is put forward as a prudent or advantageous method of dealing with an opponent. This approach has been discussed under the name GRIT, an acronym for "graduated reciprocated reduction in tension." It is argued that unilateral initiatives might be used to call forth similar initiatives from the opponent and that, if pursued in a gradually "escalating" but always prudent and cautious fashion, major improvements in the relationships between two such opponents as the Soviet Union and the United States might be obtained.[1]

Aftermaths of De-escalation from the Lower Rungs

I ended the last chapter with a discussion of the instability of the current international system and suggested that escalation might play a large role in precipitating a change. However, it seems

[1] Further discussion of these measures and their rationale can be found in Charles E. Osgood, *An Alternative to War or Surrender* (Urbana, Ill.: University of Illinois Press, 1962), and Amatai Etzioni, *The Hard Way to Peace: A New Strategy* (New York: Collier Books, 1962), Chapter IV.

unlikely that escalation involving only the lower rungs of the ladder would be an effective agent of change. More likely is the possibility that such an escalation would have its aftermath restricted to one or more of the following: (1) fear and relief; (2) anger, tension, and hostility; (3) rigidity, soberness, and demoralization; (4) education for innovation; (5) preparations, reorganization, and mobilization; (6) arms race, competition, *détente,* entente, agreement, alliance, or condominium; and (7) new alignments.

The most obvious reactions to de-escalation are fear and relief: fear because the crisis could have been worse, and relief because it was not. Partly as a result of the fear generated and partly because of the actual permanent damage done—if any—during the escalation, there is likely to be a great deal of anger, tension, and hostility remaining as a legacy. The two sides have been threatening to destroy each other, and many will remember this. Some will be rigidly determined not to give in if similar issues arise again. Others will have been sobered by the approach to the brink and will move toward more prudential and moderate attitudes in future situations. Finally, there will be many who will have been demoralized and who will be desperately anxious to avoid such strains in the future at any cost. Indeed, a crisis in which thermonuclear war enters as a possibility may impose an almost unbearable strain on a decision-maker or the population and leave some very dangerous residual effects after it passes. Having passed one crisis, a decision-maker, or important segments of the public, may resolve never under any circumstances to permit such a critical situation to arise again. This reaction may occur even if the crisis has been dealt with successfully. To quote a modern British historian:

> The annals of history can rarely have afforded so remarkable an example of successful Powers terrified at their own success as that presented by Britain and France after the May 1938 crisis with Hitler's Germany. What had been generally believed to be a threat of aggression had been met, and apparently deterred, by an outstanding display of united action on the part of the European Powers concerned. This might reasonably have been accepted as a cause for satisfaction and for the further cementing of those bonds

of cooperation which had already proved salutary, at any rate as a warning. The French Government might have been expected to follow up the long-deferred Soviet proposals for consultation between the French, Russian and Czech General Staffs for the possible implementation of their common treaties, and it would not have been extraordinary if the British Government had encouraged them to do so. In any case, in view of the intensified military preparations which Germany had undertaken, and of which there was ample evidence and information to hand, it would have been only common sense for Britain and France to overhaul their own war machines.

In effect, none of these things happened. Instead Mr. Chamberlain, appalled at the chasm of war which had seemingly opened suddenly at his feet, became more and more determined that never again should he be placed in such an unhappy position, and, instead of taking practical measures to strengthen the powers at the command of those who were opposed to the potential aggressor, he set about weakening still further the position of the victim of aggression.[2]

This is only one example of this phenomenon in recent history. And while we may never again have to contend with a master of escalation like Hitler, it would be worth while to be prepared for such a rigorous test if it could be done at modest political and financial costs. The objective would be to provide the nation with some theory of more than minimal survival, as well as carefully defined options for an effective course of action in the event of a crisis. Having such planned options could well prevent a collapse of will or confidence during—or, perhaps as important in some situations, after—the crisis. For this purpose, the emergency-readiness programs and tension-mobilization bases (discussed in Chapter VIII) might serve admirably. Such capabilities could not only strengthen the will and increase the capabilities of their possessor, but could also tend to demoralize an opponent and deter continued or future provocation.

In addition to the emotional legacy of a crisis, there are likely to be actual internal and external changes. At the minimum, the

[2] John Wheeler-Bennett, *Munich: Prologue to Tragedy* (New York: Duell, Sloan and Pearce, 1963), p. 62. There has been some disagreement among historians about the degree to which Daladier and Chamberlain personally were frightened by the advents of May, 1938, but less doubt about the effect on large numbers of French and British citizens.

crisis is likely to have disclosed certain inadequacies in the government's organization or preparations, and there would be pressures to fix these. But for some there would also have been education in the need for other innovations. How intense and widespread this education might become would depend on the outcome of the crisis. In the Cuban crisis, for example, most of the West was satisfied with the outcome and therefore felt that the existing system was satisfactory. In some sense, there ensued an actual reduction in pressures to reform the system. The impetus given to such programs as arms control in the post–Cuban-crisis period was probably due less to the shock of that crisis than to the general conditions of Soviet-American *détente.* But equally typical of a possible outcome of a crisis was the organization of NATO in 1948 after the Czechoslovak *coup d'état* and the Berlin blockade; another possible outcome was exemplified after the outbreak of the Korean War, in 1950, when U.S. and European defense budgets were raised to a permanently higher plateau.

In general, the inertia that is characteristic of such large organizations as governments is greatly diminished during a crisis; almost everybody looks for ways to improve a situation, and "nonconservative" behavior (as discussed in the next chapter) becomes very possible. Unless an escalation has been spectacularly successful, the possibility of doing again in the future what has been done in the past becomes decidedly unattractive. There will be preparations for new policies, the organization and streamlining of the government machinery, possibly even mobilization (as discussed in Chapter VIII).

Perhaps most important of all, the pre-crisis relationship between the two opponents is likely to change. If tension has been increased by the crisis, there will be an arms race or at least arms competition. Or both sides may become intensely aware of the great threat presented by nuclear "chicken" and decide that the gains to be made by probing and pushing are either less plausible or less worth while than had been thought. Particularly if a previous sense of "nuclear incredulity" has been shattered, there will be a strong impulse toward *détente*—if not entente. Thus, the results of a crisis might include increased cooperation in solving international problems. It is even conceivable that a crisis could be the catalyst for an alliance between one-time enemies, or at least for a "condominium" covering some restricted area of mutual interest.

Finally, the aftermaths to be prepared for include changes in relationships other than those between the opponents. As we know from experience, serious crises can disrupt alliances or undermine morale to such an extent as to render ineffective seemingly adequate capabilities. On the other hand, the cohesiveness of alliances could also increase as a result of increases in tension. Morale, determination, and resolve can go up as well—depending on the course of events and factors of national character.

It is advisable, then, for a nation to be, as much as possible, in a position to take full advantage of all of these possibilities. If there is to be a *détente,* it can try to exploit this *détente* to achieve a more lasting structural change in the situation—perhaps some kind of arms control or real political concessions. If there is to be an arms race or arms competition, a nation should presumably be in a position to attempt to achieve "superiority" if it believes this to be necessary or desirable. The preparations made by a defense establishment can only provide a flexibility in the system that can give a President real choices in escalation, de-escalation, and their aftermaths. Some, of course, feel that to give a President choices is to give him the opportunity to choose unwisely. It still seems advisable to give him the choices.

Aftermaths of De-escalation from the Upper Rungs

De-escalation from the upper rungs would, by definition, be de-escalation from major death or destruction. It would probably involve formal cease-fires and peace treaties. As a result of both the casualties and destruction and the formal character of the de-escalation, as well as the great emotional impact of the crisis, lower-rung aftermaths would be intensified. In addition, formal cease-fires and peace treaties would make greater changes in the international system than informal cease-fires. Outside of the formally negotiated changes, there might be other drastic social and political changes, both internal and external, resulting from the bizarre and frightening events that would have taken place.

There might be "disjunctive" solutions to the conflict that had precipitated the crisis, solutions that could not or would not have occurred through evolution from the existing system, solutions that represented a sharp break with the past. Such solutions might not, of course, be desirable, and they might only lead to new troubles; but they might also represent at least a temporary resolution to the particular crisis and could provide more or less permanent improvements in the international order. Thus, in *Thinking About the Unthinkable*,[3] I discussed a scenario, which did not seem to me to be wildly implausible, in which an accidental war resulted in the creation of a world government.

[3] See pp. 145–50.

XIII

Other Aspects of Escalation and Crises

The Problems and Value of "Conservative" Behavior[1]

Whether a particular situation is or is not a crisis is, in some measure, "in the eye of the beholder." A "have" nation might perceive a situation that threatened its possessions as a crisis. A dynamic or expanding nation might look on war or violence as a tool of expansion and (rightly or wrongly) have little or no fear of the advent of some levels of crisis or even of war, considering them normal phenomena of change. Thus, revolutionary or revisionist powers may want, and be able, to provoke crises for others at times and places of their own choosing. Moreover, they may believe that they can control the level of violence in such situations, especially against passive or compromising opponents— i.e., that they will have de-escalation as well as escalation dominance. In practice, their judgment of the course of events may easily be wrong; and even if they have not misjudged their opponents, a manipulated crisis may get out of control.

It is normal that *status quo* nations will tend to be crisis-avoiding nations, while nations with more dynamic programs or needs may tend to be crisis-seeking nations. While by no means inevitable, this does seem to be a fair generalization. In addition, if crises actually occur, the first class of nations is very likely to

---

[1] I am indebted at this point to Anthony J. Wiener; see Wiener and Kahn, *Crises and Arms Control,* for more detailed discussion of this concept. The report also discusses in more detail other topics covered in this chapter.

prefer "conservative" (or prudent) behavior, while the second may be interested in designing new and ingenious ways of creating and using crises; the second group might easily take a much more creative interest in the strategy and tactics of crises.

By saying that *status quo* nations are characterized by a tendency to prefer "conservative" behavior, we mean that they have a tendency to prefer passive rather than active behavior, familiar rather than novel methods, retrenchment rather than expansion of activities and obligations, defensive rather than aggressive strategy and tactics, the maintenance of the *status quo* rather than interest-advancing goals, loss-minimizing rather than gain-maximizing options, and efforts to reduce risks and uncertainties.

Nothing is necessarily wrong with these preferences if they are expressed appropriately and flexibly. But they may be adhered to with too much rigidity, and too little awareness of their long-run inadequacies and wastefulness. Moreover, an attempt to be conservative in some respects may preclude being conservative in other respects that ought to be more important. For example, a reluctance to use unfamiliar methods may create tremendous risks; similarly, an insistence on maintaining the *status quo* may, in some situations, necessitate aggressive tactics and active behavior detrimental to one's national interest.

Various Ways of Viewing Crises and Escalation

Crises are complex phenomena, and there are a number of ways one can approach their study. One may emphasize:

1. The specific possibilities and options available in various situations.
2. Prototype scenarios for different crises.
3. The strategy and tactics of crises and escalation.
4. Crisis-management problems and techniques including human factors, administrative arrangements, and the command, control, and communications needed for different situations.
5. How crises and escalation interact with the problem of arms control and conflict management.
6. The role or use of crises as historical transition points.

I have focused in this book on the first possibility in the list, although I have briefly discussed the second and third; while occasional references have been made to the last three, they have been largely ignored. I will try now to put these into context, although treatment of them here will necessarily be not much more than superficial. All the items on the list are important, however, and have been the subjects of studies at the Hudson Institute and elsewhere.

Strategy and Tactics

Our discussion of escalation has really been a discussion of escalation and negotiation or escalation and persuasion. Thus the tactics and strategy of escalation are, to some degree, the tactics and strategy of negotiation and persuasion in a context of coercion, and the various rungs of the escalation ladder might be thought of as tactical options to be chosen when one side is trying to negotiate with and persuade another. Relevant discussions of the tactics of such negotiation and persuasion can be found in books like Schelling's *Strategy of Conflict, How Nations Negotiate* by Fred C. Iklé,[2] and my *On Thermonuclear War* (Chapters IV, V, and VI).[3]

A confusing thing about tactics and strategy in a balance-of-terror situation is the great reliance on messages, symbols, demonstrations, and even "spectacles," as opposed to acts and objective capabilities. As force becomes less usable, the more the "threat" of force, whether explicit or implicit, becomes important.

Some years ago, I said, with a certain degree of contempt, that "some . . . seem to view the deterrence of a rational enemy as almost a simple philosophical consequence of the existence of thermonuclear bombs." I recognize today that these people may have been much closer to the truth than I then thought reasonable. While the fact that façades and "charades" may be effective instru-

---

[2] New York and Evanston, Ill.: Harper & Row, Publishers, 1964.

[3] I will not discuss this general subject further here, or the specific military tactics that may be appropriate and their relationship to procurement policy and national objectives. Some discussion of these can be found in Kahn (ed.), *A Paradigm for 1965-1975 Strategic Debate* (HI-202-FR [Rev.], November 22, 1963); and in Kahn and Irwin Mann, *Techniques of Systems Analysis* (Rand Report RM1829-1, June, 1957).

mentalities of national power ought not confuse us as to the difficulties that can arise from lack of objective and usable military capabilities, this fact cannot be ignored either. Luigi Barzini has said this of war in Renaissance Italy:

> It was an elegant and practically bloodless pantomime. Highly paid condottieri, at the head of picturesque but small companies of armed men, staged the outward appearance of armed conflict, decorating the stage with beautiful props, flags, coloured tents, caparisoned horses, plumes; the action was accompanied by suitable martial music, rolls of drums, heartening songs and blood-chilling cries. They convincingly maneuvered their few men back and forth, pursued each other across vast provinces, conquered each other's fortresses. Victory was decided by secret negotiations and the offer of bribes. It was, after all, a very civilized and entertaining way of waging war.[4]

This method of "waging war" is today no longer characteristic of the weak. Even the powerful—but the deterred powerful—must indulge in such tactics. Stratagems, ruses, a "bloodless pantomime" may increasingly become the currency of international conflict, since a resort to force itself is so dangerous. One danger, of course, is that not all will agree to this civilized substitute for war. Mr. Barzini adds:

> In normal times, after all, when there are no conflicts, power and the show of power can be considered equivalent. The mere shadow of power, if convincingly projected, can be as frightening as power itself. By its use, one may gain a few years or decades of tranquility, and that is all one wants. In a crisis, of course, only real power can defend one. But crises are rare, seldom come unannounced, and can be delayed or avoided by a tactful change of policy. This is a risky game. It may last a certain length of time, perhaps a very long time, but not forever. At some point, real power destroys make-believe power and everything ends in catastrophe. But the show is better than nothing, better than the supine acceptance of immediate defeat.[5]

There are, I think, several comments that can be made about this: that performances based on façade can indeed be effective;

---

[4] *The Italians* (New York: Atheneum, 1964), p. 91.
[5] *Ibid.*, p. 83.

that making do with unnecessary façades may end up in unnecessary disasters; and that gambling with huge stakes on high odds for small gains normally results in wins, with the gambler finding his judgment vindicated, but that when there is a loss, it is a catastrophic loss.

The "show" and the reality of force today are deeply entangled with one another. In escalation, even more than in war, "the moral is to the physical as ten to one," since in any escalation-prone situation so much depends on each side's commitment to achieving specific objectives and on its estimate of the probability that its course of action would produce a confrontation, that this confrontation would lead to hostilities, and on the additional probability that such hostilities might lead to further escalation—perhaps to eruption. Each side tries to probe and estimate the other side's degree of commitment and fears. Such estimates of the "psychological" condition of the opponent in turn affect the other's estimates. Because such estimates are crucial, each opponent is likely to wish to appear more intense and reckless than it is—i.e., to appear so "blind," "drunk," or "without a steering wheel" that confrontation and escalation would be judged inevitable if the other side did not give way. All the while, each side would be hedging its position so as to be able to avoid both confrontation and escalation. Each sign of such caution in the opponent is likely to be taken as evidence that the opponent wants to avoid confrontation and fears the consequences; and this, of course, could then increase the morale and resolve of the other side.

Many have assumed that one of the reasons the Soviets put missiles into Cuba in the fall of 1962 was a feeling, derived from previous U.S. actions (including the Bay of Pigs fiasco and the person-to-person meeting of Khrushchev and Kennedy in Vienna), that the U.S. President feared a direct confrontation. (Earlier, reasoning in part from the Guatemala revolt of 1954, the Soviets and Communists generally seemed to have believed that the U.S. would not shrink from confrontations to prevent Communist domination of any Latin American country.)

If this was true, the Soviets may have expected little more than an ostensible crisis to result from their initiative in Cuba. Many now believe that the firmness and resolution of U.S. actions during and after the Cuban crisis convinced the Soviets that they could not gain from such confrontations.[6] The current *détente* is presumed to be based on this change in Soviet estimates. I have quoted Khrushchev at length (in the previous chapter) to the effect that he did indeed learn much from the Cuban confrontation.

An interesting aspect of the Cuban crisis and its display of U.S. determination was that the U.S. in fact was carefully concerned to limit, if not avoid, direct Soviet-American confrontations. Thus, when the Navy made its first interception of a Soviet ship, the oil tanker *Bucharest,* the vessel was allowed to proceed to Cuba without search because the Navy was "satisfied it carried only petroleum." Similarly, when five Soviet ships loaded with missiles were intercepted on November 10, the only verifications on which the U.S. insisted were photographs and an alongside inspection; the tarpaulins covering the missiles were not removed to verify that there were missiles under them, and there was no boarding of the Soviet ships. Throughout the crisis, the U.S. allowed the Soviets the most graceful exit possible. We decreased the intensity of the confrontation as much as possible within the limits set by the minimum requirements of the crisis.

The above is not said in criticism. While I believe that it might have been possible to establish the valuable principle that no Soviet troops would be allowed in Cuba (or any Latin American

[6] There seems to be much confusion, particularly in Europe, about the nature of the Cuban missile crisis. It was not really a thermonuclear confrontation in the sense that the Soviets feared that the U.S. would make a nuclear attack on them if they did not back down in Cuba. No such threats were made or intended. The pressure on the Soviets came from the blockade, their fear of having their nationals or equipment seized in a U.S. attack on Cuba, and, of course, the well-advertised and apparently serious military preparations being made in Florida for a conventional invasion of Cuba. It is plausible that Khrushchev made a pre-emptive accommodation to prevent the invasion.

There was, of course, fear by many in the U.S. that Khrushchev would either insist on U.S. concessions in Berlin or Turkey as part of the crisis settlement or just introduce other elements into the crisis by retaliating locally in these areas (compound escalation) for any U.S. acts in the Caribbean. Had he done either of these, he would have caused a variety of problems, not the least among them a severe strain on the NATO alliance. He was probably deterred by fear of escalation; and only in that degree can Cuba be thought of as a thermonuclear confrontation.

nation), I quite agree with the general policy that only the minimum U.S. demands be pursued in such a situation. "Thermonuclear confrontations" are too open-ended to be exploited to the limit, even if many judge that such an exploitation might be a better or even a safer strategy in the long run. The short-run risks are too intimidating to be accepted. Optimal strategies and tactics will almost always allow for graceful retreats by the opponents.

However, it is also worth noting that it was U.S. willingness to accept confrontations in the Caribbean and the implied (but rather explicit) willingness to use the lesser degrees of force represented by the troops in Florida that brought the Cuban crisis to a successful close. Today's *détente* is thus based, at least in part, on Kennedy's willingness to escalate to Rung 12, large conventional war (or actions). This willingness to go to Rung 12 may have sharply decreased the probability of a future escalation to much higher rungs.

In general, the escalation–de-escalation continuum has many resemblances to the coercive-contractual continuum in that both are spectrums of rewards and punishments that are manipulated in order to influence another's behavior. The difficulties arise from the two-sided bargaining and signaling nature of the process, with each player attempting to "look" rigid so as to persuade the other side to adapt to his system of punishments and rewards, and at the same time trying to maintain sufficient flexibility to limit his losses if the other side does not adapt. Every technique and trick that can be used to make more likely the other's adaptation may be important if the escalation grows sufficiently intense.

In discussing possible strategies and tactics for escalation it is convenient to divide the options of the ladder into these three overlapping groups: (1) upper rungs—civilian central wars, military central wars, and exemplary central attacks; (2) middle rungs—exemplary central attacks, bizarre crises, and intense crises; and (3) lower rungs—traditional crises and subcrisis maneuvering. Note that I have placed exemplary central attacks in two categories; for some purposes it belongs in the middle rungs, and for others with the upper rungs.

There is probably more emphasis on nerve, skill, and courage in the middle rungs than in the upper rungs, paradoxical as this may seem. In the middle rungs, the competition in risk-taking probably dominates all else, while at the upper rungs the symmetry or lack of symmetry of the threats, and the actual military capabilities and postures, may loom larger. In so far as we study these upper rungs, I have suggested that escalation paths to them that go through the middle rungs first be emphasized, and that these kinds of "outbreak scenarios" are very different from those now studied.

Normal diplomacy is concerned almost completely with the lower rungs. To the extent that most decision-makers worry, or even are informed, about the upper rungs, they tend to aggregate all the possibilities into two options, limited war and all-out war. Even President Johnson, in the 1964 election campaign, said that there "would" (rather than "might") be 200 million deaths in the first exchange of a nuclear war. But, as I have suggested, there are really a very large number of possibilities at these middle and upper rungs—perhaps more than at the lower rungs.

At the lower rungs, bargaining tends to de-emphasize coercion and use instead the customary language of politics. While force and violence are always in the background, they tend to be thought of as ultimate but somewhat unreal sanctions. The issues are more political than military, since the political limits and the political maneuvering are as likely to determine the outcome as narrow military considerations. In particular, bargaining at the lower rungs tends to use such themes and bargaining tactics as: "It is in your interests," "My last demand," "One of us has to be reasonable," "My partner won't let me," "Only you can reform me," "Put yourself in my place," "Let's meet halfway," "I am too X to give in," "Let's not complicate the issue," and "Let's not oversimplify the issue."

These bargaining tactics have been discussed elsewhere,[7] and I will not go into them here as the phrases themselves should be evocative enough so that readers will understand their gross characteristics. My main purpose for mentioning this list is to contrast this kind of bargaining at lower rungs with the kind of bargaining needed at the higher rungs of the ladder. These are the kinds of stark confrontations discussed in Chapters IX and X; escalation

[7] See Wiener and Kahn, *op. cit.,* pp. 255–61.

at this level of the ladder is conducted in a world of naked coercion and constitutes a test of nerve, skill, and recklessness.

The current situation of *détente* not only provides no opportunities for decision-makers or the public to experience this kind of test, it does not motivate them to consider the possibilities even hypothetically. But how important is it that decision-makers be competent at this level? In terms of current political estimates, many will argue that it is not very important at all. Even over the rest of this century, this kind of stark crisis might occur only once or twice. But such a crisis could still be the most important event of the century in its consequences—whether or not it erupted—and it might be crucial that one possessed sufficient skill to keep down the level of escalation while furthering other national interests and values. Thus, it is possible that the lack of discussion, thought, and planning for the middle and upper rungs, and resulting weaknesses in actual physical planning and preparations, could lead to disaster.

The four columns of Figure 6 are intended to illustrate four patterns of skill that current decision-makers might have at various rungs of the escalation ladder. The first column presumably corresponds to current realities, in which anything much above Rung 10 is uncharted and largely undifferentiated territory. The second column could correspond to what might happen if decision-makers tried to become equally skillful at all rungs. Presumably, because of the various costs in doing so, their skill and capability at the lower rungs would go down. There are costs that would be paid in developing competence at all levels of escalation, including: diversion of resources; rigidification of response; undermining of morale; dissipation of support; aggravation of dissension; and unpleasantness. In a Hudson Institute study previously referred to, *Crises and Arms Control,* these costs are analyzed, as well as the benefits of such preparations, including: an improvisation base for handling the unexpected; specific planning and preparations; dilution of costs through routinization; and a more creative and efficient over-all approach.

The third and fourth columns of Figure 6 are intended to illustrate the point that as a result of these benefits—particularly the last one—the costs of such planning might be greatly reduced. It is

FIGURE 6

VARYING DEGREES OF SKILL ON DIFFERENT RUNGS

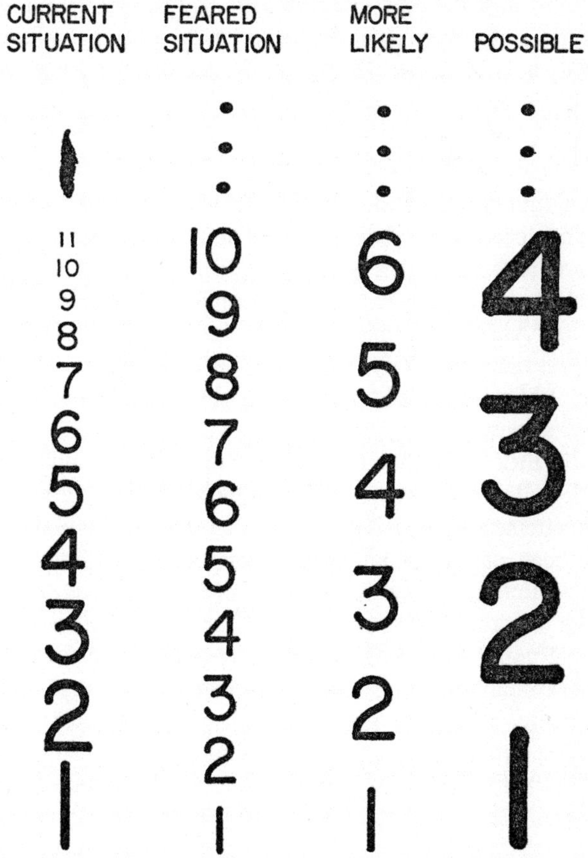

CURRENT SITUATION	FEARED SITUATION	MORE LIKELY	POSSIBLE

even conceivable, as suggested in the fourth column, that capability on the lower rungs would be improved over the current capability because of the many valuable reforms that would inevitably be carried out. Yet these problems are neglected. Principles of sound planning, well known to all, are simply not applied to such issues. In regard to the problem of the "worst" case or the bizarre situation, everyone understands that there can never be an absolute guarantee of security. Yet, worth-while preparations are often neglected because they might not work or because the situation is simply too hypothetical for action to be motivated—although the unmotivated "bureaucrat" would not really want to acknowledge the lack of preparation. It is even forgotten that a contingency program cannot properly be judged by asking, "Can we afford to risk its not working?" This is equivalent to asking for a guarantee that it will work.

The more useful criterion, and the one that would unquestionably be adopted if we had actually experienced these nuclear crises rather than considered them hypothetically, would be to ask, "Can we afford to be completely unprepared?" or "How much do we give up for a certain capability, compared with what we may gain?" or "Are the contingencies sufficiently likely, and the results useful enough, to justify the costs and disutilities of the program?" While few would argue with the assumptions implied in these questions, or dispute the likely value of crisis-management programs, little more than lip service is in fact paid to the concepts.

Damage-limitation programs are a case in point, in which there is little attempt to provide capabilities to exploit varying kinds and degrees of short- and long-term crisis "warnings." In the current situation, it may well be better to acquire additional capability for the rapid improvement of our posture than to acquire additional capability in being, yet such a criterion for evaluating and discriminating among systems or postures is almost never used.

Obviously, there are important advantages in not relying on tactics and strategies that require special actions during crises and tension, but these advantages are not decisive. And it is not likely that we will have damage-limitation programs or many crisis options in existence as part of our normal peacetime posture that give us much capability. Yet it is often valuable to be able, in escalation and crisis situations, to initiate impressive and significant actions, not only for prudential and preparatory reasons but as messages to the opponent—i.e., for bargaining purposes. Even if these purposes did not exist, I would argue that the disadvantages, while still large, were more than compensated for by the increased capability, viewed from a purely prudential point of view; the kinds of threats and situations for which emergency-readiness programs and tension-mobilization bases are designed seem significantly more likely than any surprise attack. And from the viewpoint of deterring crises and tension, emergency-readiness and tension-mobilization programs could be as crucial as military capabilities in being.

But would there be time for a useful program to be carried out? Our current posture is probably far from optimal for doing so. For these reasons, explicit plans and preparation for either emergency readiness or tension mobilization would be required to achieve the best results from our inherent capabilities.

Many or most U.S. analysts and policy-makers would agree with this. Nevertheless, in practice, the implications have been largely ignored. Planning and policy-making continue to be preoccupied with scenarios that emphasize the two extremes of a Soviet surprise attack on the United States and a mere ostensible crisis. These deserve attention, but so do the great variety of other crises that could produce both the credible threat or the actuality of limited nuclear attacks. Scenarios in which emergency-readiness and tension-mobilization programs would play central roles should probably be the "design cases" for both current posture planning and contexts for the study of tactics. Large-scale surprise attack against civilians should be thought of as an off-design, though a not-to-be-ignored contingency; and, from the military point of view at least, practically anything will handle ostensible crises satisfactorily so long as escalation is not too probable.

Having this kind of tactical flexibility could be of extreme importance in regulating Soviet behavior. Thus, while there are many reasons why the Soviets do not seek to carry out their millenarian program by rapid military action or intense nuclear blackmail, one important one may be due not only to fear of U.S. military confrontation and escalation but also to the probability—as happened in Korea—that the U.S. and its allies would greatly increase both their military strength and their resolve at the onset of provocations, and that they would improve over time their general military advantage over the U.S.S.R.

Crisis-Management Problems

Each rung of escalation is important in itself as an alternative or possibility, and each must be considered in the context of what may have preceded it and what may follow it. Because each tactic must be considered in a broad context, quite detailed decisions must often be made at the national level. This goes counter to an American military tradition of giving the commander on the spot the utmost flexibility and responsibility. Under current conditions, though, detailed and accurate knowledge of conditions at the scene of action may often be far less important than an informed understanding of broad national and international issues. However, to the extent that decision-making is hampered because the upper-level decision-makers lack authority, decisions are likely not to be made at all—or, more accurately, are likely to be made by default.

In this book, I have tended to de-emphasize these extremely important problems of crisis management, of administration and command, control, and communications. There has been much interest in them in recent years, but much remains to be done. Indeed this is one of the areas in which better preparation and skill are most urgently needed. I fear, though, that the 1962 Cuban missile crisis and the recent crisis in the Bay of Tonkin in the summer of 1964 may have given some government policy-makers and their staffs a greater sense of skill and capability in command and control than is completely justified, even if some feeling of increased "technical" competence is not completely misleading. There have been important crisis-management improvements made in recent years, but these two particular crises were not adequate tests of current capabilities since they were relatively simple from the command-and-control and decision-making points of view. It is still possible that a complex crisis (as described earlier, in Chapter IV), in which many things happened at the same time, could overload the system.

Let me list some of the operational requirements for command and control during a crisis. A system adequate to deal with crises should be able to perform the following functions:

I. Prepare for crises by:
   A. Gathering data.
      1. *Know whom and how to ask for information.*
      2. Determine allocation of effort in gathering information.

     3. Gather and accept information.
     4. Process it.
     5. Store it in a retrievable condition.
     6. Request more information and cross-check information already obtained.

  B. Disseminating data.
     1. Display relevant data.
     2. Distribute timely information to proper recipients.
     3. Answer questions.
     4. Perform other "library"-type activities.

  C. Developing and using evaluation indicators.
     1. Preliminary decisions.
     2. Warning-and-reaction (a unified concept).
     3. Immediate coordination.

II. Assist decision-making during crises in:
  A. Administration.
     1. *Know whom and how to ask for information.*
     2. Provide for emergency teams.
     3. Provide "battle stations."
     4. Coordinate internal and external information and activities.
     5. Facilitate special conferences and consultation.

  B. Planning.
     1. Update or devise alternative emergency plans.
     2. Make preliminary evaluations and collect comments.
     3. Same for contingency plans.
     4. Cover as much of the peacetime planning cycle on both emergency and contingency plans as seems desirable.
     5. Help decision-makers choose emergency and contingency plans.

  C. Execution.
     1. Monitor activities.
     2. Provide continuous evaluation and prognostication.
     3. Make creative suggestions.
     4. Aid bargaining and communication with opponent.

This may give the reader a notion of what the future man-machine combinations now being designed and installed in the various command-and-control systems must be able to do, and what the human staffs and decision-makers are attempting to cope with. All these functions are, of course, performed by any decision-maker no matter how large or small his staff, but when we consider the same functions at the government level each item on the list becomes separately a major piece of equipment or a sizable activity. In a sense, it is a major purpose of current command-and-control efforts to facilitate the "routinization"—paradoxical as it may seem—of the various aspects of crisis management.

Despite the current *détente* and the hopes that are entertained for decreasing the role of force in world affairs, it seems likely that for the foreseeable future we will confront a series of crises in which command-and-control systems may be strained. The most important response is not the obvious one of increased use of data-processing and data-display equipment—which can sometimes even be counterproductive—but of intellectual preparedness. Both leaders and followers (but presumably leaders before followers) must look and plan ahead for a range of contingencies. They must expect crises as such, and have some ideas about managing them in the national and/or world interest. Then, and only then, can it be possible to handle technical details. This means that a significant group, at least including the top echelons of decision-makers, military planners, political leaders, and some scholars, analysts, reporters, and interpreters of news and events must concern themselves thoughtfully with medium- and long-range future possibilities and the role of crisis as an agent of change.

It is not that there is not great interest in and acceptance of these concepts in the U.S. Indeed, President Johnson said in his defense message to the 89th Congress:

> Our military forces must be so organized and directed that they can be used in a *measured, controlled, and deliberate way* as a versatile instrument to support our foreign policy. [Italics added.]
>
> Military and civilian leaders alike are unanimous in their conviction that our armed might is and always must be so controlled as to permit measured response in whatever crises may confront us.

We have made dramatic improvements in our ability to communicate with and command our forces. We have established a national military command system, with the most advanced electronic and communications equipment, to gather and present the military information necessary to top-level management of crises and to assure the continuity of control through all levels of command. Its survival under attack is insured by a system of airborne, shipborne and other command posts, and a variety of alternative protected communications.

We have developed and procured the post-attack command control system of the Strategic Air Command, to assure continued control of our strategic forces following a nuclear attack.[8]

Despite the unanimity of which the President spoke, it is not likely, unless there is a vigorous program, that there will be adequate preparations.

Several aspects of our experience with the 1962 Cuban crisis suggest how useful a study of crises can be when a real one comes along. It is clear that the exact action we took in response to the particularly Soviet action could not have been preplanned; it depended on the special circumstances of a major shipment of "offensive weapons" being in transit. This is probably typical of most crises; the particular tactics to be used are likely to depend on details of the particular circumstances, and it will not be possible to determine them in advance.

Secondly, it is important to note that our actual decision evolved over several days. President Kennedy subsequently asserted that if the decision had had to be made much more quickly, it would have been a different and probably a less adroit one. It follows that one advantage to be sought from studies and simulation of hypothetical crises is that they may enable us to make an at least equally sophisticated decision even in a crisis in which we have less time to act. In support of this hope, I would observe that, although our actual response could not have been planned in advance, it was an almost perfect example of "principles" that are basic enough to be developed in crisis studies. One would not be surprised to find an analogous action—one that had basically the

[8] *The New York Times*, January 19, 1965, p. 16.

same elements—used in crisis games or crisis scenarios developed at high levels in advance of the Cuban crisis.

In improving intellectual preparedness, the first and most important problem is to escape the inertia that tends to hold us captive to obsolete notions. There are a number of ways to gain a grasp of alternatives, possibilities, and probabilities, ranging from the use of scenarios and gaming exercises and the study of historical examples, to the more usual scholarly and policy-research techniques. Yet, no busy person is likely to spend his time in such activities unless he is first convinced that much of what he knows or thinks he knows is probably outmoded and untrue, and that what he might learn today is almost certain to become obsolete in a short time. This is an uncomfortable notion because it means that one's education has to be continuous just to keep from falling too far behind to have a relevant opinion, let alone make an intelligent decision. It is also disturbing because one cannot allow oneself the luxury of many areas of certainty.

Once the need for unending and even accelerated education is recognized, the means for organizing it systematically can be considered. Unfortunately, the people who most need to make room for it in their calendars have the least time. Yet, at least at the middle and lower echelons of government, personnel could be continually involved in systematic training, which would result in better information and proposals being sent up to higher echelons.

Conflict Management, Crises, Escalation, and Arms Control

Most people will accept without argument the fact that there will always be conflict. It is as inevitable as death and taxes. But conflicts need not inevitably lead to the kind of crises and escalations that lie on the rungs of the ladder I have discussed in this book. It is presumably a major objective of arms control to prevent conflicts from creating the kinds of crises in which the options on the escalation ladder would become important, and if escalations did occur to limit the options available and the damage that could occur if the available options were used. One important aspect of escalation control and crisis management, then, is simply conflict management.

Crisis and escalation also have an important effect on arms control. A tense crisis or escalation is quite likely to accelerate the tempo of the arms race in many ways. Indeed, as I have suggested (in Chapter VIII), the U.S. should have available emergency-readiness programs and tension-mobilization bases to facilitate its capability to react in this way to a tense crisis. In examining any particular arms-control measure, one should inquire systematically into its interrelations with crises, such as the stability of the measure and its potentialities for crisis situations. We should examine the ways in which arms control might emerge from crises and, in general, the kinds of arms-control measures that might improve our abilities to handle crises and improve the stability of the international system.

Probably the most important kind of arms control that exists today is a great body of more or less shared conventions and expectations. Since 1945, the two major actors in international affairs have observed certain conventions or "rules" that serve their interests and individual security, and limit their conflict. (See, for example, President Kennedy's remarks quoted in Chapter IV.) These conventions, in so far as they have affected the employment of force, derived from the dangers of nuclear war and the realities of conventional power in the several areas of conflict and rivalry. They are in part a typical example of systems bargaining—without such rules or shared understandings and expectations the Soviet-American competition could have become intolerably dangerous. In part they have endured because there appeared to be no net advantages to be gained by their violation.

The conventions that have come to exist have included the following major restraints.[9] With the exception of the exemplary attack on North Vietnam in August, 1964, the United States has refrained from overt interventions within the areas militarily held by the Communist bloc at the end of World War II (and, as in China and North Vietnam, in areas that became part of the Communist bloc as a result of disorder created during World War II and left unresolved in 1945). The force of this "rule" of restraint

---

[9] The following remarks are largely taken from a Hudson Institute study by William Pfaff.

was evident in the American failure to intervene to prevent the consolidation of Communist power in Czechoslovakia in 1948, and in its reluctance to exploit the events in Poland and Hungary in 1956. The Soviet Union has been even more restrained in the warlike use of its conventional forces and has refrained from overt interventions beyond the line of Soviet military control (even, as in Finland, Austria, and West Berlin, when it could make some legal claim to a right to intervention and when, as in Finland in 1945–46, it faced no blocking Western power).

There has been no necessary symmetry to the conventions; in part they have reflected the realities of power—the assumed capacity for escalation dominance that existed in each area of conflict. And the U.S.S.R. has employed tactics the U.S. has avoided. Some have described this situation as one of a Soviet-defined "peace zone" where Western intervention is barred, and a "war zone" in which the Soviet Union presses its attack against established Western interests. This, however, is a conception which, while it expresses a partial truth, gives rather too much credit to Soviet capabilities and too little to the limitations and power inhibitions within which the U.S.S.R. must operate. The U.S.S.R. sponsors foreign Communist movements professing revolution, and it has extensive subversive operations, but with the partial exception of Cuba it has invariably refrained from overt Soviet national or military commitments to revolutionary movements or uprisings in states noncontiguous to the Soviet bloc. And a Western right to employ direct military intervention to deal with events outside the Soviet bloc has never met more than verbal or diplomatic objections from the U.S.S.R.: hence Guatemala, Suez, the Lebanon landings, the Thailand landings of 1962, the French and American involvements in Vietnam, British actions in Malaya and elsewhere, America's two Cuban interventions—all of them acquiesced in by the U.S.S.R.

The U.S.S.R. has also tolerated hostile bases on its borders with no action of escalation or retaliation, while it has—although reluctantly—accepted the fact that Soviet missile power was physically confined to the Eurasian Communist bloc and international waters.

These conventions of international conflict have been possible because of the "conservative" behavior of the existing great powers; and conservative behavior has, as we have argued, in part reflected the facts of power and risks of escalation. In the world we foresee, some degrees of nuclear parity will exist among the two or three great powers, and effective minimum deterrence may exist among several other states. This would appear to tend to block off the topmost rungs of the escalation ladder. The highest reaches of military power available to the great states would—as useful power in the traditional sense—be to some degree negated. That is to say, the very sophisticated instruments of force actually or potentially available only to them or, in the next decade or so, available to them and possibly to a European power or power grouping, would normally be restricted to an even narrower range of useful applications than now seems the case.

But the need for such use might decrease even further since the major nations might also experience a lessening of their commitments. States that had depended upon the Soviet Union and the U.S. would act independently; areas of the two great nations' commitment today—in Europe and in Asia—would be pre-empted by these new actors. The alliances of the 1950's, no longer responding to the needs and interests of the new international structure, are likely to lapse. The United States and Russia might continue to have interests in the areas pre-empted by the new powers—as the United States would obviously continue to have a vital interest that Western Europe remained free of Soviet control. But the two great states would no longer enjoy the capacity to influence or control events in these areas that they do today. This is likely to create both frustrating and potentially dangerous situations for them, since the several powers—new and old—with interests in an area would not have the same interests or the same perceptions of interest.

The combination of tendencies that would negate the usefulness of the largest means of force—an apparent rise in the nuclear threshold—and tendencies to reduce the great states' power and commitments, while new political actors arose with divergent perceptions of interest, could also mean an increase in the situations in which conventions would be unknown, misunderstood, or not yet established. A rise in the incidence of low-level violence and an increased activity on the nonnuclear levels of the escalation ladder would, then, appear quite possible. The *occasions* of conflict might then increase significantly, although this is by no means inevitable.

Some tentative appraisals may be suggested. The political demands of this world would be for a closer definition of national interests and political commitments—and thus of military commitments. Conflicts would no longer be evaluated in terms of a bipolar world and Cold War competition. There would be some need consciously to define and to attempt to assert new conventions governing violence and to replace those which would have been destroyed by events. And these new conventions would have to address themselves to the new realities of power.

There would be conflict, but the possibility of escalation to the middle and upper rungs would set the context for this conflict rather than resolve it. To a first approximation, strategic and nuclear weapons systems would tend merely to negate each other's offensive capability while investing any tense crisis with an enormous potential for disaster, thereby increasing the pressure for "conservative" behavior and reducing the willingness of cautious nations to accept risks of eruptions. However, an investigation of the nuances of the balance of terror might disclose that various asymmetries might have a significant—or even a dominating—influence in special cases—a subject which, by and large, remains to be investigated.

European Defense Policy—A Suggestion for a Proportionate Nuclear Reprisal Force

Any reader of this book interested enough to persevere this far is likely to be more than familiar with the argument over the credibility of the U.S. deterrent as a protection for Europe. He will certainly be aware of the spectacular challenge that President de Gaulle has made to the reliability of this deterrent. As long ago as November, 1955, De Gaulle asked:

> Who can say that if, in the future, the political background having changed completely—that is something that has already happened

on earth—the two powers having the nuclear monopoly will not agree to divide the world?

Who can say that, if the occasion arises, the two, while each deciding not to launch its missiles at the main enemy so that it should itself be spared, will not crush the others? It is possible to imagine that on some awful day Western Europe should be wiped out from Moscow and Central Europe from Washington. And who can even say that the two rivals, after I know not what political and social upheaval, will not unite?

More recently (January 14, 1963), he said:

In these conditions, no one in the world—particularly, no one in America—can say if, where, when, how, and to what extent the American nuclear weapons would be employed to defend Europe. . . . In 1945 two bombs, then elementary, led Japan, who was not able to answer back, to capitulate. I do not want to evoke here the possibilities in which Europe could suffer nuclear actions that would be localized, but whose political and psychological consequences would be immense, unless there is a certainty that retaliation, to that extent, would be immediately unleashed.

Thus De Gaulle argues that even if the United States were willing today to live up to its guarantee to Europe, despite the fact that it might entail destruction or even national annihilation, this surely could not reliably be our long-term policy. Indeed, it would hardly be astonishing if some future President of the United States were to conclude that no foreign obligation really called for the United States to risk committing suicide. In any case, one could hardly imagine a European nation committing suicide for the sake of the United States (see the previous discussion of pre-emptive and preventive surrender, in Chapter VI); and thus, by mirror-imaging, Europeans come to doubt our resolve as well. One judges that our European allies are to be pardoned if they believe that the U.S. policy itself may eventually include some degree of pre-emptive or preventive accommodation. The American sense of responsibility toward allies sometimes makes us unwilling to look at objective possibilities and the need for programs that can substitute for sheer resolve.

It is not that the problem of the deterrent's credibility is currently urgent. Given the current *détente* and the disarray in the Warsaw Pact, it seems likely that, barring an unexpected and unintended crisis (e.g., our Chapter I scenario), any kind of European defense system would work reasonably satisfactorily for the rest of the 1960's. The problem, as De Gaulle has said, is that "the future lasts a long time." It seems important to create a European defense policy that is consistent with the changes to be anticipated in the world and with a reasonable arms-control policy—in particular, with the nuclear consensus suggested in Chapter VI. Clearly, no defense system would be completely satisfactory.

I would like to propose here a European Strategic Defense Community (ESDC) based on a tactical doctrine that could be called "proportionate nuclear reprisal." The following scheme seems to meet some of the objections that are usually raised. The general— or headquarters—in charge of the armed forces of the European Strategic Defense Community might be given standing orders (i.e., a firing doctrine) to reply to any nuclear attacks on the Community with a tit-for-tat response, at some fixed number of hours later, against the aggressor. The announced doctrine need not be precise as to what the commanding general's instructions are. In particular, he might actually be given instructions to underescalate rather than to match the provocation exactly so that there should be little or no question of an upward spiral of escalation arising out of simple ambiguities or misunderstandings of what constituted equivalence. The slight possible decrease in deterrence would likely be more than made up for by the increase in stability. There would, of course, need to be some method of overriding the commander-in-chief's standing orders. This could be done by having a committee to counter the orders if it so decided by a preassigned majority—say, two-thirds or three-fourths. But unless such a group agreed by such a voting rule and by the deadline either to cancel the retaliation or extend the time, the general would proceed.

Special arrangements could be made to make the command and control quite reliable. For example, one could add a deterrent against attacks on command and control by making the system to some degree "fail-dangerous." That is, if the forces of the European Strategic Defense Community were to receive positive affirmation that a very large-scale attack against command and control had occurred, they would then have orders to fire a much larger salvo, perhaps a spasm attack, at the aggressor. One would then have made it both hard to destroy the command-and-control system and unproductive to try. While many details remain to be discussed, I would judge that with proper design and deployment and such a targeting doctrine, one could probably solve most if not all the command-and-control, vulnerability, and credibility problems of an ESDC.

In addition, it is plausible that the member governments of the Defense Community could agree ahead of time to such a doctrine. Compared with any other committal policy, this doctrine is relatively defensive and prudent, and seems otherwise acceptable—in part because the possibility of use would seem so remote, at least in normal times, when tensions were low.

Provisions might also be made to the effect that any country could, if it wished, withdraw its forces from the Defense Community, but only on sufficient notice so that such withdrawal would not weaken the basic defense or otherwise cause a serious deterioration of the Community's position during an intense crisis.

There are, of course, many other ways in which a nuclear force might be used by a single European state or by a joint Defense Community. I merely want to point out briefly that possibilities do exist that have not been fully articulated by those who discuss these problems, and that such a community could come about in stages. Of course the particular device being suggested is something of a "gimmick," but it could play the same role in enhancing the political and technical feasibility of an ESDC that another gimmick, the bicameral legislature, played in forming the United States. Because I wanted to illustrate the role that gimmicks and ingenuity could play rather than seriously to advocate specific policy recommendations, I have not discussed such basic problems as the role such an ESDC could play in defense against conventional attacks, relations with NATO, and in the European Economic Community, Western European Union, a possible European Political Community, and so on.

Even without settling such questions, one is demanding a great deal of explicit policy-making from any country—much less an alliance—that it create as a unit a carefully articulated, systematic policy in such a hypothetical, emotional and politically sensitive area as the control and use of nuclear weapons. It seems more likely that a young nuclear power would merely adopt a kind of muddling-through policy, according to which it might or might not care very much how nuclear weapons might actually be used; it might even seek to avoid a systematic debate on the question since it might believe—perhaps incorrectly—that so far as deterrence was at issue, ambiguity paid. Or a nuclear power might simply procure weapons for objectives that in some sense had little to do directly with immediate or even possible uses.

Thus policy-makers might not feel under pressure to explicate awkward and controversial decisions and doctrine. They might simply argue, or feel, that if they got into a tight situation the government could invent a tactic as necessary. This last policy should not be derided: almost all the seemingly sophisticated and esoteric tactics discussed by analysts today are not really as sophisticated or esoteric as usually believed. If a country has a basic nuclear capability, it is almost certain to invent an appropriate tactic under pressure of specific necessity (a much simpler thing than to attempt to think through—in an atmosphere of "nuclear incredulity"—a large number of hypothetical situations, even if each one separately is simple). At least, it is true that players in games—and fiction writers—regularly come up with such inventions without much training or "education." The nuclear power might also possess the capability of improvising whatever necessary special equipment or command and control its last-minute plans may need, but this is not so certain. This is always one of the main arguments for discussing possible crises ahead of time—simply to be able to "plan" the muddling-through, to build-in the necessary flexibility. Muddling-through policies need not be blind: they can be thoughtful, and it is possible that a European nuclear power might follow such a planned muddling-through policy in a thoughtful and responsible fashion.

The most likely plan, of course, is that a country would declare a committal policy—to the effect that if the nation were attacked or the nation's vital interests threatened, "whatever nuclear force necessary would be used." This policy tends to be relatively incredible; but it is possibly credible enough for deterrence in a world of *détente*. It is possible that a country could or would lock itself in, either psychologically or physically, so that such a committal policy would in fact work—even if it were not quite credible.

The efficacy of such proportional deterrence can be made even more persuasive if one notes that if there were a war between the two superpowers (the United States and the U.S.S.R.) and one of them won, the victor would, in effect and in the short run at least, have conquered the world. No such result could be expected of a war between a superpower and an ordinary power. If victorious, the superpower would still have to face the other superpower (or perhaps the Chinese or a resurgent Europe). Therefore, whatever damage was suffered in the war might be compounded by the new risks to be run in the postwar world. This concept is quite similar to the "risk theory" developed by Admiral Tirpitz before World War I, in which he argued that Germany did not need a large enough navy to *beat* the British, only a large enough navy to guarantee seriously damaging the British fleet, so that surviving British forces would not be able to deal with the second largest navy—the French. (The British handled the problem, be it noted, by forming an entente with the French. One of the difficulties rising nuclear powers have is that, if they use their nuclear power too aggressively, they may face a similar solution. To some extent, the current test ban is both a step toward such an entente and a warning of the possibility.)

How Will Escalation Be Handled in the Twenty-first Century?

The thirty-five years between now and the year 2000 seem to be a long enough period to allow, or make likely, some large changes in both current alignments and the international order generally. An early attitude common among many, particularly technologists —that drastic changes in the international order of the either/or type were inevitable[10]—is now no longer so widely or strongly held. On the other hand, many conservative individuals in both Europe and the United States are now more willing to consider

[10] Their basic attitude was that at the current rates of development, just ordinary technology might be almost as destabilizing as the $10 "doomsday machine" (discussed in Chapter XI).

the possibility of important changes. It is difficult to decide among the various possibilities, but it is clear that a very large range should be considered. Some of the possibilities might be:

I. The *status quo* is continued with minor modifications. While the practice of nations will be marked by many of the limitations on war and much of the communal decision-making described in II (and perhaps III) below, in essence each nation remains sovereign judge of the justice and practicality of its cause and of the methods and the intensity with which it chooses to forward its interests.

II. While international relations continue to be based on national sovereignty, strong restraints on the use of violence are developed, and the all-out war system essentially withers away. In particular, the use of weapons of mass destruction is felt to be, and in practice is, effectively and reliably abolished.

A. Warfare is continued but:
   1. A careful, "instrumental" style of warfare is adopted by the great powers. Combatants pursue limited goals and are restrained by calculations of self-interest and fear of violating important thresholds.
   2. Or warfare is limited by "agonistic" restrictions—normative considerations of chivalry, honor, religion, ethics, or sacred customs.

B. Limited contests are widely substituted for large-scale violence. Thus, great-power competition is primarily expressed in:
   1. The power struggles of factions within third countries. Bullets and external support are used as "ballots," but major powers can exert only limited leverage, and will accept a *fait accompli.*
   2. "Potlatch" wars. Competitions in conspicuous consumption of resources or spectacular successes in such areas as space, economic growth, and "showy" military systems are employed to gain prestige and influence events, or at least to "sublimate aggressions."

3. Very limited contests—personal or diplomatic duels, arbitration conferences, foreign-aid competitions, U.N. maneuvering, publicity battles, and so on.

C. Or, presumably most desirable of all, a rule of law is widely accepted. Most issues have reached formal or *de facto* settlement, and most nations are willing to respect these settlements. Remaining disputes are not so intense that they cannot be handled legalistically by arbitration, international law, or the U.N.

III. Or there may be a very basic change in the current system. Some possibilities are:

A. A relatively stable bloc system in which there might be a small number (perhaps between three and ten) of stable regional or continental blocs that among them virtually cover the world. They could deal with confidence among themselves by restrained and ritualistic techniques. These restraints and rituals are not subject to great strain because the stability of the blocs and the lack of disputed areas remove many or most grounds for major conflict.

B. Limited "condominiums," most likely between the U.S. and the U.S.S.R., though other powers are not excluded, in which the major portion or all of the world finds its freedom to pursue violence or develop modern weapons systems limited by restraints imposed by the joint control, which would probably be limited to specific issues having to do with the control of war. Because fear of the arms race is so widespread, at the outset there might be substantial voluntary acceptance by the rest of the world of such a condominium, especially if it did not seem to change the present order very much, beyond forcing control of nuclear weapons. In the long run, such cooperation is likely not only to transform the basic relationships between the members of the condominium but also to change the relationships of all states in ways as yet not understood.

C. A system of community sanctions in which nations use modern technologies (perhaps anonymous or official missiles launched by private or internationalized Polaris submarines) to punish infractions of the peace or moral standards. This might be done by lynch law or an international vigilante committee, or it might be more formally organized as below.

D. A concert of the large or small powers that has great influence in the world. The original conception of the United Nations was, in effect, such a concert of large powers (the intended role of the Security Council). And in some ways it is developing into something very close to a concert of small powers (the current role of the General Assembly).

E. What might be called a "classical world government" (i.e., some kind of federal system embracing at least all major countries with common citizenship, but not necessarily all having the same privileges and rights), all having direct relations between the citizens and the central government, and federal retention of a near monopoly in military power. There are, of course, many variations on such a model, and this is a situation in which even "minor" variations may be of decisive importance. (Systematic studies of this possibility are important not only because they may have direct practical significance for foreign-policy proposals, but also because conceptions about the nature of such systems are very influential, in many quarters, on both policy formulation and the public debate.)

F. Creation of one or more "world empires." The 6,000 years of recorded history provide many examples of "world empires," but no stable, federal system for governing the known world. Such a world empire would probably develop eventually into some sort of legitimatized community, more or less accepted by all its citizens. But, initially at least, it would be imposed by one or a small group of nationalities on other nationalities. As always, its creation would most likely involve war and violence.

G. Controlled or uncontrolled disarmament, with the international order otherwise largely unchanged, at least initially. There is today much official, scholarly, and popular discussion of this possibility, so it should be included in any list of topics and systems to be investigated. It seems likely, however, that disarmament would require some fundamental changes in the present international order, and the nature of these changes should be explored further.

H. Some degree of setback to civilization as a whole. One cannot, in the light of the existence of modern weapons systems, foreclose this possibility. While it is unlikely that this would take the form of a world-wide thermonuclear war (including, for example, Africa and Latin America), it is clear that even this possibility cannot be excluded. Therefore, the prospects for such an event and the possibility of alleviating some of the consequences should also be included in any systematic study of possibilities.

Almost any item on this list of possibilities will seem so implausible to some that they may wonder why I included it. There are those, for example, who do not believe the current system is stable in the medium or long run. Others, who feel almost certain that the current system will change radically, will still find all the suggested alternatives implausible. But if there is to be a change in the current order, as seems probable to so many, then it is almost inevitable that a seemingly unlikely possibility (but not necessarily one of those on the list above) will become reality. The apparent implausibility of any specific possibility focuses attention on the next question.

Wherever we get by the start of the twenty-first century, how will we have gotten there? Some possibilities are: (1) "peacefully," by natural evolution, aided evolution, or negotiation; and (2) "violently," by crises and small wars, "controlled" wars, uncontrolled but "successful" wars, "unsuccessful" wars, or "Armageddons."

As much as we would like to negotiate the route peacefully, it somehow seems unlikely that the second group of possibilities will not, in fact, play an important role. As Karl Marx once said, "War is the midwife of history." We might substitute "escalation" for "war." The phrase is a good one. The midwife does not make the baby; that is a question of conception and slow development. But the skill of the midwife may make a great deal of difference to what happens to the baby.

We can regard our military and foreign policies as giving the United States a voice in determining what the future international order will be like. Obviously, we cannot expect that the United States alone can determine these issues; but since the United States can influence events, we ought to know what our values and preferences are, and how strongly we feel about them. Perhaps of greatest moment is the need to analyze and evaluate a range of possibilities so that we do not simply and unthinkingly attempt to perpetuate the *status quo* into the indefinite future—at least not without having made a thoughtful decision that there are no other possibilities we care to risk.

APPENDIX

Relevant Concepts and Language for the Discussion of Escalation

National-security discussions—particularly those dealing with escalation—often suffer from a terminology that is conceptually inadequate, imprecise, inconsistently used, or emotionally biased. Terminological difficulties and ambiguities affect professionals as well as the public. Much too often, for example, terms that represent simple concepts have to be explained at great length even at conferences of experts, or tentative definitions have to be established and relatively simple distinctions made or elaborated, and as a consequence the major purpose of the conference often is impeded or frustrated.

The situation can be improved. Most of the concepts, terms, and distinctions can be made clear and useful. Where new concepts and distinctions are needed, they can be developed. The number of shared understandings and explicit formulations can be increased. Ideally, what is required is a language and set of concepts that are: (1) precise enough to describe and communicate accurately; (2) comprehensive enough to cover comfortably the relevant universe of discourse and discoursers; (3) simple enough to be usable; and (4) acceptable to the relevant communities. Although such a program is only part of the task of developing a comprehensive analytic framework for escalation, it is an indispensable step. It is also a difficult one—so difficult that it is unlikely that any single organization will produce a satisfactory language and set of concepts, although it is a major aspiration of the Hudson Institute to do so.

I have, inevitably, used many terms in this study that may be ambiguous or possess unfortunate connotations. Where it has seemed useful, new concepts and issues have been named and defined, and some of the problems and issues raised by some old concepts and terms have been discussed. This Appendix represents a further attempt to improve the strategic vocabulary. Obviously, it risks proliferation of the kind of jargon that can obscure rather than clarify ideas, but it was a useful and educational task to compile it, and it has been included here in the belief that some readers —lay or expert—may find that examination of it supplies some additional light on strategic issues, whether or not they make use of the terminology themselves.

I will consider the terms and concepts in ten related categories (as listed below for reference). If a term is enclosed in parentheses, that term is *not* part of the category.

1. Deterrence vs. Denial, Warning vs. Threat, Force vs. Violence, Spasm War vs. Controlled War, Ostensible vs. Real Crisis, Barely Workable vs. Stark Deterrence, Escalation Spectrum vs. Limited or General War

2. Deterrence, Types I, II, III; Types A, B, C, D
   Active and Passive Deterrence
   Deterrence Only, Minimum Deterrence, Finite Deterrence, Pure Massive Retaliation, etc.

3. Accidental War, Unintended War, Inadvertent War, Unpremeditated War
   (War by Miscalculation)
   Catalytic War, Escalation, Eruption

4. Deliberate War, Premeditated War
   Preventive War, War by Calculation, Calculated Win, Preemptive War
   (Calculating, Controlled, or Controlled-Response War)

5. Attack-Threatening Strategies, Type II Deterrence, Graduated Deterrence, Deterrence by Reprisal, Symbolic Attacks
   Impose Fear of Inadvertent Eruption
   War-Threatening Strategies

6. Escalation, Escalation Ladder, Escalation Dominance, Eruption
   Show of Force, Demonstration of Force, Demonstration Attack, Exemplary and Reprisal Attacks
   Controlled Reciprocal Reprisal, War of Resolution

7. Improved War Outcome, Damage-Limiting, War-Fighting, War-Controlling Forces
   Counterforce, Counterforce Targeting, Counterforce Strategy, Counterattack, Military Attack, No-Cities Strategies
   Countervalue, Civilian, Retaliation, Devastation Attacks
   Insurance, Deterrence plus Insurance, Extended Insurance
8. Stability, Stability to External Forces, First-Strike-Only Forces
   Parity
   Stable Deterrence, Multistable Deterrence, Nuclear Stalemate
   No-First-Strike, No-First-Use
9. Local War, Localized War, Noncentral War, Limited War
   Central Confrontations
10. General War, Central War, All-Out War, Spasm War
    Limited General War, Controlled War, Calculating War, Controlled Counterforce War, Controlled Response, Bargaining War, Damage-Limiting War
    Controlled Reciprocal-Reprisal War (Symbolic Attacks)

Some Important Distinctions Made with Special Significance in the National-Security Area

DETERRENCE VS. DENIAL: A now customary distinction is that between deterrence and denial, although it is sometimes phrased as "deterrence vs. defense." Deterrence prevents an enemy from doing something by making him fear the consequences that will follow. The prevention, therefore, is psychological, although it may make use of physical or material factors. Denial involves putting a "physical" barrier in the way of the enemy. A denial policy or capability may contribute to a deterrence policy or capability, and vice versa (since the denial policy may force the opponent to escalate more than he wants or to exceed a threshold, and the deterrence policy may result in the other side's not using capabilities that could overwhelm the denial capability). Despite the interrelation, the distinction is a real one and is widely recognized, even though it is sometimes neglected or confused.

WARNING VS. THREAT: We use this distinction in two ways. In the first, which is drawn from Schelling, a warning involves calling the opponent's attention to the fact that one will react in a way that the opponent will not like, simply because, on a cost-effectiveness or gain-loss calculation, one's reaction will be reasonable and justified. A threat, by contrast, is defined as a commitment to do something that it might be unreasonable to do if the threat or commitment had not been made.

We also use warning vs. threat in a sense which, while conceptually more complicated, can more easily be applied to many practical cases. Warning here is a general drawing of attention to the fact that the aggrieved party will not stand idly by if he is provoked, and a threat is a specific statement as to what the counterreaction will be, whether or not the counterreaction includes a rationality-of-irrationality commitment.

FORCE VS. VIOLENCE: Again a distinction drawn from Schelling. Force is the use of physical compulsion in a way that directly carries out or furthers the end to be desired. Violence is the use of pain for punishment, coercion, bargaining, or signaling purposes. The pain that is caused or threatened may have little or no direct relationship to the objectives in view, but may depend on "psychological" reactions rather than direct effects to achieve its ends.

SPASM WAR VS. CONTROLLED WAR: This distinction is, of course, one of degree, rather than of kind. Spasm war presumes a pre-set plan which, once the buttons are pressed, cannot be changed. Usually, it involves the launching of every available weapon against the enemy. Control implies that information is constantly being received and evaluated, and that a war is waged through a series of conscious decisions with a competence to react to changes.

OSTENSIBLE VS. REAL CRISIS: An important distinction because so often people use the language of crises when they do not actually mean it. The difference in the behavior of the antagonists might be expressed as that between a willingness to exchange, at most, vituperation and threats or to cause economic or political damage, and a real intention, even if a conditional one, to resort to violence. The real crises since World War II have almost all been restricted to the relatively low region of traditional crises; because we have not experienced anything like the full range of possible crises that involve nuclear violence, there are systematic tendencies to overestimate the intensity of the crises that are experienced. Paradoxically, because most people recognize—at least unconsciously— that there is a large gap between the traditional-crises rungs on the escalation ladder and the upper rungs, they may have a false sense of security, their imagination being insufficient to see how the middle rungs might bridge that gap.

BARELY WORKABLE VS. STARK DETERRENCE: These are the end points of a set of distinctions. Various studies and heuristic arguments have convinced the author that one needs at least a five- or six-point scale for measuring degrees of deterrence. The points on a reasonable scale might be: minimum, workable, "adequate," "reliable,"[1] approaching absolute, and stark. Very briefly and inadequately, these can be defined as follows:[2]

Minimum: A relatively small deterrent threat that depends on unreliable mechanisms, sanctity of thresholds, nuclear taboos, or even the "inconveniences" that might have to be accepted by an opponent.

Workable: A capability that gives a nation a reasonable probability of inflicting several million casualties on an attacker or of destroying important kinds of property. No nation, even the largest, would lightly risk the deaths of a million citizens; and it would take a very large issue indeed to cause one even to run a major risk of such losses.

"Adequate": Any deterrent threat that promises, with some modest degree of reliability, to kill 5–10 per cent of the opposing nation's population. (This would be about equal to or slightly greater than the losses suffered by major belligerents in World Wars I and II.) Under many conditions, a single large-yield, ground-burst bomb might be able to inflict on Moscow or New York (if the populations were not evacuated or protected) fatalities in the 5–10 per cent range; and two or three large-yield bombs dropped on two or three cities with unprotected populations would certainly do it. Such a capability should deter attack in any crisis characterized by the rungs of traditional crises. But it could fail to give a nation the deterrence, much less the confidence, it might need to negotiate an intense or bizarre crisis.

"Reliable": Any deterrent which could, with high probability, kill more than a third of its opponent's population or destroy the

---

[1] The quotation marks are necessary to make clear that it is not being claimed that these deterrents can really be adequate or reliable.

[2] A discussion of an abstract model with some scenarios that illustrate the differences between the various degrees of deterrence named can be found in Kahn (ed.), *A Paradigm for the 1965–1975 Strategic Debate,* Chapter XI.

opponent's major urbanized areas (even if evacuated) could probably be called a "reliable" deterrent, with "reliable" understood as meaning that it is almost impossible to imagine a realistic scenario in which the other side would be willing to accept this kind of loss, whatever the provocation—short of an all-out attack. In other words, even a city-trading tactic might be "feasible" if both sides possessed deterrents of this character.

Approaching absolute: A capability to kill somewhere between half and "200 per cent"[3] of the opponent's population. For all practical purposes, decision-makers would regard such an eventuality in terms of an end to history, and presumably would judge that no rational objective could justify accepting this kind of damage.

Stark: Overkill by a factor of ten or more, so that even the blind, fanatical, or stupid would understand the situation; a deterrent so stark that misleading calculations or wishful thinking would be impossible. Such a deterrent might, in a large range of circumstances, even deter an insane leader, or at least make so absolutely certain the destruction of an attacking nation that subordinates would understand the necessity of overthrowing such a leader. One would be tempted to call this an "absolute" deterrent, but of course even such a deterrent could fail.

In summary, there is a broad range of circumstances in which even a minimum deterrent might work, and there are conceivable circumstances in which a stark deterrent might fail. Other things being equal, it is probably better to be higher on the scale than lower—but, of course, other things are not ordinarily equal. Thus, the common question "How much deterrence does a nation need?" can be answered only by examining a range of scenarios, asking the who-whom-why kind of question discussed in Chapter I, and, most important of all, assessing the degree of assurance one feels necessary for various situations and the costs of going higher on the scale of deterrence.

ESCALATION SPECTRUM VS. LIMITED OR GENERAL WAR: The usual dichotomy between limited war and general war tends to be misleading, since there is in fact a spectrum of possible violence, as indicated by the escalation ladder, and each level of violence has a place in that spectrum. It is particularly worth noting that while limited war is often stated to be more like a Cold War than general

---

[3] Representing overkill by a factor of two. Presumably, decision-makers would not distinguish between 50 per cent and an overkill factor of two.

war, general war itself is also more like Cold War than the image of general war popularly held. This is true because, once the possibility of mutual suicide, or Pyrrhic victory, is introduced into the system, it is vital that even the victor show enough restraint and diplomatic skill to prevent the loser from being driven to irrational or suicidally defiant measures. The term "escalation" focuses attention on the fact that each side can almost always increase the stakes, and that bargaining is almost always crucial: that deterrence continues to function during and after an attack as well as preattack, and is likely to be as important as denial in preserving a country.

Deterrence, Types I, II, III; Types A, B, C, D
Active and Passive Deterrence
Deterrence Only, Minimum Deterrence, Finite Deterrence, Pure Massive Retaliation, etc.

Strictly speaking, the word "deterrence" means dissuasion by terror; and most modern usage of the term describes a situation in which there is a motivation to refrain from an action because of a fearful threat (explicit or implicit) or a warning of fearful consequences. However, the term also is now much used for situations in which a person refrains from doing something simply because he believes the consequences will not be desirable, whether or not terror or threat is involved. We will generally stay within the narrower definition.

The classification of deterrents into Types I, II, and III is a device found useful by the author for some years. As illustrated in Table A, deterrent situations may be divided into six categories. This classification focuses attention on two major issues. The Type I–Type II distinction takes note of the difference between deterring attacks directed at the United States or its major forces, and deterring extreme provocations, such as nuclear or even conventional attack on Europe. The Type II–Type III distinction indicates the inappropriateness of threatening massive attacks to deter relatively minor or moderate provocations. A different classification has been suggested by Donald G. Brennan[4] (see Table B). His A and D are similar to I and III, while his B refers to the deterrence of extreme nuclear provocations by threat of nuclear attack.

[4] In *Arms Control, Disarmament, and National Security* (New York: George Braziller, 1961), p. 25.

TABLE A
DIFFERENT DETERRENT SITUATIONS

U.S.S.R. ACTION / U.S. COUNTER-THREAT	MAJOR STRIKE AGAINST U.S.	EXTREME PROVOCATION	OTHER PROVOCATION
SOME KIND OF "ALL-OUT" ATTACK ON S.U.	Type I Deterrence	Type II Deterrence	Old Massive Retaliation Policy
LESSER VIOLENCE, OTHER ACTIONS, OR THREATS	Unnamed, but sometimes included in Type I Deterrence	Graduated Deterrence (Exemplary and Reprisal Attacks)	Type III Deterrence

Finally, Type C deterrence refers to the deterrence of extreme nonnuclear provocations by threat of large but nonnuclear attack. The motivation for Brennan's breakdown is his belief that provocations which do not use nuclear weapons are, at least for arms-control purposes, very different from provocations which do—no matter how extreme the nonnuclear provocations may be; he wishes to focus attention on the importance of such things as a no-first-use agreement. It thus is convenient for him to have a terminology that distinguishes easily between nonnuclear provocations and extreme nuclear provocations.

Brennan's deterrence diagram is of special relevance to the idea of trying to organize the world so that it will, in effect, "pretend" that nuclear weapons do not exist. As we observed in Chapter VI, the U.S. and other nations could attempt to create precedents and expectations, and follow foreign and defense policies that assumed that the only purpose of nuclear weaponry was to negate other nations' nuclear weaponry—i.e. to fulfill the same purpose that a disarmament agreement would perform, and no other purposes. This plan would also call for a self-denying ordinance to refrain from the use of nuclear threats, and *a priori* from use of nuclear weapons, for any purpose other than retaliation to nuclear threats or attacks.

TABLE B

BRENNAN'S DETERRENCE DIAGRAM

U.S.S.R. ACT / U.S. RESPONSE	STRIKE ON U.S.	NUCLEAR PROVOCATION	EXTREME PROVOCATION	OTHER PROVOCATION
STRIKE ON S.U.	A	B_1	--	--
LOCAL NUCLEAR WAR	--	B_2	--	--
LESSER VIOLENCE OR THREATS	--	--	C	D

A distinction is sometimes made between active and passive deterrence. Active deterrence involves a threat which, to be carried out, requires an act of will, a conscious decision. Passive deterrence is so arranged that if provocation occurs, the carrying through of the threat is more or less automatic or involuntary.

Type I deterrence is often thought of as passive. It is assumed that if the United States or its major forces were struck, there would be no question about the decision to strike back with the surviving forces. Similarly, Type II deterrence is often thought of as active. If, for example, the Soviets attacked Europe with conventional forces and overran Allied conventional forces, it would require a conscious decision (and a very difficult one) for the United States to live up to the NATO obligation as it is normally understood and to attack the Soviet Union with strategic forces.

These correlations should be thought of as propositions rather than as definitions. Indeed, one notes that neither proposition is true for all interesting cases: one can write many plausible scenarios in which the United States is deterred from striking back at the Soviet Union on a large scale, even though it has suffered a major attack. One can also write plausible scenarios in which a Soviet conventional attack on Europe inadvertently erupts into central war through a U.S. attack on the Soviet Union, without such an attack's really being deliberate or premeditated. If such scenarios describe what are, under some circumstances, plausible possibilities, then it is better not to think of Type II deterrence as active and Type I as passive, but rather to ask to what extent Type II deterrence is active deterrence, and to what extent Type I deterrence is passive deterrence.

"Deterrence-only" forces are designed on the assumption that deterrence can be made certain enough so that it is not necessary (worth the cost) to plan for a failure—or that it is positively undesirable to plan for a failure because of the various deleterious effects of such planning. Thus, deterrence-only advocates sometimes argue that planning for situations in which deterrence fails can show a lack of confidence in deterrence and subtly affect the chances of deterrence actually failing. At other times, an emphasis is placed on the possible bad effects of such planning on the arms race or on the psychology of decision-makers. In any case, deterrence-only forces are for "show" (to threaten) and not for use.

Deterrence-only is the opposite of "war-fighting," as described below. Thus, deterrence-only forces are those which are not designed to fight effectively by rational post-attack criteria.

The following kinds of strategies would be deterrence-only strategies: (1) finite deterrence strategies; (2) massive-retaliation strategies, which use the threat of a resolute or uncalculating first strike and make no provisions for limiting the consequences of the opponent's response; and (3) other war-threatening strategies that make use, implicitly or explicitly, of the possibility of unintended war, but do not make preparations for alleviating the consequences of a war if there really should be an eruption.

Of course, since the ability to retaliate massively can, in fact, always be converted into an ability to fight a military central war at some rate of efficiency—however low—a pure deterrence-only force can never exist. However, the phrase "deterrence-only" is reasonably accurate in some cases—particularly when applied to intentions or to the concerns of those designing the force.

Accidental War, Unintended War, Inadvertent War,
Unpremeditated War
(War by Miscalculation)
Catalytic War, Escalation, Eruption

In some ways, this group of terms is of the utmost relevance to strategic discussion in a stable balance-of-terror environment, since many believe that it contains the most likely possible causes of war and thus constitutes the category of problems most important to deal with. Accidental war denotes a special kind of inadvertent, unintended, or unpremeditated war. The other three terms carry slightly different connotations but as a category include all wars that start without explicit decisions by the responsible leaders of the participating nations. They would, however, include wars in which the causal chain of events included some explicit responsible decisions, provided the incident that triggered the events immediately leading to war was accidental or contained a very large accidental element.

The term "accidental war" has often been used to mean essentially the same thing as inadvertent or unintended war. However, it can be used in a narrower sense to refer to a particular class of inadvertent wars, those which start as the result of misunderstanding, equipment failure, etc. The term would not include any war started as a result of a mistaken belief by the attacker that it could achieve more of a success than was in fact possible. This would be called "war by miscalculation" and (as discussed below) would fall in the class of deliberate wars.

Note that there is an inherent causation problem in the concept of accidental war. Since accidental war focuses on a "triggering" incident, it raises the question of how important the role of the "trigger" must be in relationship to other factors causing the war. It is clear that the same triggering incident could cause a war in one situation and not in another. The problem is to decide when one wishes to emphasize the triggering incident, and when to emphasize the context within which the incident is sufficient to cause war.

All accidental wars are inadvertent and unintended, but not vice versa. The larger class, for example, also includes catalytic wars—wars started as a result of the actions of a third country that is not one of the primary opponents.

A war can also be called inadvertent, unintended, or unpremeditated if it results from an escalation process in which each side keeps escalating over the other until an eruption takes place that was not itself "intended." In general, the category also includes any war that is caused by a chain of "self-fulfilling prophecies" so long as the chain does not include an explicit decision to go to war made at a time when war could still have been averted. (A self-fulfilling prophecy could occur as follows: One side's temporizing action is observed by the other side and misinterpreted as being aggressive rather than defensive, thus causing the other side also to make some temporizing defensive move. This second defensive move could in turn be misread by the side originally alerted as confirming its suspicions, so it might make further moves. Under some conditions, it is possible for reactions and signals to be set into motion which trigger off further reactions and signals by both sides until a point of no return is reached, all without either side's making an explicit decision to go to war.)

A borderline case between this category and that of deliberate war would be a war that occurred as a result of reciprocal fear of surprise attack. This would be an example of self-fulfilling prophecy possible if there were an intense crisis and both sides had vulnerable forces. Each side might then fear that the other side was going to strike, mainly because it knew that the other side was afraid of the first side's strike. Thus each side might become convinced that it should attack not because it wanted to, but only because it believed that the other side might attack simply to preempt a supposed attack by the first—itself launched as a pre-emptive attack. A similar situation, but clearly one that would not be in the unintended category, would be war as a result of reciprocal fear of preventive war. In this situation, one or both sides plan an early strike. While each side wishes to get in the first blow, the situation is not tense enough for either to feel that its plans must mature immediately. Both sides feel they have months or years, but sooner or later the process matures.

Deliberate War, Premeditated War
Preventive War, War by Calculation, Calculated Win,
   Pre-emptive War
(Calculating, Controlled, or Controlled-Response War)

The first two terms are, of course, antonyms of unintended and inadvertent. In most cases, the word "war" by itself means "deliberate war," but sometimes it is useful to make the issue explicit.

A preventive war is a special kind of deliberate, premeditated war. It is started because the nation feels that war is, in a particular situation, the least undesirable alternative available. It is a war for prudential reasons: the decision-makers believe they are preventing a greater disaster later. It is normally considered that this greater disaster is a war at a less opportune time or in some other way more disastrous than immediate war. It is conceivable that there could be a just, or justifiable, preventive war. But preventive war also includes wars without moral justification. It can result from decision-makers' judgment that the probability of a worse war or other disaster is high enough for them to take their chances with an immediate war, timed to their own choice.

A pre-emptive war is also a deliberate war, even though the decision to go to war may be made in a rush. It denotes an attack made because of a belief that the other side has determined to make an attack on the pre-empting party and that such an attack is either imminent (probably less than twenty-four hours away) or actually under way. In this case, the war is basically the result of the opponent's war preparations.

The word "pre-emptive" should be reserved for attacks that are made because it is believed—correctly or not—that there are advantages in striking first. There are at least four possible rational motives for pre-emption:[5]

First, because the pre-empting force would be destroyed or disproportionately reduced if it waited for the attack.

Second, to blunt or prevent an attack. This might be done, even when a count of weapons indicated that it was disadvantageous to attack, so long as the pre-emptor hoped that unexpected weapons effects or other results of the attack might make the blow more effective than ordinary calculations indicated.

Third, for subsequent bargaining or tactical advantage. The side that strikes first is likely to have more and better information about the status of both sides than the one that goes second. By his tactics, the attacker may determine or strongly affect the subsequent course of the war. He makes the first "proposal" about which weapons or capabilities to use. For example, he chooses which of his forces to use in his first strike and which to withhold. He also chooses how to allocate his first strike among the various targets of the defender. Finally, the attacker has a psychological and timing initiative that he might be able to exploit in the subsequent bargaining or tactical campaign.

Fourth, to reduce the collateral damage to his civilians by conducting most of the war on the other side's territory. This last

---

[5] It is also possible that future decision-makers, familiar with the vulnerability problems of the 1950's and early 1960's and not realizing the full implications of the newly procured "invulnerable" forces, would be tempted to pre-empt for the first two reasons even when they no longer held true.

motive might lead to pre-emption even when, from the purely military point of view, it would be disadvantageous.

"War by calculation" is a phrase that expresses the thought that decision-makers, after due analysis, may correctly conclude that war is advantageous, for either offensive or defensive reasons, for their nation. Common belief, of course, holds the opposite: that deliberate war could arise only as a result of miscalculation. It is possible for decision-makers to miscalculate, but it is also possible that they could calculate correctly and that events would vindicate their calculations.

The three terms "calculating," "controlled," and "controlled response" do not belong in this group. They refer to wars in which, at each step and turning point, the decision-makers analyze what is the national interest and try to implement tactics and strategy that will advance this national interest. Such wars are to be contrasted with an emotional or uncontrolled war, or with the carrying through of a committal strategy (as explained below).

Attack-Threatening Strategies, Type II Deterrence, Graduated Deterrence, Deterrence by Reprisal, Symbolic Attacks
Impose Fear of Inadvertent Eruption
War-Threatening Strategies

Attack-threatening strategies use explicit threats of a first strike or exemplary attack to achieve such major foreign-policy goals as the protection by the U.S. of Western Europe from massive Russian attack. There are three kinds of attack-threatening strategies:

1. Threat of a disarming first strike. Such strategies would probably need to have large or very large war-fighting forces, and might or might not have first-strike-only forces as part of the posture.
2. Threat of exemplary attack (a version of graduated deterrence). This strategy principally requires a secure Type I deterrent to discourage deliberate eruption by the defender.
3. Threat of a resolute or uncalculating first strike of any size.

Obviously, even a country with only one weapon can threaten to make a first strike, and if it is a country with a record of erratic behavior such a threat would not be entirely incredible. Hence, in a sense, there are no posture requirements for a strategy that threatens an uncalculating first strike: the possibility that the attack may be made on committal or resolution, regardless of calculations, can be enough to make the threat effective. The common form of this strategy is "massive retaliation," and normally it would be expected to involve large or very large forces, but the forces need not be war-fighting and could include major first-strike-only forces.

Attack-threatening strategies thus use tactics designed to achieve Type II deterrence and graduated deterrence. Type II deterrence involves the threat of a large attack in response to an extreme provocation, while graduated deterrence involves threat of a high-level symbolic attack (reprisal or exemplary) in response to some provocation, but one that is not expected to lead to war. The symbolic attacks also include low levels of force (show of force or demonstration attack).

The category "war-threatening" might be understood in two ways. One would be mutually exclusive with "attack-threatening strategies" and would thus include only strategies that threatened war in some other way than by threatening attack (generally by manipulating the apparent risk of inadvertent war or by threatening to do so). This would usually be done by escalatory moves. The second interpretation would make "war-threatening" and "attack-threatening" overlapping categories, the former including all strategies that used any kind of threat to make war more probable. This second definition seems preferable and thus includes Type II deterrence.

Escalation, Escalation Ladder, Escalation Dominance, Eruption
Show of Force, Demonstration of Force, Demonstration Attack, Exemplary and Reprisal Attacks
Controlled Reciprocal Reprisal, War of Resolution

I have pointed out that in a typical escalation situation there is "competition in risk-taking" or at least resolve. Either side could win the particular conflict by intensifying the conflict or increasing its efforts in some other way, provided the other side did not match the increase. Furthermore, in many situations it would be clear that if this increase were not matched and victory were thus achieved, the cost of the increased effort would be low in relation to the benefits of victory. Thus, escalation is generally deterred by the fear that the other side may react, indeed overreact, rather than by the undesirability or cost of the escalation itself.

In some escalation situations, it is possible to make escalatory moves as a war-threatening tactic. These moves might not by themselves bring victory, even if the other side did not counter-escalate, but they might bring victory or acceptable compromise by increasing the opponent's fear of eruption. In this last case, the confrontation might be reduced to a pure, stark "competition in risk-taking."

In talking about the escalation process, it is convenient to use as a metaphor some physical analogue such as "escalation ladder," without trying to make a rigorous analogy. A typical escalation ladder for the U.S. was illustrated in Chapter II (Figure 3) and for the Soviet Union in Chapter XI (Figure 5). The justification for using such models of escalation is, in part, that the structure being displayed has important and useful implications, but mainly that it makes it possible to use such metaphors as "regions of the escalation ladder," "steps up the ladder," "rungs of the ladder," etc.

An important concept in a discussion of the tactics of escalation is escalation dominance. This is a capacity, other things being equal, to enable the side possessing it to enjoy marked advantages in a given region of the escalation ladder. Escalation dominance thus is a function of where one is on an escalation ladder. It depends on the net effect of the competing capabilities on the rung being occupied, the estimate by each side of what would happen if the confrontation moved to other rungs, and the means each side has to shift the confrontation to these other rungs. One variable affecting escalation dominance is each side's relative fear of eruption. That side which has least to lose by eruption, or fears eruption the least, will automatically have an element of escalation dominance.

Some of the tactics used to contribute to an escalation confrontation are: spectacular show of force, demonstration attacks, exemplary attacks, reciprocal reprisals, and so on. The reader will note that these tactics range from Rung 18 to Rung 31 of the ladder. In other words, though technically on the middle rungs, they are, relative to "normal" crises, very high. They are used in what can be called a "drive toward a showdown."

A war of resolution—the naked matching of resolve with resolve in an exchange of exemplary attacks and reprisals—is a very important concept in the analysis of controlled wars, since even controlled counterforce wars can develop into wars of resolution while still remaining controlled. In fact, one basic and important way of viewing the counterforce phase of a war is as an attempt by each side to put itself in a better military and threat position to fight a war of resolution.

*Improved War Outcome, Damage-Limiting, War-Fighting,
    War-Controlling Forces
Counterforce, Counterforce Targeting, Counterforce Strategy,
    Counterattack, Military Attack, No-Cities Strategies
Countervalue, Civilian, Retaliation, Devastation Attacks
Insurance, Deterrence Plus Insurance, Extended Insurance*

Improved war outcome denotes the strategic aim of limiting war damage to the population and resources of one's own nation and its allies and of improving, so far as possible, the military-political outcome of a war. Forces that can contribute to this are damage-limiting, war-fighting, or war-controlling. Because such forces have some degree of flexibility, the decision-makers would presumably have the option of using the offensive part of the force in either a counterforce (military) attack or countervalue (civilian) attack, or in some mixture of the two. Typically, the side that strikes first and expects to win would wish to limit, as much as possible, the risk of damage from the defender's retaliation. It would therefore prefer to keep the war to a purely military attack and counter-attack, and would be likely to start with counterforce targeting and hope that the defender would respond with the same kind of targeting. In such a case, the attacker and defender would be following a no-cities (or no-cities-except-in-reprisal) policy. The defender could, of course, also respond with an attack against cities, a re-taliation attack (also called countervalue, civilian, or devastation attack).

We normally use "retaliation" to refer to a large countervalue attack in response to an extreme provocation (including a large initial attack). The definition has the advantage of being commonly understood; it has the disadvantage of allowing continued slurring of the difference between responding to an attack on the U.S. and responding to an extreme provocation (the difference between Type I and II deterrence). Thus, a retaliation attack is thought of as large; or, if it is small, it is nevertheless close to a maximum effort (most of the force may have been disarmed in an attacker's first strike, or it may be that the nation did not have many weapons to begin with). It is launched out of motives of revenge or punishment, or in fulfillment of a committal policy.

While all retaliation attacks are civilian attacks, not all civilian attacks are retaliation attacks. The category of "civilian or counter-value attacks" also includes aggressive attacks and attacks with instrumental motivations.

A counterforce strategy is one that aims, among other things, at improved war outcome, but emphasizes counterforce targeting as a method of gaining this (i.e., offense is the best defense). It may, of course, be that active and passive defenses are as important as, or even more important than, counterforce targeting in getting improved war outcome: the term "counterforce strategy" tends to prejudge some important issues. Historically, of course, the term and the philosophy are often associated with the Air Force's interest in destroying an enemy on the ground. Partly as a result of this association, the term also has another connotation: that of a particular kind of counterforce strategy that argues that enough weapons should be available to target every military installation in the Soviet Union, in either a first or a second strike.

Improved war outcome or damage-limiting can be pursued for its own sake and without seeking collateral benefits in the areas of foreign policy or deterrence. We call this the "insurance" purpose; its assumption is that, despite all efforts, war could occur, and that if war occurred, it would be better to survive it than not, and furthermore, that it would be better to win than to stalemate, and better to stalemate than to lose, and that the best outcome of all would be to have the least number of people killed and the smallest amount of property destroyed—while still obtaining one's political objectives. That strategy which emphasizes improved war outcome as a major purpose in its own right, but simultaneously rejects all war-threatening purposes is called deterrence plus insurance.

Stability, Stability to External Forces, First-Strike-Only Forces
Parity
Stable Deterrence, Multistable Deterrence, Nuclear Stalemate
No-First-Strike, No-First-Use

Stability here refers to the manner in which a person, system, or piece of equipment responds to surprise, stress, strain, or shock.

For our purposes, a strategic system is stable when stresses or shocks do not tend to produce large and irreversible changes. This does not mean that the system does not react when subjected to stress or shock. For example, a crisis may change strategic forces enormously by putting them on a state of alert. Stability means that the reactions are of a limited, and perhaps predictable, nature, and that they are reversible or lead to a new balance not essentially different from the original. One necessary, but not sufficient, condition for stability is that neither side be under overwhelming pressure to attack because of military requirements based on the nature or deployment of his own or the enemy forces—i.e., that no party be under extreme pressure to act because of the advantage of pre-emption.

Thus, stability is partly, but only partly, measured by the degree of advantage that any side may obtain by acting first, relative to his situation if he is attacked. We have already discussed the classic unstable situation, reciprocal fear of surprise attack, where each side, if it were attacked, would be so very much worse off than if it struck first that there is a motivation on each side to pre-empt because of fear of the known pressure to pre-emption of the other side—as well as out of knowledge of the other side's fear of its own pressure for pre-emption. Stability would be increased if one side became indifferent, in terms of military considerations, as to whether it struck first or second. Stability would be further enhanced if both sides became indifferent. Stability would become greater still if the difference between first and second strikes remained the same, but the absolute level of the balance of terror were raised. Although this seems true of stability against pre-emption or first strike (as will be discussed below), stability against other threats may decrease as the level of deterrence increases. Compare, for example, two situations in which 50 per cent of the casualties to be expected if the enemy struck first would probably be prevented by pre-emption. There probably would be more stability against pre-emption if the expected number of casualties from a first strike were 50 million rather than 1 million. Even greater stability would exist if all parties would gain great military advantages from striking second as compared with striking first. This would obtain theoretically if there were two parties with roughly equal numbers of weapons, and more than one weapon were required to destroy a weapon.

The above condition of little or no first-strike advantage is desirable for stability, but neither sufficient nor necessary. It is not sufficient because there can be instability with no first-strike advantages. For example, there can be a situation in which one side has 1,000 missiles and the other side has no strategic forces. Both sides would be militarily indifferent to which struck first. Yet, the side with the 1,000 missiles could, from the military point of view, afford to be aggressive. Unless the unarmed side submitted completely, the situation would obviously be unstable if the superior side had aggressive policies; and vice versa—there would be greatly increased stability if the superior side were a devoted defender of the status quo. The degree of stability against pre-emption and surprise attack is measured mostly by the advantage a side may obtain by striking first relative to a situation in which it is attacked, by the absolute level of the Type I deterrence of both sides, and by political considerations. Many discussions of stability tend to overemphasize the technically destabilizing effect of having some first-strike-only forces[6] or of asymmetry. Today, for example, the United States has many forces that can be thought of as being first-strike-only, and it has a much larger total force than the Soviet Union; yet few are concerned that the Soviets might strike

---

[6] "First-strike-only," of course, describes forces that are vulnerable to enemy attack and therefore are not likely to be available after an enemy first strike. "First-strike-only" can also be used to describe tactics or systems that are only justified on a basis of their utility for a country which makes or threatens a first strike.

The term "first-strike-only" is almost necessarily an oversimplification. The following are some of the difficulties of the concept:

1) Even a vulnerable weapon is of some use to the victim of an enemy first strike because at least its draws off some enemy fire.

2) Bombers and perhaps other weapons are more or less first-strike-only depending upon their degree of alertness. An airborne bomber is not first-strike-only. Whether a ground-alert bomber is first-strike-only depends on the quality of the warning system and the willingness of its command to put bombers in the air.

3) Some systems that are not thought to be first-strike-only may turn out to be so because of some unexpected weapon effects or weaknesses.

4) It may be important to distinguish between weapons systems whose first-strike-only characteristics are a by-product of some other special purpose. For example, fighter bombers based in Europe for tactical use in connection with land warfare in Europe may be first-strike-only strategic weapons in relation to a possible attack against Russia. An example of weapons that are deliberately first-strike-only may be a special increment to the missile force which deliberately saved money by not being hardened or dispersed. Such a force would provide a very economical way to get sizable increases in first-strike ability, but would be truly first-strike-only.

the U.S. even though a large force-reduction attack is possible. This is because, even though the Soviets might obtain a greater relative advantage if they struck first, the results of their first strike would still not be good enough.

Thus, the sources of stability need not be the same on all sides. There can be stability in a situation in which one side is very much stronger than the other, but is passive for internal reasons. A situation may also be unstable if two sides have equal strength but one is much more aggressive than the other.[7]

The term "parity" is shorthand for "nuclear parity" or "strategic parity." Parity exists when neither side obtains any important strategic technical advantages or options from its central war forces. Parity does not imply stability, or vice versa. For example, it may be that in a situation in which parity exists there is an advantage to be obtained by striking first. However, if there is parity, the degree of advantage from striking first must be roughly the same for each side.

One of the most important criteria by which parity is judged is the size of the retaliatory blow each side is capable of delivering after being attacked by the other. Parity does not exist unless the size of such retaliatory blows is roughly equal—measured, presumably, in a purely technical fashion by something like percentage of destruction from the retaliation. Another possible dimension by which to measure Parity is the effect each side could achieve from its best first strike. We would say that parity did not exist if one side could achieve substantially more military advantage by its best first strike than could the other.

Because it is defined in terms of narrow military considerations, the concept of parity does not imply that each nation obtains equal benefits from its strategic forces. That nation which is more reck-

---

[7] Winston Churchill made the following comment on the situation in 1938 in *While England Slept* (New York: G. P. Putnam's Sons, 1938), p. 13:

I should very much regret to see any approximation in military strength between Germany and France. Those who speak of that as though it were right, or even a mere question of fair dealing, altogether underrate the gravity of the European situation. I would say to those who would like to see Germany and France on an equal footing in armaments, "Do you wish for war?" For my part, I earnestly hope that no such approximation will take place during my lifetime or that of my children. This does not in the least imply want of regard or admiration for the qualities of the German people, but I am sure that the thesis that they should be placed in an equal military position to France is one which, if it ever emerged in practice, would bring us within practical distance of almost measureless calamity.

less, more determined, more willing to accept damage, or enjoys greater freedom in making threats could have important superiorities in a parity situation, both in its foreign policy and in its capability for escalation dominance. The situations in which there are both parity and stability are referred to as enjoying either stable deterrence or multistable deterrence.

Multistable deterrence exists when each side is judged by its opponent to have: (a) the ability to respond to the enemy's best first strike by delivering retaliation that would in normal times be unacceptable, or (b) the ability to deliver a first strike that would disarm the enemy to such a degree that he would probably not be able to deliver a retaliatory blow that would be "unacceptable" in extreme or desperate circumstances.[8]

The basic characteristic of a situation in which there is multistable deterrence is that both sides have a good deal of Type I deterrence, but in addition they have an ability to threaten a nuclear attack in order to deter extreme challenges to their existence. That is, where multistable deterrence exists, the threat of a calculated nuclear attack will serve to constrain the political conduct of both sides.

While this definition has been framed in terms of the *size* of possible retaliatory blows, essentially the same situation can be achieved on the basis of the *probability* of very large retaliation. That is, multistable deterrence could exist if each side (a) had a 50 per cent chance of delivering an overwhelming retaliatory blow if it were attacked, and (b) had a 50 per cent chance of escaping without overwhelming damage if it made a first strike against the other side. In practice, multistable deterrence will represent a mixture of the quantitative and the probabilistic factors. It may be unstable from the point of view of arms-race considerations, in that it could be relatively sensitive to technological and force changes.

On the other hand, it is important to note that a deterrent situation that is very stable against pre-emption or first strike may, in some sense, actually encourage extreme provocations. A situation in which there is multistable deterrence, although it is somewhat less stable to surprise attacks and unintended war, has a larger stability against provocations; that is to say, provocations do not increase from a lack of central war dangers to deter them.

The concept of multistable deterrence implies that it is possible for two opponents to possess, simultaneously, reasonably satisfac-

[8] See Kahn, *On Thermonuclear War,* pp. 141–42.

tory levels of Type I and Type II deterrence. This seems paradoxical because, to some extent, one side's Type I deterrence is measured by the inadequacy of the other side's Type II deterrence. A partial resolution of the paradox lies in the fact that nations tend to be conservative and to look at the reasonable worst that might happen to them. Thus, the calculations made by both sides will be inconsistent because both sides will hedge. To the extent that nations tend to make optimistic calculations, it is more difficult to have multistable deterrence.

A nuclear stalemate (of the Cold War) exists when the balance of central war forces is such that neither side is capable of making a disarming first strike. That is, a nuclear stalemate exists when neither side has a clear theory of how to win a central war mainly through counterforce operation.

One of the important things to notice about this use of the term "nuclear stalemate," which is clearly not the only reasonable way to use it, is that even when a nuclear stalemate exists there may be an important role for nuclear weapons. For example, all of the symbolic attacks and threats of escalation of various sorts which I have already discussed remain possible. Thus, the word "stalemate" should not be understood as carrying the connotations it possesses in chess—i.e., the *end* of the game. A nuclear stalemate is *not* an absolute deadlock in which neither side can move; it is a situation in which neither side is in a good position to win a nuclear central war through counterforce operations. Nor does nuclear stalemate necessarily imply parity or symmetry.

Many strategists and arms-controllers believe that stability would be greatly enhanced if both sides explicitly adopted a no-first-strike or a no-first-use policy, either by agreement or unilaterally. A no-first-use policy is one that renounces the option of being the first to use nuclear weapons; a no-first-strike policy is one that renounces the option of being the first to make a major strategic attack. (Of course, these simple definitions do not deal with the distinctions among various forms of declaratory and internal policies.) A no-first-*strike* policy is different from a no-first-*use* (of nuclear weapons) policy in that the latter would renounce the introduction of tactical nuclear weapons into a conventional war, while the former would not; and if the enemy used tactical nuclear weapons, the former policy would still preclude a major strategic attack—although of course it would not preclude use of tactical nuclear weapons—while the latter would not.

Local War, Localized War, Noncentral War, Limited War,
Central Confrontations

All these terms refer to wars fought within geographical limits.
There may or may not be other constraints. The limits may be
inclusive or exclusive. That is, the war may be limited to a single
area such as Korea, or it may be limited only by the exclusion of
certain territory—such as the Soviet Union and the United States.
In the latter case, "noncentral war" seems more appropriate. However, if the U.S. or the Soviet Union were directly involved, rather
than by proxy, we would call even a local war a central confrontation.

It is important to understand that the word "local" does not
imply that the war is fought over local issues or that it is not part
of a world-wide conflict. This point is emphasized in the term
"localized war."

The expression "limited war" has recently acquired some ambiguity because of the realization that there are many ways in
which wars might be limited. The use of the term as a synonym of
"localized war" wrongly implies that any wars not within the definition are necessarily unlimited. On the other hand, the term
"limited war" has gained wide currency among both laymen and
professionals, and it is difficult to believe that it will be dropped.

General War, Central War, All-Out War, Spasm War
Limited General War, Controlled War, Calculating War,
  Controlled Counterforce War, Controlled Response,
  Bargaining War, Damage-Limiting War
Controlled Reciprocal-Reprisal War (Symbolic Attacks)

The terms "general war" and "central war" are basically synonymous. The first, which is sometimes preferred by the Army and
Navy, emphasizes that all forces and branches of service are engaged; the second, which is sometimes preferred by the Air Force,
emphasizes the fact that strategic attacks upon enemy homelands
are probably going to dominate the outcome, although if the
strategic exchange is inconclusive, the cease-fire is likely to be
influenced by or simply recognize the *ad hoc status quo*, which in
turn may be dominated by the war fought by the general-purpose
forces.

A general war or a central war is usually thought of as all-out war, and this is not very misleading if the term "all-out" is used to refer to the effort—that is, to the forces committed or available to the enterprise. But "all-out" sometimes connotes undiscriminating targeting and, in this case, can be misleading as a description of general or central wars. Undiscriminating or uncontrolled war is only one special kind of general or central war.

Large wars that are fought within limitations are generally given such names as limited general war or controlled war. Again, the two terms are synonymous but have different connotations. Limited general war implies some modification of general war. Controlled war has the implication of even greater modification. Wars that involve war-fighting forces with flexible war plans, adequate command and control, the use of pre-attack and post-attack coercion, and a discriminating use of force to facilitate post-attack blackmail, intrawar deterrence, and bargaining are controlled wars. Various forms of controlled wars are given such names as controlled response, bargaining war, controlled counterforce war, and damage-limiting war.

All these terms are in sharp contrast to the "spasm" or "insensate" war. They were deliberately invented to discredit a fairly common picture of thermonuclear war as inevitably an orgiastic spasm of destruction in which all the buttons are pressed and the commanding officers go home, their duty done. Spasm war now has acquired the technical significance of an attack in which there is a maximum effort in the first strike and little or no concern over later strikes. The objective is to achieve as much destruction as possible in the first strike without compromising other considerations. There are circumstances in which this might be a preferred tactic, although normally this tactic is associated with an uncontrolled or insensate war—blind and irrational.

There are two basically different kinds of controlled war—the controlled reciprocal-reprisal wars (wars of resolution) and controlled counterforce wars. A controlled reciprocal-reprisal war indicates a series of reciprocal "tit-for-tat" reprisals carried out in the hope that the other side's morale or purpose will weaken first. The controlled counterforce war envisages strictly military attacks by each side until one side or the other gives up or deliberately or inadvertently changes to some sort of countervalue attack, possibly a controlled reciprocal reprisal. Controlled reciprocal-reprisal wars may, and usually would, be wars of resolution—a naked matching of will against will.

Finally, there are symbolic attacks. These are hostile, violent, and usually illegal acts, but acts that are not necessarily accompanied by any intention to wage war or create a state of war in the legal sense. Of course, a legal state of war can exist without hostilities if the parties have expressed an intention to deal with one another as belligerents, or even if they act as belligerents without explicit declaration. But if hostile actions are not treated as war by either contestant or by outside parties, then such hostilities do not in themselves create a state of war. In our language, they may constitute shows of force, demonstration attacks, exemplary attacks, or reprisals. Sometimes the dividing line may be difficult to draw. One or two reprisals clearly do not constitute a controlled reciprocal-reprisal war. Ten or twenty clearly do.

Index

301

Beichman, Arnold, 59
Brennan, Donald G., 143, 281–83
Brodie, Bernard, 132, 198–99
Brown, Allen, 99n
Brown, William, vi, 154n, 155n
Buchan, Alastair, 132

Calculated win, 286
Calculating war, 288. *See also* Controlled response
Caranfil, Andrew, ix
Central sanctuary
defined, 142–43
and European "neutrality," 177–78
De Gaulle's views on, 264–65
Central war, versus general war, 298. *See also* Civilian central wars, Controlled response, Military central wars
Chamberlain, Neville, 20n, 27, 30, 240
"Chicken," game of, metaphor, 10–15
Schelling's criticism of, 225–26
Churchill, Winston S., 30, 33, 295n
Civilian central wars, 179
and unilateral arms control, 160–62
unlikelihood of, 167–70
see also Controlled response, Systems bargaining
Coercive aspect of national conduct. *See* National conduct
Cold War, 40, 53, 74, 106n, 113n, 165, 208, 264
Command and control
communicating with the enemy, 222–23
dead reckoning, 212
in exemplary central attacks, 147–48
fog of war, 211
functions of, 256–58
requirements of in war, 258–59
unexpected weaknesses, 187
Committal strategy
as tactic in game of "chicken," 11
use of declaration of war tactic, 171–72
as used by Khrushchev, 72

Congressional resolutions
on defense of Formosa, 56
on Gulf of Tonkin, 57
on SEATO, 57
Conservative behavior, 244–45
and systems bargaining, 133
Contractual aspect of national conduct. *See* National conduct
Controlled response
implications for current U.S. programs, 181–82
layman's understanding of, 185, 186n
Johnson's views on, 258–59
McNamara's statement on (1962), 168
McNamara's statement on (1964), 169–70
in slow escalation, 168
Soviet attitude toward, 68–69, 169, 180
symbolic attack, 300
see also Deterrence, National conduct, Rationality
Controlled war, 288. *See also* Controlled response
Crisis
common characteristics, 62n
context, importance of, 149–54
intense, 83
Korea, as example of, 84
ostensible, 53
ostensible vs. real, 278–79
seven basic tactics for, 155
Crisis and Arms Control, 62n, 244n, 252
Crisis management, 255–59. *See also* Command and control, De-escalation, Escalation, Systems bargaining, Tactics
Crisis termination. *See* De-escalation
Cuban crisis, 74–82, 87, 226, 241, 248–50, 256, 259–60
not a thermonuclear confrontation, 249

Damage limitation (and crisis), 153–54, 292. *See also* Emergency-readiness, Evacuation, Improved war outcome, Tension mobilization, War-fighting

Davey, William R., 168n
Dead reckoning, 211–13. *See also* Command and control
Declaration of war
an overlooked possibility, 26–27, 47, 170
"phony war," 168–69
purpose of, 88, 171–72
De-escalation (crisis termination)
aftermath, from lower rungs, 238–42
aftermath, from upper rungs, 242–43
approaches to, 233
as escalation in reverse, 231
need not be "friendly," 237
requires shared understandings, 236
typical gestures, 232
see also Crisis, Escalation, Tactics, War termination
De-escalation dominance, 231
Deliberate war, 286. *See also* Controlled war, Unintended war
"The Delicate Balance of Terror," 192
Détente, U.S.-Soviet, 69, 125, 157, 163, 224, 241–42, 249, 258
as aftermath of crisis, 241
exploitation of, 242
possibility of escalation, 53
study of crisis neglected, xi, 54–55
weakens blocs, 237
Deterrence
degrees of, 279–80
as highest priority task of strategic forces, 153
multistable, 296
offensive, 98n
types A-D, 281–83
types I-III, 281–84
by uncertainty, 125
see also Balance of terror, Controlled response, Systems bargaining
DEW Line, 92
Dobrynin, Anatoly F., 81
"Doomsday machines," 227–28, 269
Dulles, John Foster, 87, 194
Dustin, Sara, vi

Emergency-readiness
defined, 154–56
pros and cons, 162
Soviet counters, 164
see also Crisis, Evacuation, Tension mobilization
Enthoven, Alain, 94–95
Eruption
defined, 7
fear of inadvertent, 63–66
see also Escalation, Unintended war
Escalation
agent of change, 273–74
"chicken" metaphor, 11–14
compound, 6
degrees of, 8
Halperin's two terms, 5
in the twenty-first century, 269–74
labor-strike analogy, 9
likelihood of eruption, 109–13
midwife of history, 274
reasons for, 3, 4, 8
Schelling's comments on, 226–27
symmetry and asymmetry in expectations, 113
tactics, 109–12, 137
term not defined in dictionaries, 3
two basic strategies, 7
two sets of basic elements, 6
two-sided situations, 7
ways of increasing, 4
see also "Chicken," Committal strategies, De-escalation, Rationality - of - irrationality, "Strike" metaphor
Escalation dominance
defined, 290
examples where militarily dominant power did not act, 24
not assured by mere military superiority, 23
see also Escalation, Tactics
"Escalation and Its Strategic Context," v
Escalation ladder
chart, 39
climbing down, 216
criteria for ordering of rungs, 216
defects of, 214

Stillman, Edmund, vi, ix, 94n
Stone, Jeremy J., vi
Strachey, John, 132
Strategic Air Command (SAC), 85,
  176, 178, 181, 259
*Strategic Considerations for In-
  creased Readiness,* 168n
*Strategic and Tactical Aspects of
  Civil Defense, with Special Em-
  phasis on Crisis Programs,* 155n
"Strategy Hits a Dead End," 198
The Strategy of Conflict, 63, 246
"Strike" metaphor, 10–12. *See also*
  "Chicken"
*A Study of Escalation: The Use of
  Force in Peace and War,* v
Suez crisis, 84
Systems bargaining
  current conventions, 261–62
  defined, 19
  Kennedy on Soviet violation of
    current conventions, 79, 261–
    62
  nuclear consensus example, 101–3
  and precedents, 133, 236–37
  see also Agonistic behavior, Agreed
    battle, Arms control, National
    conduct

Tactics
  for crisis management, 253–55,
    256, 258
  current neglect of, 149, 196–99,
    252–53
  lower-rung bargaining, 251
  pre-emptive, 80–82, 287–88
  purpose of, 274
Taylor, Maxwell D., 59
Techniques of Systems Analysis,
  246n
Technological and Doctrinal Lags,
  ix
Teller, Edward, 99, 123
Tension mobilization
  analyzed, 156–57
  Korea, an example of, 165
  Soviet reactions to, 164–65
  see also Crisis, Declaration of
    war, *Détente*

Thant, U, 76–77
Thinking About the Unthinkable,
  v, 100n, 243
Thresholds
  likelihood of being observed, 136
  saliency of nuclear, 94–97
  see also Agonistic behavior, Cen-
    tral sanctuary, Central war,
    Systems bargaining
Tirpitz, Admiral, "risk theory" of,
  269

Unconditional surrender, dangers
  of, 200, 204. *See also* War termination
Unintended war, 64–66. *See also*
  Accidental war, Escalation, Inadvertent war
United Nations, 149n

Versailles Treaty, 33
Vietnam, war in
  Gulf of Tonkin crisis, 54, 256,
    261
  leaks and announcements, U.S.
    and Chinese, 56, 59
  reprisal plan and targets, 60
  threshold crossed, 73
  third escalation, possibility of, 112
Vocabulary
  important distinctions in, 277–81
  requirements for, 275
Vulnerability
  by assumption or by analysis?,
    192, 192n
  current U.S., 151n, 192–94
  doctrinal lag, 287n
  possibility of, 192–94
  unexpected, 187

War termination, 200–205
  five basic options for each side,
    202
  insufficient thought in U.S. about,
    201
  see also Unconditional surrender
War-fighting, 196–213
  Antonym of "spasm" or "deter-
    rence only," 196
  see also Controlled response, Dam-